FIELD SPORTS LIBRARY

SHOTGUN SHOOTING:

TECHNIQUES & TECHNOLOGY

Other Books Available

The Pheasants of The World
Dr. Jean Delacour

Pheasants and Their Enemies
Dr. J. O'C. Fitzsimons

Gamekeeping and Shooting for Amateurs
Guy N. Smith

Ferreting and Trapping
Guy N. Smith

Ratting and Rabbiting
Guy N. Smith

The Notorious Poacher
G. Bedson

SHOTGUN SHOOTING:

TECHNIQUES & TECHNOLOGY

by

JOHN BRINDLE

With line drawings by the author

Distributor:
NIMROD BOOK SERVICES
PO Box 1
Liss, Hants, GU33 7PR
England

Second Impression 1985.

For George and Jolyon

Publisher:
NIMROD BOOK SERVICES
Fanciers Supplies Ltd
P.O. Box 1
Liss, Hants, GU33 7PR

DEDICATION

DEDICATED TO THE MEMORY OF

G. T. TEASDALE-BUCKELL

WHOSE KEEN OBSERVATIONS AND
ASTUTE PERCEPTIONS OF THE
SPORT OF SHOOTING MAKE HIS
BOOKS AND ARTICLES OF A
VALUE AND AN INTEREST THAT
TIME CANNOT DIMINISH

Quote...

"The *Bristol Mercury* relates
the case of a man who, at
one shot, killed three pigeons,
wounded a fourth, broke seven
panes of glass, and cured a
rheumatic cripple by frightening
him into the use of his limbs."

The Illustrated London News
June 15, 1861

CONTENTS

LIST OF TABLES

FIGURES

Figures *(continued)*

FIGURES *(continued)*

FIGURES *(continued)*

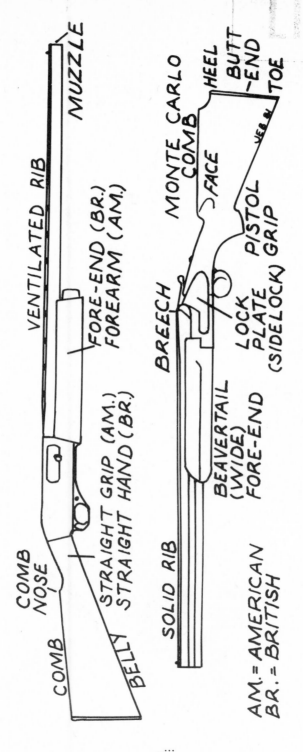

Figure 1 Gun Nomenclature

Chapter 1

Definitions and
some fundamentals

BASIC TERMS

The Third Edition of the Shorter Oxford English Dictionary defines the term shotgun as follows:

> **"Shot-gun, shotgun, orig. U.S. 1828
> A smooth-bore gun (fowling piece)
> used for firing small-shot, as dist.
> from a rifle for firing a bullet."**

This definition will serve us admirably. The primary purpose of the shotgun is indeed the firing of "small-shot" (usually at birds) and only a miniscule minority of shotguns have rifling in their barrels. American readers will be gratified that the term is American in origin (as are many other things in shotgun shooting). British readers may be surprised that this is so!

In the minds of the public at large, the term "shotgun" conjures up the double-barrelled gun with side-by-side barrels. Proof of this is to be found in virtually any cartoon with a shotgun in it in any general-circulation newspaper or magazine. However, many types of shotgun are in current regular production and use. Most are breechloaders, these including single-shot guns with many different kinds of breech-actions, double-barrelled guns with barrels side-by-side or one above the other, manually-operated single-barrel repeaters (mainly "pump guns") and self-loading repeaters with a variety of mechanisms. Some muzzleloaders, single and double-barrelled, are still made for those who like to shoot them. Nor do they exhaust the list. But such things as three and four-barrelled guns (which are occasionally made but have not proved generally useful), bolt-action repeating shotguns (which, though reloading from a magazine, are too slow in the repeating function for this feature to be useful in the field), guns with rifled barrels and smooth-bore barrels in combination, and punt and other guns too large to use from the shoulder without a rest, or too heavy in recoil to be shot without some kind of device to absorb this, will not be dealt with in these pages.

The nomenclature in general use for the external features and measurements of shotguns is shown in Figures 1 to 5.

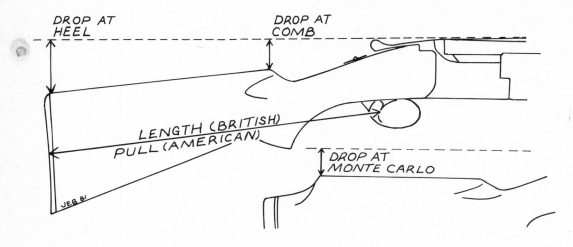

Figure 2 Stock Measurements

Gun gauges are measured by the internal diameter of the barrel, generally at a point some nine inches from the face of the breech. The following table shows this dimension for the five gauges and the single calibre in general use in the world:

Gauge	Diameter in Inches
10	.775 (.751 − .802)
12	.729 (.710 − .750)
16	.662 (.637 − .685)
20	.615 (.596 − .636)
28	.550 (.543 − .567)
.410 cal.	.410 (.405 − .430)

The range of figures for each gauge shows the considerable spread in actual dimensions of barrels chambered for ammunition of that gauge. In North America guns larger than 10 gauge are everywhere illegal for waterfowling (and usually for game shooting of any kind). Guns of larger gauges (principally 8's) are still used in waterfowling in some places on the east side of the Atlantic. The gauge system does not go below 50. In North America the .410 is called a ".410 bore". It would be a 67½ gauge if the gauge system went as small as that. In Europe it is erroneously referred to as the 12mm (which is the diameter of its chamber) and sometimes as the 36-gauge! In Britain, guns entitled to the gauge-terminology are usually called so-and-so bore: 12-bore, 20-bore and so on. Which matters not in the least, providing we each know what everyone else is talking about. There are some examples of differences in British and American terminology in Figures 1 to 3.

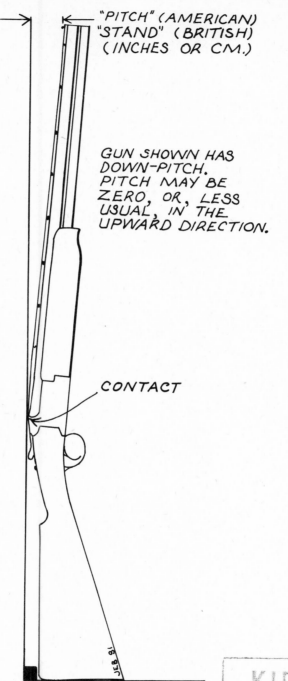

"PITCH" (AMERICAN)
"STAND" (BRITISH)
(INCHES OR CM.)

GUN SHOWN HAS
DOWN-PITCH.
PITCH MAY BE
ZERO, OR, LESS
USUAL, IN THE
UPWARD DIRECTION.

CONTACT

Figure 3 Pitch

   Shotgun barrels are usually internally constricted to some degree at the muzzle end, this being the sole important way by which the *gun* may be modified so as to affect the spread of the shot after it has left the muzzle. Within limits (discussed later in this book) increasing the constriction (in a suitably shaped conical taper) decreases the spreading of the shot. Such constriction is termed "choke". Paradoxically, enlargements of the barrel-bore at the muzzle are also termed "choke"! Such enlargements are fondly hoped by their users to increase the spread of the shot to dimensions greater than those produced by a barrel which is cylindrical to the muzzle (i.e. without constriction) but none has yet, I think, been shown to do so. Various forms of choke are shown in Figure 6. The total length of the choked portion of a barrel may be a fraction of an inch or as much as four inches for normal chokes (those with constriction) and up to eight inches for enlarged "bell" and "trumpet" "chokes", reflecting the different ideas and practices of their manufacturers.

   In the vast majority of shotgun barrels the breech end is internally enlarged in the form of a cylindrical chamber to take what is called in Britain a cartridge and in North America a shotshell. This chamber (Figure 7) is usually long enough to hold the full length of whichever you call it, *after* it has been fired. It is connected to the barrel bore by a cone, the "chamber cone" which may be as short as ¾-inch or as long as four inches, reflecting, again, differences in manufacturers' theories and procedures. A tiny minority of shotguns have no perceptible enlargement within the breech end of their barrels. These are usually intended for use with ammunition having thin, brass cases, so little different in external and internal diameter that the wads which are a tight fit in the case behind the load of shot form a good seal in the barrel when the gun is fired, since only a little lateral expansion of the wad is required to effect this.

   More usual, present-day, shotgun ammunition (Figure 8) has a plastic or paper body, and the head alone reinforced with metal. The metal head is formed into a rim which fits into a corresponding recess at the rear end of the chamber, thus retaining the head close to the face of the breech when the gun is closed. Some plastic-cased ammunition now lacks all metallic reinforcements as superfluous.

   Internally, there is a charge of propellant at the rear end of the case, ignited by the primer in the base of the case when the gun is fired. The wads between the propellant and the load of shot cushion the latter from the blow delivered by the gases of the burning propellant, as well as forming a sealing piston behind the shot during its passage up the barrel. Wads used traditionally to be combinations of card and fibre (felt or felt substitutes) in the form of discs. Such wads are still the norm in many British and European game cartridges. However, in American ammunition for every purpose, and in competition ammunition from all countries, wads are now usually of pliable plastic with a skirt facing the propellant (which, expanding under pressure of the gases, forms a seal first against the walls of the case and then against those of the barrel). There is a central, cushioning section, and, more often than not, a split sleeve extending forward around the sides of the shot-load to protect the outer pellets from abrasion on the walls of the barrel. When card and fibre wads are still used, the card over the propellant is often in the form of a rearward-facing cup, and the shot is often protected by thin sheet-plastic wrapped into a cylinder without ends.

   The end of the case is nowadays usually closed by inward folding of the walls of the case itself into six or eight regularly-spaced folds, which are themselves folded down on top of the shot. For obvious reasons this is termed a "folded crimp". In former years closure was by means of a thin top-wad (usually card) held in place by rolling down the top edge of the case, thus forming a "rolled crimp". This is still seen on some

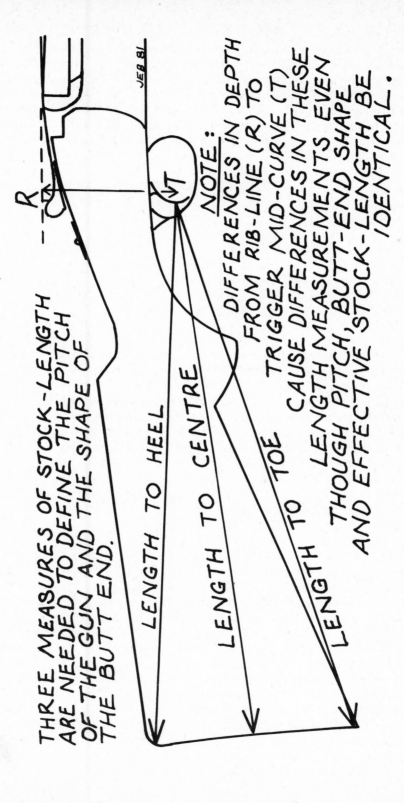

THREE MEASURES OF STOCK-LENGTH ARE NEEDED TO DEFINE THE PITCH OF THE GUN AND THE SHAPE OF THE BUTT END.

LENGTH TO HEEL

LENGTH TO CENTRE

LENGTH TO TOE

NOTE:
DIFFERENCES IN DEPTH FROM RIB-LINE (R) TO TRIGGER MID-CURVE (T) CAUSE DIFFERENCES IN THESE LENGTH MEASUREMENTS EVEN THOUGH PITCH, BUTT-END SHAPE AND EFFECTIVE STOCK-LENGTH BE IDENTICAL.

JEB 8L

Figure 4   Defining Stock Length and Pitch

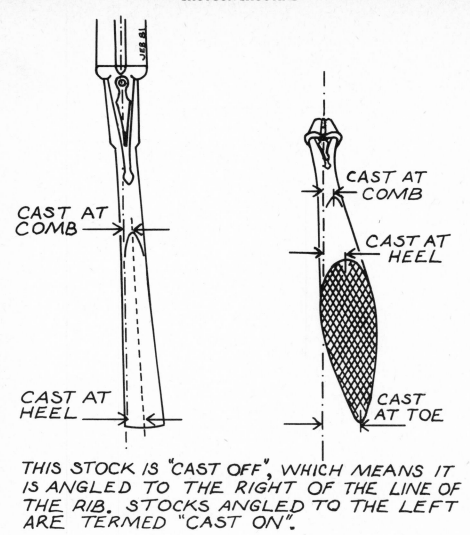

THIS STOCK IS "CAST OFF", WHICH MEANS IT IS ANGLED TO THE RIGHT OF THE LINE OF THE RIB. STOCKS ANGLED TO THE LEFT ARE TERMED "CAST ON".

Figure 5 Cast

ammunition. Figure 8 shows two possible combinations of case construction and components.

The normal range of commercial loads, American, British and European, are encompassed by the following limits:

10 gauge Magnum (3½ in): 2 to 2¼ oz.
10 gauge (2⅞ in): $1\frac{7}{16}$ to 1⅝ oz.
10 gauge (2⅝ in): $1\frac{5}{16}$ to 1⅞ oz.
12 gauge Magnum (3 in): 1⅝ to 1⅞ oz.
12 gauge (2¾ in): 1 to 1½ oz.
12 gauge ("2½" in, 65 and 67.5 mm): ⅞ to 1¼ oz.
16 gauge (2¾ in): 1 to 1¼ oz.
16 gauge (shorter than 2¾ in): $\frac{15}{16}$ to 1 oz.

TRUE CYLINDER

CHOKES

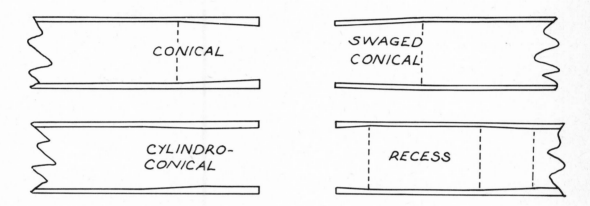

CONICAL

SWAGED CONICAL

CYLINDRO-CONICAL

RECESS

"SKEET" "CHOKES"

"SKEET" "CHOKES" INCLUDE ALL TYPES SHOWN ABOVE
(INCLUDING TRUE CYLINDER) PLUS THOSE BELOW
AND A VARIETY OF OTHERS!

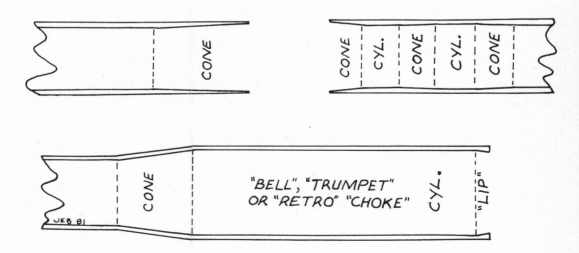

CONE

CONE CYL. CONE CYL. CONE

CONE "BELL", "TRUMPET" OR "RETRO" "CHOKE" CYL. "LIP"

JEB 81

Figure 6 Chokes

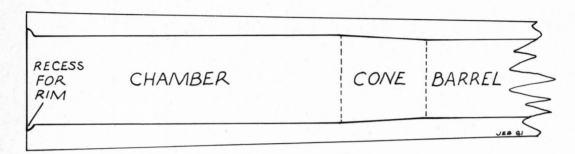

Figure 7   Chamber details

20 gauge Magnum (3 in): 1¼ oz.
20 gauge (2¾ in): ⅞ to 1⅛ oz.
20 gauge (shorter than 2¾ in): $\frac{13}{16}$ to ⅞ oz.
28 gauge (2¾ in): ¾ oz.
28 gauge ("2½" in, and 65 mm): $\frac{9}{16}$ oz.
.410 (3 in): ⅝ to $\frac{11}{16}$ oz.
.410 (2½ in, and 65 mm): $\frac{7}{16}$ to ½ oz.
.410 (2 in, and 50 mm): $\frac{5}{16}$ oz.

For any of the above, loads lighter than the range shown can be assembled easily by handloading (following tested and approved recipes!) but it is difficult to load more shot than the maxima shown at acceptable (i.e. not too high) pressures, except at muzzle velocities lower than that of the heaviest factory load for a certain case.

Muzzle velocities of commercial, factory-loaded, ammunition range from a low of 1150 to 1200 feet per second (f.p.s.) for loads for American-rules trap and skeet, to as high as 1450 f.p.s. for some International rules skeet loads. Loads for International-rules trapshooting (Trench) are often about 1250 f.p.s. muzzle velocity. Ammunition intended for game and waterfowl shooting in 10, 12 and 16 gauges is usually in the 1250 to 1350 f.p.s. range, while that in 20 and 28 gauges and the .410 is usually between 1150 and 1250 f.p.s. The pressures produced by shotgun ammunition are low compared to those encountered in modern rifles, but are kept within strict limits. Higher-pressured ammunition would not only be unsafe to use in many of the countless millions of shotguns scattered over the world, it would also result in greater deformation of shot on its way to the muzzle, and uncontrollably wide spreads beyond the muzzle, which is to say poorer performance.

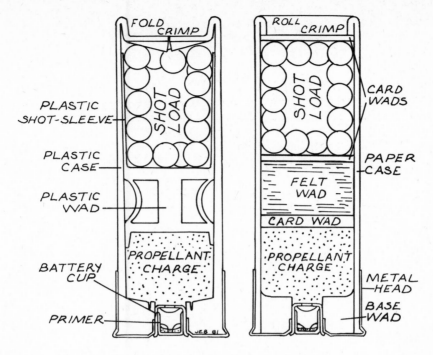

Figure 8   Shotgun Ammunition

So much for definitions and a few generalities. Now for the three fundamental factors in shotgunning: the three the beginner finds himself immediately up against (for "himself" in this book please read "himself or herself" of course). These are:

1. **Gunfitting**
2. **Recoil**
3. **Lead** (or, if you prefer: Forward Allowance).

Without further ado I propose to deal with each of these in turn.

GUNFITTING

By "gunfitting" is meant the process of finding the dimensions and shape of the gunstock needed to "fit" a certain shooter, so that the gun he uses *actually* shoots where it *seems* to the shooter he is pointing it. Two things must be said at once. One is the obvious one that gunfitting cannot compensate for errors in lead (forward allowance) given to a crossing bird. The other, less obvious, is that it cannot compensate for errors in gunmounting, either, and in the above there is a supposition that the shooter will dispose his head, arms, shoulders and trunk in a certain way, consistently, relative to the gun each time he puts the latter to face and shoulder to shoot. Note that the human body is quite highly contortible, and hence more than one such disposition is possible for any shooter (almost any disposition seeming "normal" and even "natural" after some repetition of it). A classification and account of current methods of gunmounting, and gunfitting for these methods, is a major component of this book.

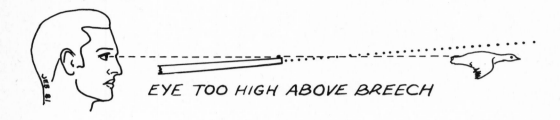

EYE TOO HIGH ABOVE BREECH

Figure 9   Missing over from Eye too High

Rifles and pistols are *aimed*. This means that a part, or parts, of them: the sights, are *looked at* by the shooter in aligning them on a target. This is true even if the sights are telescopic, for the telescope brings an image of the target into the same plane as something attached to the rifle: the reticle of the sight, and the shooter looks at both together.

Shotguns are not aimed. Shotguns are *pointed*. Perhaps I should say "merely pointed", though to do so might give an erroneously-low impression of the accuracy thus obtainable. At any rate: in all shotgun shooting the first act is to concentrate the vision on the *target*, and it is this, and this alone, which is *looked at*.

The upper surface of the gun, from breech to muzzle/s is *seen* by the shooter, though out of focus (the muzzle end of the barrel/s less so than the breech) and much foreshortened. Indeed, he could not help seeing it, for, with the target, it is in the centre of his field of vision as the trigger is pulled.

But the gun is *not* looked at.

In practice it is the muzzle end of the gun, virtually alone, which is used, consciously or subconsciously, in pointing the gun. Usually if the breech of the gun is laterally out of the line eye to muzzle to bird the shooter receives no visual warning of this state of affairs, and no form of rib, or "eye-catching" feature on the breech end of the gun, seem to be of perceptible help (if the reader will pardon the unintentional pun!). Ribs are useful in achieving constant *elevation* of the barrel or barrels relative to the eye. If by being placed too high above the breech the eye sees more than is normal to it of a matt-surfaced rib, or less or none of it by being placed too low, this usually registers sufficiently on the consciousness of the shooter that he makes the necessary correction in the relation of eye and rib. The presence of a rib of this kind does make errors of elevation far more obvious to the eye than they would be had the latter in view merely the smooth curved surfaces of the top of a barrel or barrels (or the latter with a smooth concave rib). It is too much to hope that slight *lateral* misalignments of the gun would

WRONG EYE FORCED TO TAKE CHARGE

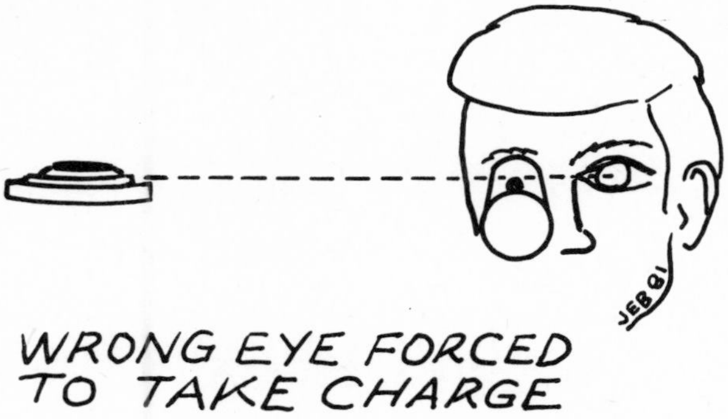

Figure 10   Cross-firing due to Eye too Low

also be made apparent to the eye without the gun being directly looked at. In fact, such lateral errors of alignment of the breech are not made apparent to the eye (fixed as it must be for success on bird or target) to any worthwhile degree by any form of rib or non-optical sights yet put on a shotgun.

In a real sense, then, the eye in charge of pointing the gun is itself the backsight of the shotgun and of the shotgunner. Though both his eyes may be (and usually are) open, usually (again!) one of the shooter's eyes takes charge of this function. This eye is referred to as his "master eye", a concept we shall return to shortly. If this eye is placed too high relative to the breech of the gun, the shot will go high (Figure 9). Conversely, if it is too low the shot will also go low, or, if it is so low that it can no longer see the muzzle-end of the gun because the breech is in the way, then the other eye will take charge of directing the muzzle, resulting in a wide lateral, and low, miss due to cross-firing (Figure 10). In similar fashion, if the muzzle-end of the gun is in the view of the master eye, but the line from eye to muzzle to bird passes to one side of the centre of the breech, the shot will deviate to that side too (Figure 11).

It is the primary purpose of gunfitting, then, to ensure:

a) At worst, that it is *possible* to place the eye in charge of pointing the gun in line behind the rib and a little above it.

b) At best, and ideally, that each time the gun is mounted correctly the shooter gets subconscious assurance that the eye is so placed because the stock is then in its usual, comfortable, contact with his face and shoulder.

In short: the eye puts the muzzle into the right relationship with the bird, and it is the function of gunfitting to put the breech of the gun in the line eye to muzzle, thus ensuring the shot goes where the shooter is looking.

If the eye is a little higher than the breech of the gun (not so high as depicted diagrammatically in Figure 9) this not only allows the shooter to see the muzzle end of the gun with that same eye and hence point the gun properly (avoiding the state of affairs

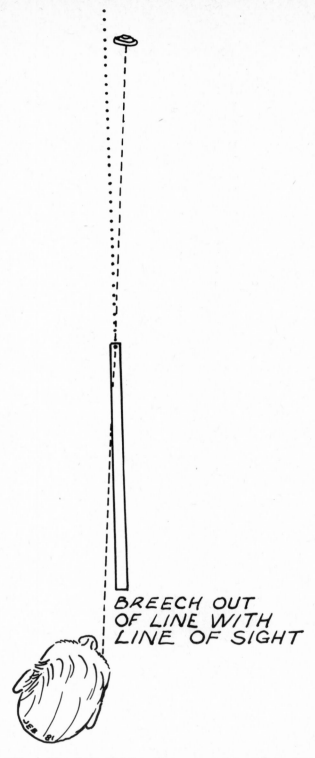

Figure 11   Lateral Miss, Eye to one side of Breech

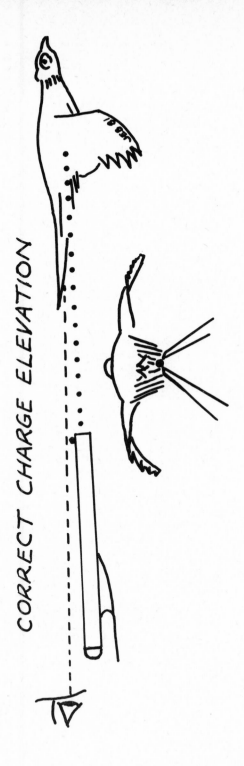

Figure 12   Line of Sight right distance above Breech

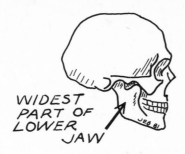

Figure 13 Showing widest part of Lower Jaw

shown in Figure 10), it also ensures that a target in level flight seen just *above* the end of the gun will be hit (Figure 12). This is an advantage, since there is always a desire on the part of shooters to see as clearly as possible that which they wish to hit. For reasons which we shall examine later, the shooter who can and does keep both eyes open when he shoots can usually still see any bird which he has had to "cover" with his barrel or barrels in order to hit it. But he does not see it so clearly as when it is the view of both eyes, above the muzzle, and for this reason a gun which for its user places its charges somewhat above the point where the frontsight would seem to indicate they would go, is an advantage for virtually every kind of shotgun shooting.

A stock which will not allow the shooter to get his eye in the right place behind the rib without conscious contortion (and perhaps not even then) due to there being "wood in the way", as it were, is a far greater evil than is the opposite extreme: a stock which does not even touch the shooter's face at all when the eye is in the right place relative to the breech. If the shooter is a consistent pointer, the former stock will cause him to miss with virtually every shot. The latter, on the other hand, will at least allow him the possibility of hitting, and perhaps consistent hitting, though in using it, since the face does not touch the stock, he lacks the tactile reassurance that he is placing the head and eye in precisely the same way relative to the breech of the gun on each shot.

Thus, the ideal remains a stock in gentle, yet positive, contact with the face when the butt is at the shoulder and the eye correctly placed relative to the breech. Where the shooter places the butt of the gun relative to his shoulder-joint, and where the comb of the stock crosses his face, can be used to classify every kind of shotgun stock and the gunmounting suited to it, and this is done in Table III (p. 185).

One feature of "average" human anatomy is of paramount importance in gun-mounting, and in shaping the gunstock as regards drop and cast to fit the user.

The feature referred to is the width of the lower jaw at its widest part on and above the rear angle (arrowed in Figure 13). Looked at from the front (Figure 14) this part of the jaw lies well outside a vertical line through the eye on the same side of the head, even when the head is turned on the neck so that the side of the jaw would lie flat against the side of the stock of a gun being pointed at the observer (as in Figure 15). I repeat that what I am considering here is the average head, and not one of that minority with jaws narrower, or much narrower, than average.

Thus, if a *castless* stock of normal comb-thickness is mounted with:

a) The butt inside the shoulder-joint of the shooter (in the "pocket" between shoulder-joint and chest) and

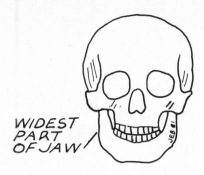

Figure 14   Skull, Front View

b) The comb of the stock crossing the shooter's face over the widest part of the jaw as in Figure 16 (the jaw being closed, not necessarily tightly) and

c) The shooter's head neither canted sideways over the stock nor turned towards it farther than will bring the side of the face parallel to the side of the stock (thus giving the maximum area of contact between them) then, if the shooter has a jaw of normal (let alone above-normal) width, and a usual, proportional, distance between his eyes (and no more) the eye on the "gun side" of his head will not be in line with the rib of the gun, but will be to one side of the centre of the breech (to the left for right-shouldering shooters, as in Figure 11, and vice versa for those who put the gun to the left shoulder).

This fact is *at the root of the existence of the cast stock* (Figure 5) which is one remedy for this state of affairs, and the one most favoured by British game shooters and their gunmakers for the past 80 or more years. It may be noted here in passing that if the jaws are closed, and particularly if the large muscles over the corner of the jaw are tensed, this effectively widens the jaw and increases the amount of cast required to put the eye above the centre of the breech over what it would be were the jaws open and the jaw musculature relaxed. As will become clear later when we come to consider shooting styles, and particularly trap vs. field shooting, this is not such a minor point as might first appear.

To bring matters home further: if a shooter had *no* lower jaw, then there could be no need for him to have cast on his stock. Such an apparition could put the stock-comb anywhere under his upper jaw that was required to put the eye in line with breech and muzzle.

The cast stock is not the only "remedy". Another one, usual in North America, but far from confined thereto, is to use a castless stock but to mount it *below* the angle of the jaw (Figure 17) thus allowing the eye to be centred above the breech.

Four other practices allow the use of a castless stock mounted over the widest part of the jaw (Figure 13) without the jaw pushing the breech out of the line from eye to muzzle. These are:

a) Turning the head towards the stock so that the comb comes under the cheekbone next to the nose. This necessitates the butt being mounted on shoulder-joint or upper arm in order that the shooter can look centrally down the gun, the line of sight passing very close to the nose (Figure 18).

b) Canting the head sideways over the gunstock comb (Figure 19). The butt may be in the shoulder pocket or farther out on shoulder-joint or upper arm.

c) Canting the gun towards the head (Figure 20).

LIES
FLAT
AGAINST
STOCK

Figure 15   Skull turned so Jaw lies Flat against Stock

    d) Shooting with the jaw (and usually mouth) open. This allows the stock comb to push the lower jaw sideways a little, thus permitting the eye to align with the gun's rib (Figures 21, 22).

Practices a) and c) are commonest among trapshooters, but not confined to them. Some shooters cant the head sideways over the comb as well as canting the gun towards the head! Observation leads me to believe that d) is confined to trapshooters, and to skeet shooters under American and English national rules which allow gunmounting before the target is called for.

All these possible combinations of gunstocks and gunmounting, their finer points, variations, and pros and cons will be considered in these pages. None of them removes the necessity of checking (and, if required, altering) the fit of the gun to the shooter for the primary purpose of having the gun shoot where it seems to the shooter he is pointing it. The secondary purpose is that the stock shall be comfortable in use, indeed perhaps it is wrong to label this secondary, for if the shape of the stock were such as to allow the shooter to hit birds, yet in doing so he received such punishment from the stock that he was unwilling to repeat the experience more than a few times, such a stock is useless to him and cannot be said to fit him.

Though it would seem logical that if gunfitting is to be done at all it should eliminate the necessity of canting head or gun, or of mounting the butt elsewhere than on the deep musculature between shoulder-joint and chest wall (which has greater recoil-resistance than the thinner coverings of muscle on shoulder-joint or upper arm) yet shooters continue to refine the fit of stocks to allow them to shoot with the butt thus mounted, or with canted head or gun. Some of these people shoot very well indeed, and it is a moot point whether or not they would shoot even better with guns which fitted them when mounted with the butt in the shoulder ''pocket'', uncanted, against an uncanted head. Most coaches and gunfitters would say that, after a period of re-adjustment, they would.

When they shoot a shotgun with both their eyes open, most people have a ''master eye'', which is to say that one of their eyes will take charge of pointing the gun (''pointing'', as we have seen, boiling down to placing the muzzle relative to the target). For this majority, shooting with both eyes open, with any normally-stocked gun, must be from the shoulder on the same side as the shooter's master eye if satisfactory results are to be obtained. If the gun is put to the other shoulder cross-firing will result as the master eye puts the muzzle on the track of bird or target (Figure 23). We have already seen that cross-firing will also result if the eye behind the breech is

COMB ON REAR
ANGLE LOWER JAW

Figure 16   Comb of Stock crossing widest part of Jaw

placed so low that its view of the muzzle end of the gun is blocked by the breech, so that the eye on the side of the face opposite the gun takes charge of placing the muzzle relative to the target (Figure 10).

The shooter's master eye is easily found. Take a big sheet (say, 4 feet by 3) of thick paper or thin card and roll it into a cone open at both ends (the long side of the paper going around the cone). The smaller opening should be 1 to 1½ inches across, the larger about 15. The person whose master eye it is wished to find takes the cone by the large end and, holding the cone out in front of him (the wide end nearest his face, the narrow end farthest from him) looks through the cone at the eye of an observer facing him a few yards away. The observer should have his other eye closed. Most people will use one eye to look through the cone at the open eye of the observer, using the same eye each time the experiment is made, and (from the observer's viewpoint) centering this eye perfectly in the circle at the narrow end of the cone (Figures 24, 25). Only the eye and a small area of the face of the person undergoing testing is visible to the observer. These, the majority, have a definite master eye, and the observer can see clearly which one it is. It is important, by the way, that the narrow end of the cone be not too large or *most* people will use *both* eyes to look through it.

A minority of people will be found who, from the viewpoint of the observer, either use one eye consistently but locate that eye away from the centre of the circle formed by the smaller end of the cone, or who use first one eye and then the other. The latter, when the observer comes closer, so arrange the cone that from the observer's viewpoint it is the bridge of their nose which occupies the centre of the circle (Figure 26). All or part of their eyes are visible on the edge of the circle according to the size of the latter. These are all people who lack a definite master eye. When they point a shotgun with both their eyes open, the optical task in doing so is shared by their eyes, often quite equally. The two images of the gun (one formed by each eye) in front of the shooter who has both eyes open and focused on the bird or target differ markedly in clarity for the shooter who has a definite master eye, and he uses only the bolder, clearer, image in pointing the gun. For the shooter who lacks such eye dominance, the two images are quite similar in clarity, and in pointing the gun with both eyes open he uses a kind of average of the two, a point somewhere between the two images of the muzzle-end being taken as the true position of the latter. He has what a gunfitter calls "central vision". Such shooters usually, and consistently, align the gun nearer to the line of sight of one eye than to that of the other, though often by not very much.

If a person with this kind of "central vision" shoots with both eyes open and with the muzzle end of the gun in the unhindered sight of both eyes, he needs a great deal of

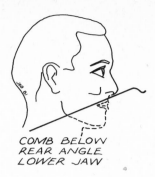

COMB BELOW
REAR ANGLE
LOWER JAW

Figure 17   Comb of Stock below Angle of Jaw

cast on the stock (Figure 27) often 1 to 1½ inches, to put the rib in line with the combined vision of his eyes. Some shooters with this kind of vision have indeed been furnished with such stocks, particularly by those British gunmakers for whose customers the made-to-measure stock is the norm. However, other means are available to solve the problem, and most shooters with central-vision use stocks which (in whatever gunmounting style they choose) align the gun perfectly with the eye on the side where the gun feels most "natural", and either:

    a) Close the other eye (note that if they can learn to delay this eye-closing until the muzzle reaches the visual vicinity of the bird or target, they can preserve the full depth-perception given by two open eyes, and their view of what is going on under the gun, until the last split second before taking the shot), or

    b) Wear spectacles with a small sticker on the lens in front of the eye opposite the gun side, the sticker being placed on the lens in such a position as to block the muzzle from the view of that eye when the gun is mounted to shoot, or

    c) Have some kind of flap or "blinder" on the gun, about halfway along the barrel or barrels, which sticks upward and outward on that side where it will block the muzzle from the view of the eye not over the rib.

Though most people have a master eye, numerous left-handed people have right master eyes, and vice versa. In choosing the side from which to shoot, natural "handedness" should be ignored if this is at all possible. The shooter should be grateful to a gunfitter who is quite strong minded about this, and should help the fitter by being quite firm with himself! If a shooter who feels more "natural" with the gun at the shoulder on the other side from his master eye is really so unadaptable as to be unable to change sides (and virtually everyone who really tries can do so) one possible solution lies in the so-called "cross-eyed" stock (Figure 28) which has enough cast (2½ inches is a common figure) to bring the breech of the gun under the master eye. When a gun is stocked thus, the recoil is supported at the shoulder well to one side of the barrel or barrels, and the stock swings noticeably into the shooter's face in the late stage of recoil, each time the gun is fired. Nevertheless, a cross-eyed stock is a necessity for the shooter with but one eye and one arm when these are on opposite sides. However, for the two-eyed shooter who insists on shooting from the shoulder on the opposite side of his body from his master eye (and who has an arm on that side, at least) remedies other than the cross-eyed stock are possible, usually preferable, and certainly more sightly. These (closing the eye not over the gun, or using a sticker on one lens of a pair of spectacles, or a "blinder" flap on the gun) are the same as those suggested above for the central-vision shooter.

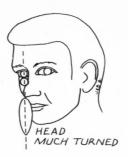

HEAD
MUCH TURNED

Figure 18 Much-turned Head

Note that when a shooter has both eyes open, the eye not directly over the gun gets some kind of view of what is going on *under* (or behind) the gun (Figure 29). As we shall see later, this is useful indeed in one kind of trapshooting. It can be useful, too, in shooting the high, approaching bird, which can be seen behind (or "through") the gun even when the gun is pointing ahead of it. However, it must be said that when there is time and opportunity to do so, it pays to turn oneself through 90 degrees right or left, as appropriate, before raising the gun and shooting at such birds as they pass overhead. This action converts the incomer into a crossing bird, directly visible at all times, including the period when the gun is pointing ahead of it as the trigger is pulled. Hence it is more clearly seen than is an incomer which is under the gun (and hence seen by one eye only) in the same period.

RECOIL

Shotguns as a whole are relatively heavy in recoil, and reducing the recoil as felt by the shooter to manageable proportions is an important and limiting factor in shotgun design. This is not simply a matter of making shooting more pleasant. Recoil heavy enough to punish the shooter makes good shooting impossible, because sooner or later the shooter begins to "flinch" in a variety of ways (hesitating before pulling the trigger, jerking the gun out of alignment with the forward hand, raising the head before or as the trigger is pulled, holding the gun away from the shoulder, and so on), any and all of which destroy accurate gun-pointing. A "flinch" thus acquired is often very hard to get rid of. The shooter may continue to flinch for a long time, even after he reverts to the use of guns of little or no appreciable recoil.

In considering how "felt recoil" may be diminished it is useful to think of the movement of the gun during recoil as divided into two periods. If a shotgun had its centre of gravity on the axis of its barrel (or the axis of the barrel which is fired) then, since the force on the breech face produced by firing the gun is also on the barrel-axis, its first movement would be straight to the rear, in line with the axis of the barrel. However, since virtually all shotguns have a centre of gravity below their barrel or barrels, their first movements in recoil are to rotate around the centre of gravity and to move bodily rearward (Figure 30). The rotational movement in this first phase of recoil is slight compared to the rearward movement of the gun.

Having moved far enough rearward to encounter more or less firm resistance from the shoulder of the shooter, the gun then rotates upward as a whole about the shooter's shoulder as a pivot, in the second period or phase of recoil (Figure 31).

Figure 19   Canted Head

The two most important aspects of recoil so far as the shooter is concerned are:
a) The speed attained by the gun in recoil.
b) The manner in which the gun recoils, most importantly:
   i) The rise of the comb of the stock in the second phase of recoil.
   ii) Whether or not any part of the gun comes into, or goes out of (and stays out of) contact with the shooter *after* recoil has started. If the former, then the shooter may be in effect *struck* rather than pushed by the gun, while the latter, conversely, tends to be an attribute of a stock which is unusually comfortable in use.

I propose to deal with a) and b) in turn.

The difference between recoil velocities that are not simply unpleasant but actually sufficient to shift the gun in (and even to sting) the hands, and lower velocities that allow the firing of all the shots that one might reasonably wish to shoot in a day (from a score or two in the case of heavy waterfowling loads, to several hundred in some kinds of clay target competition, shooting driven game in Britain or Europe, or hunting crows in North America) is remarkably small. Assuming that the shooter is not especially sensitive to recoil, the position is somewhat as follows:

20 f.p.s.: unpleasant, "punishing", recoil, gun moves in the hands.

18 f.p.s.: normal upper practical limit, usable for a limited amount of shooting if gunmounting is in a style giving a great degree of recoil resistance to the shooter (which will be a recurrent subject in this book) and the gun is fitted to the shooter for this style.

16 f.p.s.: upper limit for field shooting other than that involving the firing of some hundreds of shots in a day, when 14 to 15 f.p.s. (and loads not more than 1⅛ oz) are the limit.

14 f.p.s.: mild recoil in game-shooting terms, upper limit for clay target competition of a maximum of 150 shots per day (e.g. International Trap and Skeet, Sporting).

12 f.p.s.: upper limit for clay target competition when many, perhaps hundreds, of shots will be fired in a day; desirable upper limit for adult beginners learning to shoot.

10 f.p.s.: Desirable upper limit for juveniles learning to shoot.

Taking a certain weight of shot at a certain muzzle velocity as the constant thing (which is about the same as saying "Assuming it is desired to use a certain load") recoil velocity can be reduced by:
a) Increasing the weight of the gun.

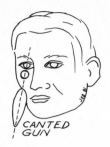

Figure 20 Canted Gun

b) Incorporating in the gun some kind of mechanism to cause it to recoil more slowly (i.e. to reach a lower "peak velocity" in recoil). If this is done, then to dissipate the energy produced when the gun is fired, the gun must recoil for a longer time. However, this longer period is not reflected in "felt recoil" nor in adverse effects on the shooter.

Table I relates recoil-velocity and gun-weight for ordinary fixed-breech guns for a variety of factory-loaded, commercial ammunition. It is, and can be, only approximate, for there are many factors involved that cause variations. Nevertheless, it is offered as a valid guide. American loads are tabulated since the velocity of these (and hence their recoil energy) is a matter regulated by the trade association to which their manufacturers belong.

	RECOIL VELOCITIES (F.P.S.)				
LOADS	**18**	**16**	**14**	**12**	**10**
10 ga. 3½ inch Magnum 2 oz	11¾	13¼	—	—	—
12 ga. 3 inch Magnum 1⅞ oz	10¾	12	—	—	—
12 ga. 3 inch Magnum 1⅝ oz	9¼	10½	—	—	—
12 ga. 2¾ inch Magnum 1½ oz	8¾	9½	—	—	—
12 ga. 2¾ inch 3¾ dr × 1¼ oz	7¼	8	—	—	—
12 ga. 2¾ inch 3¼ dr × 1¼ oz	6¾	7¼	8½	—	—
12 ga. 2¾ inch 3¼ dr × 1⅛ oz	6¼	7	8	—	—
12 ga. 2¾ inch 3 dr × 1⅛ oz	6	6½	7½	8¾	—
12 ga. 2¾ inch 3 dr × 1 oz	5¼	6	7	8	—
20 ga. 3 inch Magnum 1¼ oz	6½	7¼	—	—	—
20 ga. 2¾ inch Magnum 1⅛ oz	6	6¾	7½	—	—
20 ga. 2¾ inch 2¾ dr × 1 oz	5¼	6	6¾	—	—
20 ga. 2¾ inch Skeet ⅞ oz	4¾	5	5¾	6¾	8¼
28 ga. 2¾ inch Game ¾ oz	4½	4¾	5¼	6	7½
.410 2½ inch ½ oz	—	3	3¼	3¾	4½

TABLE I — Weights in Pounds of Ordinary Fixed-Breech Shotguns for certain Recoil-Velocities with American Factory Loads (approximate)

Figure 21   Closed Jaw   **Figure 22**   Open Jaw

The heavy type in Table I is in areas where ordinary fixed-breech guns of the normally obtainable range of weights for that ammunition would require weight to be added to them to reduce the recoil velocity to the level for that column. Few fixed-breech guns chambered for the 3½ inch Magnum 10-gauge exceed 10½ lbs and few 3 inch chambered 12-gauge guns or 2¾ inch chambered 12-gauges intended for field shooting 8 lbs, yet in ordinary fixed-breech designs heavier guns than these are necessary for comfortable shooting with the 10 and 12-gauge Magnum loads listed above. At the other end of the scale, 20 and 28-gauge fixed-breech guns much heavier than those readily available would be needed to bring recoil velocities down to levels desirable for juvenile beginners when using, for example, the 20-gauge skeet load, or the only 28-gauge commercial load readily available in North America. These, then, are the immediately obvious areas for the use of guns which, by reason of their design, spread out the recoil energy over a longer period, so that the peak velocity reached by the recoiling gun is lower. It must be said, though, that reducing recoil as felt by the shooter benefits the performance of all shooters (all other things: gun-fit, sharpness of trigger-pull, etc., being equal) under all circumstances (even when the recoil is reduced from ''very low'' to ''negligible'') and thus there is a case for the use in all kinds of shotgun shooting of guns which incorporate some kind of mechanism that reduces apparent recoil.

The principle of all such mechanisms is to use part of the energy generated by firing the gun to drive some movable part rearward against friction and spring pressure at the same time that the charge of shot is proceeding forward within the barrel. Instead of all the mechanical energy produced being transferred immediately to the shooter as in ordinary fixed-breech designs (my continual harping on the ''ordinary'' fixed-breech gun has a reason which will become apparent very shortly) part of it is lost to friction in the mechanism and part is stored as spring pressure. When the mechanism is in balance with the forces produced in firing the gun, or is adjusted to be so, the ''fixed'' parts of the gun (which always include the buttstock and the fore-end) are not able to reach the peak velocity of an ordinary fixed-breech gun of the same weight firing the same ammunition. Relaxing of the spring produces a relatively gentle ''push'' against the shooter after the, now lower, peak recoil velocity of the gun has passed.

The most usual guns of this type are various kinds of autoloader. In these, the reciprocation of parts during recoil is used to eject the fired case, to cock the lock, and

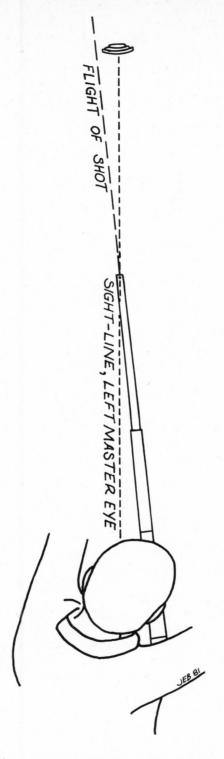

Figure 23 Cross-firing, Master Eye not over Gun

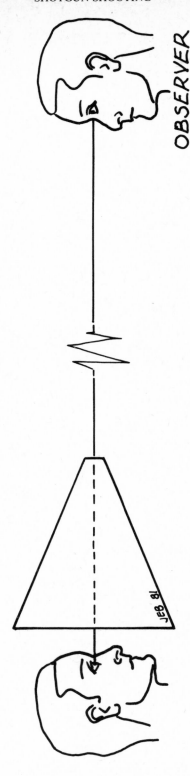

Figure 24   Testing for Master Eye

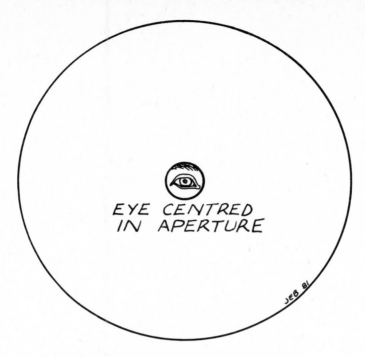

Figure 25 Observer's view of Master Eye

to close the breech bolt on a new cartridge from the magazine, the gun being then ready to fire again. The most successful autoloaders in terms of reducing the recoil-velocity of the gun (and perhaps the most successful in any terms) are those in which gas is tapped from the barrel into a separate cylinder where, expanding, it drives a piston actuating the mechanism. These gas-operated autoloaders are not particularly sensitive to variations in gas-pressures produced by the ammunition used in them, and not at all to the degree by which rearward movement of the gun as a whole is restricted by resistance from the shoulder. These last two properties are not common to all other (mainly older) types of autoloader, not gas-operated, and with these, to produce certainty of function with the occasional cartridge producing less than average pressure, or when they are not held as tightly as normal to the shoulder, it can be necessary to allow their moving parts to recoil against spring pressure and frictional drag less than those which would give correct functioning and maximum recoil attenuation with ammunition of normal pressure, and with the gun held firmly against the shoulder. With such guns, then, this may result in recoil velocity of the gun as a whole *greater* than that of a fixed-breech gun of the same weight firing the same load, though it must be said that this is an extreme case combating extremely irregular ammunition, or highly inconsistent gunmounting, or both.

Tapping of gas from the barrel to drive a piston rearward against spring pressure and friction, thus decreasing the peak recoil-velocity of the gun, is not confined to autoloaders. The same principle is used in the Remington Model 870 single-shot trap gun, a pump-action gun which has a gas-cylinder containing a piston and spring in the same position as the magazine tube on other pump guns. A Japanese over-and-under gun, not yet in production, has two tubes, each with piston and spring, one on each

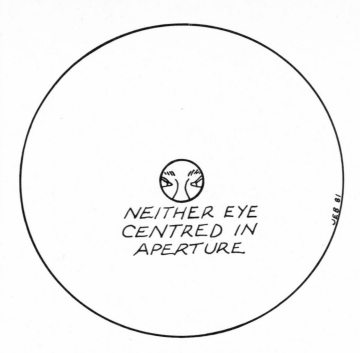

Figure 26   Observer's view, Central Vision

side of the barrels and concealed by the fore-end when the gun is assembled. Both barrels are connected by ports with both cylinders. Both the Model 870 single-shot and this Japanese over-and-under gun are fixed-breech types (i.e. the breech remains fixed until moved by the operator) but are quite different from ordinary fixed-breech guns in respect to recoil-velocity, and this is the reason for my use of the term "ordinary fixed-breech guns" for fixed-breech guns other than these.

The manufacturers of gas-operated autoloaders often claim that their gun "halves recoil" and, as they may be presumed to be referring to recoil energy (which is proportional to the square of the velocity of the recoiling gun) this would indicate that the recoil velocity of their particular autoloader is about 70 per cent of that of an ordinary fixed-breech gun firing the same ammunition. This accords well with published figures for measured reduction of recoil velocity. Table II has been calculated using this 70 per cent figure, together with typical weights for gas-operated autoloaders of the gauges and chamber-lengths in the heavy type areas of Table I. Also shown are figures for typical autoloading clay target guns with their usual loads. Note that:

  a) The recoil-velocities of the 10-gauge Magnum, the 3 inch case 12-gauge, and the 2¾ inch 12-gauge with the 1½ oz load, are all quite manageable.

  b) The 20-gauge and the 28-gauge with ⅞ oz and ¾ oz loads respectively, produce recoil velocities sustainable by the juvenile beginner from guns of a weight he or she can handle.

  c) The gas-operated 12-gauge clay-target guns all produce very low recoil velocities with typical loads. This has great advantages for the competition shooter.

Figure 27 Cast-off Stock for Central Vision

Figure 28 Cross-eyed Stock

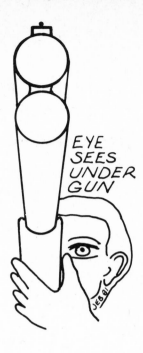

EYE
SEES
UNDER
GUN

Figure 29   View under Gun by Eye not above Breech

LOADS	GUN WEIGHT (lbs)	RECOIL VELOCITY (F.P.S.)
10 ga. 3½ inch Magnum 2 oz	11½	13
12 ga. 3 inch Magnum 1⅞ oz	9	14½
12 ga. 3 inch Magnum 1⅝ oz	9	13
12 ga. 2¾ inch Magnum 1½ oz	7½	14
12 ga. 2¾ inch 3¾ dr × 1¼ oz	7½	12
12 ga. 2¾ inch 3¼ dr × 1⅛ oz (International Trap & Skeet)	8	10
12 ga. 2¾ inch 3 dr × 1⅛ oz (American & English Skeet)	8	9½
12 ga. 2¾ inch 3 dr × 1⅛ oz (American & British Trap – DTL)	8½	9
20 ga. 2¾ inch Skeet ⅞ oz	6¾	8
28 ga. 2¾ inch ¾ oz	6½	8

TABLE II — Recoil-Velocities of Gas-Operated Autoloaders (approximate)

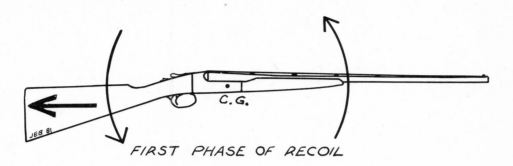

Figure 30   First phase of Recoil

Rubber recoil pads (or the better-designed ones!) decrease recoil as felt by the shooter by cushioning the shoulder. The principle involved is, again, to spread the force of the recoil over a longer period, thus reducing the peak velocity (this time of the rear face of the pad where it contacts the shooter). They are not so effective in this as is the mechanism of the gas-operated autoloader. Most pads are ribbed or roughened on the rear face, and this helps keep them, and hence the gun, in place at the shoulder for repeat shots. It is arguable that this is the most important property of the recoil pad. It is not one shared by those pads covered wholly in leather. In any case, it is the shooter's face and not his shoulder which is normally the greatest sufferer from excessive recoil, and it is now time to say something of the way in which recoil as felt by the shooter is affected by the manner in which the gun recoils and the effect of such factors as stock-shape on this.

In what I have called the "second phase" of recoil (Figure 31) the gun rotates upward about the shoulder as a pivot. It does this because the rearward movement of recoil is moving the centre of gravity of the gun in a direction which would carry it above the point at which this rearward movement is resisted by the shoulder of the shooter on the butt of the gun. In the terminology of Mechanics, a "couple" is created by the force of recoil and the resistance of the shoulder (R and S respectively in Figure 32). The greater the distance D between these forces the more the gun will rotate upward about the shoulder in recoil (all other things being equal). This depends partly on how much the gun has already rotated around the centre of gravity in the first phase of recoil (note that the direction the gun is moving rearward is not now parallel to the barrel/s) and partly on the drop at the heel of the stock, both of which tend to increase D. In using most shotguns this rotational component of the second phase of recoil,

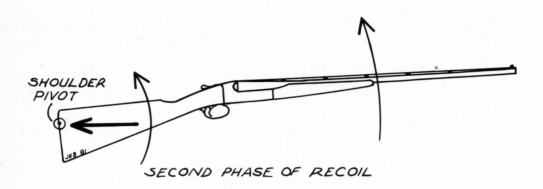

Figure 31 Second phase of Recoil

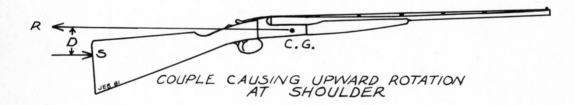

Figure 32 Couple causing rotation about Shoulder

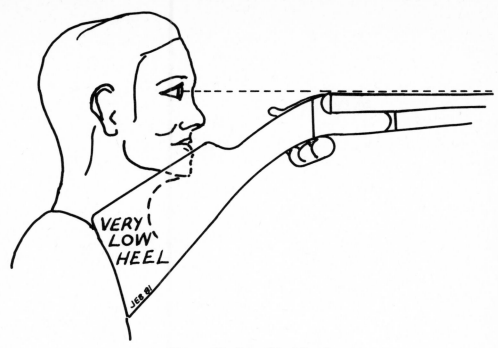

Figure 33 Low-Heel Stock

which tends to bring up the comb of the stock into firmer, and even sometimes forcible, contact with the shooter's face has greater potential and is more directly important in causing discomfort to the shooter than is the rearward movement of the gun. Of course, if the gun is very light indeed in relation to the load being shot from it the rearward movement of the gun as a whole may also be noticeably objectionable, as discussed above under recoil velocities.

The upward rotation of the gun about the shoulder is resisted by the weight of the gun, the more so the farther forward this weight is distributed. Having to lift the weight of the shooter's forward arm, too, helps to reduce the upward rotation of the gun. Obviously, the higher the heel of the stock can be made, and the shooter still be able to hit what he is shooting at (by adjustment of the other dimensions of the stock and modification of gunmounting technique to suit) the less will be the upward rotation of the stock and the less the discomfort arising from this.

Such modifications can take either of two forms, and both work in concert with the decreased upward rotation of the comb against the face just alluded to, to increase the shooter's comfort. In understanding this let us consider first the case of a stock with a very low heel. This is (indeed, can only be) used with the head held upright as viewed from the side, on a fairly well extended neck (Figure 33) thus allowing the eye to see over the breech when the gun is at the shoulder. Recoil of the gun drives the shoulder back, and if the recoil is heavy enough, causes the head to pivot downward and forward. This brings the face (and in particular the sensitive area under the cheekbone) down harder on the comb, at the same time that the comb itself (due to the low heel of the stock) is rising toward the face (Figure 34). The two tendencies therefore work together, with possibly painful results on the shooter unless the gun is quite heavy relative to the load being used.

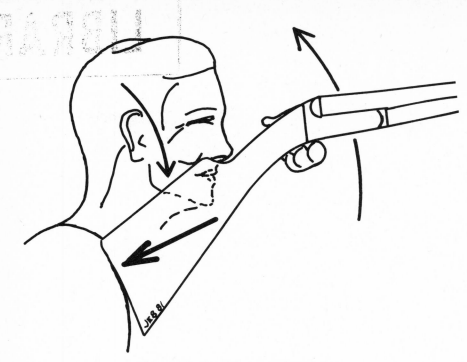

Figure 34   Recoil, Low-Heel Stock

By contrast, the high-heeled stock is shot in one of two ways, the shooter either bending forward (e.g. Figure 124, p. 168) or by shrugging up the shoulders and stiffening the musculature of the neck (e.g. Figure 102, p. 125). In the former attitude the shock of recoil from the rearward movement of the gun has little or no tendency to cause the head to rotate farther downward against the comb since the weight of the head is now a smaller vertical distance above the pivot. In the latter attitude, the stiffened musculature of the neck tends to prevent any forward dip of the head, and the head is farther back on the comb where actual upward rotation is a smaller quantity. And, in both instances, the high-heeled stock has less tendency than lower heeled types to rotate upward to boot! Again, we have two things working together, but this time for, rather than against, the comfort of the shooter.

With most stocks in use today a bruised cheek is usually the signal that the shooter has taken one or more shots with an upright head on an unbraced neck, and his face well off the comb prior to pulling the trigger (perhaps an inch or so). Note, however, that the comb of a stock may be so high (often it is an unmodified trap stock) that in order to shoot accurately (i.e. not to miss by overshooting, Figure 9) a particular user is forced to press his face down *hard* on it, so that the flesh under his cheekbone is already tightly sandwiched between bone and wood before he pulls the trigger. If so, then unless the design of the gun and the weight ratio of gun and load are such that recoil is very light and causes virtually no upward rotation of the gun, the results are likely to be very painful. A flinch, hard to eradicate, is in fact a certainty, and such a stock cannot be said to fit the user in any sense.

It is possible to design stocks that *reduce* the pressure on the face of the shooter during recoil, and the comfort given by such a design is a powerful incentive to seeking

LITTLE OR NO SPACE

Figure 35   Incorrect Grip, two-trigger Gun

such a stock in dimensions that fit the user and in learning to mount a gun so equipped. Such designs are particularly important when a shooter fires hundreds of shots in a day, as can happen in driven game shooting and American trapshooting and skeet-shooting. We shall look into this matter again where appropriate in the following parts of this book.

Really we have already begun to consider our second part of the way in which a gun recoils as this affects the shooter, this being whether or not some parts of the gun come into, or lose, contact with the shooter *after* recoil begins. If the former, then what he receives from them is a blow rather than a push. We have already seen how the stock comb may act thus. So may the butt of the gun if the stock is too short for the shooter (either totally, or for the style of gunmounting he uses). A stock that is actually, or effectively, too short is often mounted with the butt either in very light contact with the shoulder, or even some distance ahead of it. The shoulder, and the wrist of the rear hand, then both suffer, a good deal of the force of the recoil being caught by the latter.

If a double-barrelled gun with two triggers is shot with the rear elbow raised side-ways (so that the upper arm is somewhere near the horizontal) the stock is then grasped from the side (Figure 35). When the elbow is kept down the stock is then grasped rather from beneath (Figure 36). The former attitude brings the middle of the middle finger close to the back of the relatively long trigger-guard necessarily fitted to two-triggered guns to accommodate the twin triggers. In this position the finger is usually struck, more or less painfully, each time the gun is fired. Rubber rings around the rear of the trigger-guard to soften the blow are no solution. The lowered elbow is. A raised rear elbow is part and parcel of some shooting styles as we shall see. Such styles are unsuited to double-barrelled guns with two triggers.

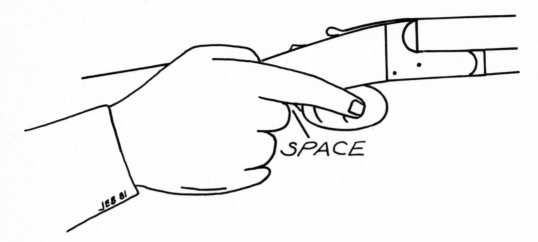

Figure 36   Correct Grip, two-trigger Gun

Further to reduce the apparent recoil of, mainly 12-gauge, guns certain specialist gunsmiths carry out such steps as porting the barrels with small holes or slots in various arrangements over a few inches behind the chokes, by lengthening the chamber cones, and by slight enlargement of the barrel-bores (often to about .740 inch in 12-gauge guns). Most of these guns are used in clay target competition, and for this kind of shooting an increasing number of new guns for this purpose embody these features. When a gun is to be used exclusively with ammunition having skirted plastic wads there seems little reason for it *not* to have long chamber cones, since these not only reduce recoil but deform the shot less and offer no problems in sealing the propellant gases when plastic wads are used, and the same applies to a slightly enlarged bore. The barrel-porting mentioned is so disposed as to keep the muzzle down when the gun is fired and hence to help prevent the stock comb rotating upward.

Before leaving the subject of the movements of the gun during recoil it is appropriate to say something of how these affect *where* a gun shoots. The shot leaves the muzzle when the gun has recoiled but a short distance, one which depends on the relative weights of gun and load, on the length of the barrel, and also on whether or not the gun is an ordinary fixed-breech type. The distance a gun recoils rearward before the shot is out of the muzzle is usually between ⅛th and ⅓rd of an inch, and very often about ¼ inch. Sufficient resistance from the shoulder is rarely encountered after so short a movement of the gun to cause it to enter the second phase of recoil (Figure 31) and begin pivoting upward about the shoulder. The shoulder is not a hard-faced object. Its musculature (or that of the upper arm if that is where the butt is resting) together with the layer of clothing that is usually over it, will generally yield these

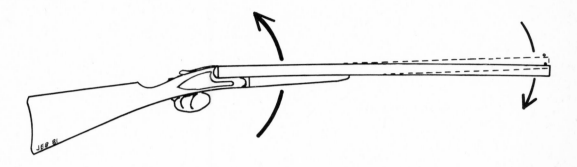

Figure 37   Downward flexing (down-flip) of Barrels

orders of distance before the butt encounters resistance stiff enough to cause the gun as a whole to pivot upward about the shoulder, and a soft recoil pad, if present will further delay the onset of this phase.

The shot generally leaves the gun, therefore, during the first phase of recoil (Figure 30). However, if the gun *is* in the second phase, pivoting upward about the shoulder, when the shot leaves the muzzle, then of course the behaviour of the gun in this second phase will affect where the gun shoots relative to the mark. Due to the firmness of contact between butt and shoulder in British styles of gunmounting (described in detail in the next chapter) the effect can be appreciable when these are used, an effect accentuated by the general lightness of guns used in Britain compared with the shot-loads often fired from them. This matter is looked into further in Chapter 2.

Returning to the general case: that in which the shot leaves the muzzle while the gun is still in the first phase of recoil, it might seem that due to the upward rotation of the barrel in this phase the charge would always strike above a point which was on a prolongation of the barrel axis at the time the trigger was pulled, in fact that the gun would always shoot high. However, this is far from being true of all guns. Of course, on its way to the target the shot drops a little way out of its original line of projection due to the effect of gravity, but more important causes of low shooting are to be found in the guns themselves. Some side-by-side double-barrelled guns have barrel-walls so thin, particularly towards their outward ends, that rotational movement of the gun in the first phase of recoil causes these barrels to flex downward to point *below* the mark by the time the shot load reaches the muzzle (Figure 37). The same tendency, arising from a different cause, is apparent in certain repeaters which have the

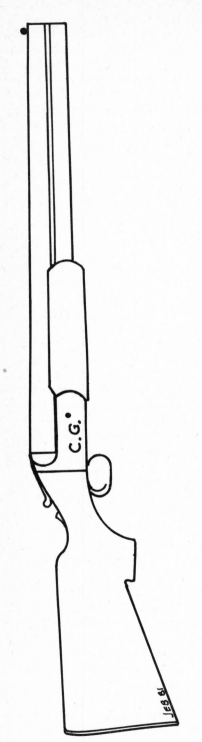

Figure 38   Centre of Gravity, Over-and-Under Gun

Figure 39   Centre of Gravity, Side-by-Side Gun

magazine tube fastened *onto* (rather than being screwed or soldered firmly *into*) the forward end of the receiver, thus affording but poor vertical support to the barrel. At 40 yards such guns often shoot a foot below a mark which was on a prolongation of the barrel-axis when the trigger was pulled. A higher-combed stock (with, perhaps, a rib especially high at the rear end) is a legitimate ''cure'' for the low-shooting double (if the shooter *must* have a gun of this type with the minimum of weight forward, it being doubtful if such a balance confers any advantage in any kind of shooting). However, repeaters with the fault in design described should simply be avoided, others being available.

The barrels of *most* over-and-under guns support each other so well that down-bending of the barrel-assembly in the first phase of recoil is negligible, and hence these guns have an inherent tendency to shoot above the mark. Since the barrels are at different heights relative to the centre of gravity of the gun (Figure 38) firing of the upper barrel causes more rotation of the gun in the first phase of recoil than does firing the lower one. To cause both barrels to shoot to the same elevation, therefore, they have to be converged towards the muzzles. You can think of this as raising the shooting of the lower barrel to coincide with that of the upper one.

Side-by-side double guns have the centre of gravity somewhere between the barrel axes in plan view (Figure 39). The barrels of most of these too, then, must converge muzzlewards to counteract the outward swing of the gun towards the fired barrel, and thus cause the barrels to shoot to a mark in line with the rib of the gun.

Some double-barrelled guns are so constructed that the barrels receive little support from each other. Often these show, and need, little barrel convergence. One example is those over-and-under guns whose barrels have no ribs between them, and are joined at the muzzles by an arrangement which allows them to slide back and forth relative to each other. The increased velocity of rotation of the gun about the centre of gravity when the upper barrel is fired, as compared to that when the lower barrel is fired, is often almost exactly counter-balanced by the greater down-flexing of the barrels under these circumstances. Note that the barrels receive much less support from each other against bending forces than they would were they securely fastened to each other from end to end. Thus, a near-parallel barrel-setting produces shooting to the same point by both barrels. Some side-by-side doubles of French origin have a light top-rib on the barrels, but nothing actually *between* the barrels except at breech and muzzle. The barrels of these guns, too, need but slight convergence to cause them to shoot together.

Barrel-convergence can only be absolutely correct for certain loads at certain velocities. With guns which are relatively light for the loads they are required to shoot (e.g. a 6½ lb, 2¾ inch chambered 12-gauge) it is often difficult to find more than one load with which both barrels shoot to the same point at, say, 40 yards (the usual testing range). Guns which are relatively heavy for the loads shot in them, being less disturbed by recoil, are less temperamental and demanding in this respect. Nevertheless, it is a good idea to test any kind of double-barrelled gun specifically to see whether or not the barrels shoot to the same point with the loads you wish, or might wish, to use in it. If it will not, there is little point in wasting time on a game or skeet gun in such efforts as fitting it with a stock that suits you: gunfitting cannot be carried out for two different points of impact from the same gun. Some double-barrelled guns are made which will not shoot both barrels to the same point with any load, and we shall return to this subject. Only in the special case of guns meant for trapshooting *may* this be intentional, as we shall see.

LEAD (FORWARD ALLOWANCE)

There is hardly a beginner in shotgun shooting who has thought about the matter at all who does not believe that leading the moving target is the thing about it that will give him most problems. The more he shoots the more certain becomes his realisation that this is not so.

Leading is actually easily learned. Willy-nilly and quite effortlessly the shooter learns how long it takes the shot charge, from whatever ammunition he uses, to cover the distance to the bird or target at all useful ranges. He learns to make use of this knowledge, knowledge that he is scarcely aware he has, with no conscious efforts at calculation, in moving the gun and placing the muzzle so that the shot charge hits the bird. He learns that under most circumstances he can (and if primarily a game, rather than a clay target, shooter probably does) hit without *conscious* reference to the relative disposition of the bird and the muzzle end of the gun at the moment he pulls the trigger (which relative disposition he certainly *sees*, though after the shot he may not remember doing so). He learns, too, that due to variations in some kind of personal factor, he needs to afford apparently identical targets more lead on some days than on others, the means of doing this depending on the method of leading he uses. Unless he belongs to the minority of "pure" Churchill-style shooters (a term which will be explained shortly and which we shall see again and again) he learns to recognise the range beyond which (due to the relatively large separation of muzzle and target needed to hit distant crossing birds) he does need to be conscious of, and to adjust, the gap between muzzle and bird. He learns that there are circumstances when he can *choose* to shoot with visible lead *or* by bringing the muzzle sufficiently rapidly from behind the bird that he can pull the trigger as the muzzle passes the bird — and hit it by either method.

A knowledge of *why* various methods of leading work does no harm and spoils nothing. Part of the analysis follows here and the rest is in the section on Churchill (the famous London gunmaker, not the statesman and politician!) in the next chapter. Nor is there anything wrong with being consciously aware, before the shot and after it, of where the gun was, and is, pointing relative to the bird or target. Indeed, it is axiomatic that to be in the top rank of clay pigeon competitors, for example, one must diligently cultivate such an awareness. It is true that many game shooters, ranked as competent by their fellows, do not *notice* where the gun was pointing at these times (they cannot avoid *seeing* it of course, for it is in the centre of their field of vision!). But after the shot many of them rarely remember where the gun was pointing when they pulled the trigger, or can only do so with a great deal of effort. But, to elevate this state of affairs into a *rule* for good shooting (by saying, for example, that good shooting depends on not knowing where the gun is pointing when the trigger is pulled) is ludicrous. Many of the most competent shooters of game, as well as virtually all of the same class in clay target competition, *do* notice the relationship of barrel to bird on virtually every shot. Those others, the ones who say, for example "You should never see the gun, or be conscious of where it is pointing relative to the bird, or you can't possibly shoot well", will, in the next breath, tell the shooter to "Shoot straight at the bird!", or, "Point at the bird all the time you are mounting the gun", instructions difficult indeed to carry out if the shooter cannot see, and obeys adjurations *not* to see, where the gun is pointing!

Leading is quickly learned, and once learned stays with one. Correct gunmounting is equally quickly learned, *if the shooter is shown how it is done* (which is part of the purpose of this book) but gunmounting differs from leading in that the very best shooters are apt occasionally to put up the gun to shoulder and face improperly, even when plenty of time is available for the purpose. They may even lapse into chronic error of this kind. This is something that every shotgunner has to guard against all his shooting life. Gunmounting styles (*how* gunmounting is carried out) depend on the type of gunstock adopted by the shooter (and vice versa) and this subject forms the greater part of the next chapter. The point I am trying to make here is this: that when a seasoned and hitherto successful shotgunner seeks a coach because, suddenly, he has started to miss birds (sometimes almost all of them) it isn't because he has suddenly forgotten how to lead. Consider how unlikely that would be when every successful shot he has made over the years has put still further data on lead into his personal "computer". Usually, in fact, he has started to err in the way he puts the gun up to face and shoulder, and perhaps consistently so, and a competent coach can see if this is the trouble within a few shots.

There is a school of writers on shotgun shooting, particularly prevalent in Britain, that worships at the shrine of the "natural shot" ("natural shooter" in American terms), a subspecies of the "gifted amateur". The typical story involving this phenomenon runs as follows: A chap turns up one day at an establishment where shotgun shooting is taught and coached, shoots a lot of clay targets, and then asks the coach how he fared by comparison with others who shoot, and have shot, there. The ancient instructor, his face full of awe and wonder, tells the shooter that seldom, if ever, in his life has he seen anyone shoot so well, and, further, that our hero should never risk flawing this naturally-perfect performance by reading in the future *anything* on the techniques of shotgun shooting, preferably not discussing it either with less-favoured people, lest *thinking* about shooting get in his way and cause him to hesitate in what he is doing, thus undermining his prowess.

The origin of the "natural shot" lies in his having obtained, by chance or otherwise, a gun with a stock that suits his, often untutored, style of gunmounting, and hence which "shoots where he looks", and in *no more than that*. Presuming normal faculties and reflexes, and a degree of practice, most people quickly learn how to point and move such a gun to hit what they are shooting at. Again: lead is not a problem. So long as nothing changes, the "natural shot" goes on his merry, successful, way. If something *does* change: a new gun not quite like the old one, a different trigger pull, a face grown fatter with the years, an unnoticed change in gunmounting — he begins to miss as consistently as he was accustomed to hit. The magic, which never existed in the first place, is gone, and then *think* he must. Let us hope that his first thought is to seek a coach capable of diagnosing what has gone wrong.

Reading will do him no harm either. He will find that there are many books in which the author gives an account, sometimes with admirable clarity, of how he personally goes about the business of hitting with the shotgun, but few which attempt to be comprehensive in at least mentioning different styles of gunmounting and the gunfitting that goes with each, as well as the different, consistently successful methods of leading the moving target which are available to the shooter. It is an objective in writing this book to be exhaustive in these matters, and to demonstrate the fundamentals of the variety of shooting styles and methods of leading in use today, comparing and contrasting those in common use in different parts of the world. These include the integrated method of gunmounting and leading associated with the name of the English gunmaker Robert Churchill. This method, allowing one to shoot, apparently, straight at any crossing bird and still hit it (despite having given it no lead discernible to oneself, the shooter) has been a source of (often bitter) controversy among shooters for over half a century, ever since it was first advocated at any length in print, in fact, in a little book by Churchill first published in the 1920's. Actually the system Churchill advocated was not new (few things in shotgun shooting are ever wholly so) but earlier advocacies in print are short and caused no great stir. Churchill's early book was incorporated into another, larger, book carrying his name which appeared after World War II and has circulated internationally.

Churchill himself said that his books were "drills" to be followed religiously. They had to be. He himself seems not to have had any scientific knowledge as to why his method, carried out properly, works. Or if he had, he was unsuccessful in conveying it to the ghost writers who put together his books. Thus, in advocating the method, and in teaching it to others, he didn't dare to leave out any detail: the one he left out might be the key to the success of the whole package! His disciples (not too strong a word) do the same today. Their influence on the literature of shotgun shooting (though not matched by that on common practice) and the attraction of the possibility of learning how to shoot, apparently, directly at a crossing bird and still hit it, have been and are so strong that in America today, for example, it is usual for writers to refer to the "Churchill" style as the "English style". In fact, it is but one of three peculiarly British styles, and the minority one at that.

Like Churchill himself, none of his followers who have appeared in print has so far analysed what he, and they were, and are, doing, let alone why, carried out properly, it is successful as a technique. Or none that I have encountered at least. Various pseudo-analyses are to be found in what they have written, but most Churchillians (particularly when it is demonstrated to them that their "explanations" and the laws of Physics cannot both be true) revert eventually to saying: "Well, just do thus and so anyway, and you'll hit". However, this happy result does not by any means always accrue, much depending on the physiology of the shooter, the interpretation he puts on the advice he has just received, and not least on the average order of range at which his targets present themselves. Unfortunately, perhaps following in the footsteps of the often testy Churchill, there is in the writings of the Churchill school a strong suggestion that theirs is the only proper way to shoot a shotgun, and that those in the rest of the shooting world who do not use it all the time (virtually everyone uses a kind of "Churchill" style on some shots as we shall see) are simply pedestrian piddlers. Which includes the majority of shooters everywhere, including Britain, and is not an attitude conducive to persuading that majority to investigate the "Churchill" method fully and to give it a fair trial. There is a fine bit of irony here, too, in that the "Churchill" method is best suited to people of somewhat slow reflexes, which is to say long reaction-times. The explanations for all this we shall get to in due time in the next chapter.

People who already shoot successfully by leading birds in what I shall term in this book the "majority method" (because it is the one used by most shooters: I shall describe it immediately) on reading accounts of the "Churchill" method advocating shooting straight at crossing birds with no lead apparent to the shooter, usually dismiss it as nonsense that just can't work, and leave it at that. If they actually do try it, unless they are in the hands of an instructor who is thoroughly conversant with the physical requirements of the style (if not always with the reasons behind these) they usually do indeed fail to "make it work", thus "proving" to themselves that they were right in believing that it couldn't.

One thing is sure: to hit a crossing bird or clay target travelling at normal speeds and

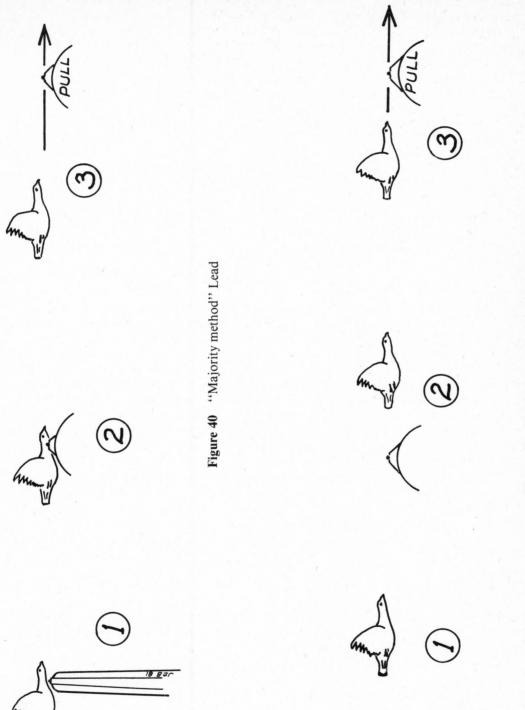

Figure 40   "Majority method" Lead

Figure 41   "Majority method" Lead modified

more than a few yards from the shooter, the gun must be pointing ahead of it when the shot leaves the muzzle or the pellets will pass harmlessly behind whatever is being shot at. This is true no matter where the gun *seems* to the shooter to be pointing when he pulls the trigger. For a bird flying at a certain speed at a certain distance from the shooter, the lead needed to hit it, measured at right-angles to the flight-path of the shot charge, is at a maximum when the bird crosses this line of fire at a right-angle, is less when the bird is quartering obliquely towards or away from the shooter, and is of course zero when the bird is a straight incomer or outgoer along any line of sight. Yet some shooters maintain, truthfully, that they shoot straight at everything and manage to hit their share of birds, including the right-angle crossers.

Mystified? So was I, even though I, too, like virtually everyone else, *did it on some shots* (point straight at the right-angle crosser and hit it squarely, I mean) specifically on short-range, fast, birds. I was determined to understand what those shooters who did it habitually on birds at all ranges, near and far, were doing, and why they were successful. Before I arrived at that understanding I had to learn to ignore what most of them said (and honestly thought) they did. In the course of watching all kinds of shotgun shooters, and learning, myself, to shoot in different styles, with stocks suited to these, on both sides of the Atlantic, I arrived at the analyses of shooting styles and gunfitting for them which constitute the next chapter of this book.

Enough of generalities!

A bird crosses in front of Mr. Average Competent Shotgunner anywhere in the world. He decides it is legitimate game and within range. Concentrating on, and hence fixing his vision on the bird, he begins to bring his gun up to face and shoulder, the muzzle visually on, and keeping pace with the bird as he does so. Without pause, as the gun comes fully up to the face and into the shoulder, he looks ahead of the speeding bird. The muzzle "follows the eye", racing ahead of the bird. The shooter then pulls the trigger while keeping the gun moving (and indeed accelerating) as in Figure 40. He may not consciously take note of the lead he uses on the shot, either as a space visible between muzzle and bird or a time-lapse between the muzzle leaving the bird and his pulling the trigger, particularly if the shot was a quick one at a close-range bird. Or he may. However, the "sight-picture" or the time-lapse, and perhaps both, do register on his subconscious, adding to his experience.

This is the "majority method" of leading (or "giving forward allowance") I mentioned above, the way that nearly all the world's shotgunners shoot nearly all of the time. It is, for example, the common method among the millions of shotgunners of America. Usually preceded by one or other of two styles of gunmounting* differing from those typical of America (and, incidentally, of the rest of the world) it is also the method of leading taught at nearly all shooting schools in Britain, all in fact except those (there may now remain only one) with a strong Churchillian tradition. It is also the approved successful method taught by the coaches of the British clay pigeon shooting associations. So much for Churchill's method being the standard thing in the United Kingdom!

Notice several things:

1. Since the gun is still accelerating as the trigger is pulled, the muzzle moving faster than the bird, the *apparent* lead needed to hit the bird (that lead seen, but perhaps not consciously noticed, by the shooter) is somewhat less than the *actual* lead given. This is because the muzzle moves still farther ahead of the bird, a distance un-

---

*Termed "Standard British" and "Modern British" in this book.

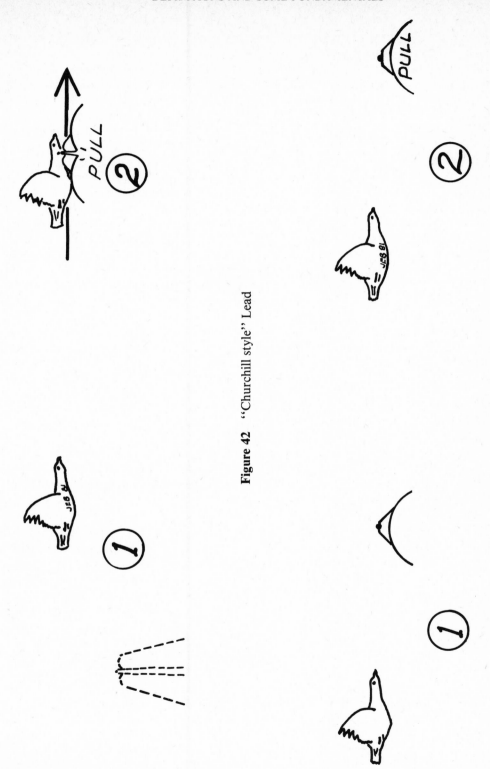

Figure 42 "Churchill style" Lead

Figure 43 "Sustained" Lead

appreciated by the eye, in the interval between the decision to pull the trigger, and the trigger actually being pulled. Thus:

a) It is possible to cut down the apparent lead needed for fast crossing birds (which starts to be a useful thing to be able to do if these are much beyond 28 to 30 yards range) if the shooter gives himself more space in which to accelerate the gun. This is achieved by pointing the gun as it is mounted, not at the bird, but at an imaginary spot a little behind (and keeping pace with) it, then looking ahead of the bird as described above, which causes acceleration of the muzzle "through" the bird and beyond it (Figure 41). Because the muzzle is now moving still faster relative to the bird, less apparent lead is needed to hit the latter than would be necessary if pointing during gunmounting had been at the bird itself.

b) Taking this a stage further (and again beginning gunmounting with the gun pointing behind the bird): if the muzzle is made to move still faster relative to the bird, a point is reached when *no* visible lead at all is required, and if the trigger is pulled as the muzzle passes the bird the latter will be hit by the shot charge (Figure 42). This is the essence of what I have called the "Churchill" method, and at this point the "majority" method has been left behind. The pure "Churchill" style differs from the "majority" method in that the vision is wholly concentrated on the bird throughout. It has a section to itself in the next chapter.

c) Conversely, if the shooter mounts the gun pointing some distance ahead of the bird, all he can do is to adjust the space between muzzle and bird to the required lead, and pull the trigger while keeping the gun moving (Figure 43). The shooter looks at the bird throughout, seeing the muzzle (less distinctly) to one side of it. There is no acceleration of the muzzle relative to the bird, and the apparent lead required is the actual lead needed to hit the bird. This is the "sustained lead" method used, for example, by many (and perhaps most of the expert) skeet shooters. Obviously, to use the method, the shooter *must* see the lead quite consciously. This is the only method in which the lead as it is apparent to the shooter does not depend on the speed with which his muscles answer the dictates of his brain. In all other methods the apparent lead needed does so depend, and hence the apparent leads a shooter needs when using them are as personal as his reaction-time. As the latter also varies a little from day to day (even from hour to hour) in the same person, it would seem to be common sense for the competition shooter to choose, when he can, a method of leading unaffected by such variations. In skeet shooting such a choice is possible for almost everyone on most of the targets.

2. Since in using any method of leading other than "sustained lead" the right apparent lead for a particular bird or target is different for different people, the correct leads to cover all circumstances (fast birds and slow, near and far, quarterers and crossers) in terms of distance for the "majority" method and variations thereof, and in the speed with which the muzzle overtakes the bird for the "Churchill" method, have to be found by each shooter for himself, thus building up an account in the bank of experience, an account from which withdrawals are usually made quite subconsciously. People with short reaction-times show little delay between the decision to pull the trigger and the action of doing so. To get a certain actual lead, therefore, they have to pull the trigger with the gun pointing visibly farther ahead of the bird and/or to accelerate the gun faster (the latter alone in the case of the "Churchill" method) than do people with longer reaction-times. In using the "majority method" they must look farther ahead of the bird as they decide to pull

the trigger. Everyone has to find their personal equation, but using the clay target this is neither a long nor a painful process. Obviously the equation is one that alters when the shooter uses a gun different in weight, inertia or trigger-pull from the one he used in arriving at his existing equation. A different gun has to be "got used to" for this reason. A famous British coach is said to instruct his pupils that, having obtained a gun that suits them, never even to pick up someone else's gun, or at least never to put it up to face and shoulder. It should be added that despite all this, and the variations in reaction-time of any particular shooter, leading methods other than the "sustained lead" are the usual thing in shotgun shooting as a whole, the one I have termed the "majority method" being exactly that.

3. In all methods except the "Churchill" method the bird is used as a moving reference point, and as we shall see later it is in this regard that the "Churchill" method may be said principally to differ from the rest. In all others the gun is always pointed first at the bird (or at an imaginary spot moving along a constant distance behind or ahead of it) and there is a very short period during which the muzzle just keeps pace with the bird while it is thus pointed. The muzzle is then accelerated, or otherwise adjusted to the right relationship with the bird, depending on their relative velocities, and the trigger is pulled while the gun is kept moving. In this, it may be observed, there is some variation possible in the timing of the full mounting of the gun to face and shoulder relative to the time at which the right lead is obtained or seen by the shooter (I am not here writing of those competitions in which it is customary for all taking part to mount the gun before calling for a target). Though in the "Churchill" "no-lead" method the gun is always triggered simultaneous with its reaching face and shoulder, among "majority method" and "sustained lead" shooters one can observe those who habitually mount the gun fully and then go about producing the right apparent lead, and others who do not put up the gun fully until the lead is right, pulling the trigger as the stock comes to face and shoulder. In these latter styles, it must be said that not fully mounting the gun until all is right to shoot gives a compact finish to the swing that tends not only to give greater accuracy than does a long uncontrolled movement of the gun, but also to keep the gun going until after the shot is away: and a good "follow through" is vital to successful shotgun shooting.

However, for birds or targets appearing to rise steeply towards 12 o'clock in front of the shooter (for example, the "springing teal" targets of Sporting clay target layouts) or which, oppositely, dive straight down towards 6 o'clock (for example, the High House skeet target viewed from Station 1) the key to success is to mount the gun fully to face and shoulder first, pointing at the target, and then adjust the lead. To do otherwise means that often the butt will be mounted too high or too low on the shoulder, and a miss will usually result from this. As might be anticipated, the "Churchill" method (we don't seem able to get away from piecemeal discussion of it, but all will be brought together in the next chapter) is inherently unsuited to such targets. In fact, when shooting high-overhead, straight-incomers (effectively rising straight towards 12 o'clock in front of the shooter if you think about it) Churchill habitually resorted to, and recommended, un-Churchillian makeshift methods we shall examine in the appropriate place.

4. In no method of leading is the gun *aimed*. The gun is *not looked at*. The focus is in the area of the target. However, in the "majority" and "sustained lead" methods, well before the time comes to pull the trigger, the gun is seen clearly enough for its direction of pointing to be discernible to the shooter. The upper surface of the gun

from breech to muzzle may in fact be wholly in the field of view right from the beginning of gunmounting proper. It is important to remember this for comparison with the Churchill method.

5. Because the shooter can see the apparent lead as he fires, and may even remember after the shot what it looked like, does not mean (I repeat!) that the apparent lead is a matter of conscious calculation, let alone one with an answer in feet and inches and undertaken during gunmounting. Experience of what are the correct apparent leads to hit the target under various circumstances is quickly acquired (very quickly if the shooter sets out deliberately to find them using clay targets) and once acquired, the right lead is given without conscious effort, though the size of the lead may be noticed by the shooter if he makes a conscious effort to do this, and if he tries to remember what it was after the shot he may find himself able to do so. He may miss the bird, note, for other reasons, even though he produced the right apparent lead! Conscious knowledge of what his leads are for a wide variety of targets is essential to the clay target competitor. And there is no harm whatsoever for *anyone* in knowing how he obtains the necessary lead on a crossing bird, nor in knowing that there are different ways in which it can be obtained. It is great fun (and a post-graduate course of great utility) deliberately to practise different methods of leading: "majority", "sustained" and the "Churchill" "no-lead" method described in the next chapter. This can be done on clay targets crossing the shooter's front at a variety of ranges and speeds, and from either side.

6. Note that if a shooter misses targets crossing left to right by shooting behind them, and targets crossing right to left by shooting ahead of them (or hits one set and not the other, and this pretty consistently) the error is not in leading. The most likely cause is a bad fit of gun to shooter, so that in the example given, for instance, the gun is simply shooting to the left (left of where the shooter looks, that is) and if this is indeed the cause proof will be obtained by shooting at straightaway targets, when the centres of the patterns will pass to the left of them. The second most likely cause is that a shooter swinging towards his gun side sometimes falls into the habit of moving the gun away from his face (by swinging with his arms alone instead of the whole of his upper body) the result being that his eye is no longer above the breech and on that side he tends to shoot behind his targets (Figure 11). The author begs the pardon of the reader for stating such obvious facts, but he has so often heard advice of the kind: "You need more lead on your targets going to the right, and less on those going left" (or vice versa) when the real trouble lay in gun-fit or the dangerous habit of swinging with the arms alone, that he felt something had to be said! There is even some advice of this kind in certain books on trapshooting, and it seems likely that the authors of these shoot a little to one side of centre with the stocks they use, or have fallen into the habit of a disconnected swing.

Chapter 2

Shotgun Stocks
and Shooting Styles

THE CROOKED STOCK

The so-called "crooked stock" is the oldest type of shotgun stock, being the type found on the flintlock fowling pieces of the late 17th and the 18th centuries: the first guns used with consistent success for "shooting flying".

The term refers to stocks having a heel-drop of 3 inches or more (4½ inches is not unknown) and a straight comb (i.e. a comb without a "Monte Carlo" step in it). The drop at the comb nose is generally not less than 1¾ inches, and 2 inches is usual.

At this point it is necessary to say something about the posture of the shotgunner. Many authors on shotgun shooting write as if there were something quite "natural" about the stance and the style of gunmounting they recommend, no matter what these are. They cannot have had much to do with beginning shooters, despite their presumption to instruct. Nine out of ten beginners lean backwards to counterbalance the weight of the gun, and almost the same proportion do not turn the body sufficiently sideways as to bring:

a) The breech-end of the rib directly under the eye (presuming the shape of the stock allows them to do this, the head being upright as viewed from the muzzle, and not canted sideways over the stock).

b) The fore-end within easy reach of the forward hand.

Any would-be shotgunner, then, has to learn two "tricks" immediately, these being not to lean backwards against the weight of the gun, and not to stand too squarely to what is being shot at.

The beauty of the crooked stock is that, even for shooting at low and fairly low birds (not a little matter as we shall see a little later in this chapter) the user needs virtually no other "tricks"! When a gun thus stocked is raised to the shoulder by anyone of fairly normal physical dimensions in the least sophisticated way possible (our two "tricks" aside): the head erect, the neck at more or less its full extension, and the shoulders raised no more than they rise naturally with the arms in mounting the gun to face and shoulder, it will be found that the deep heel-drop of the stock allows the butt to meet the shoulder in the "pocket" between shoulder and chest, and the comb to cross the jaw, while the barrel (pointing horizontally or at a slight upward angle) lies a trifle

HEAD AND
BODY ERECT

JEB 81

Figure 44 Shooter with Crooked Stock

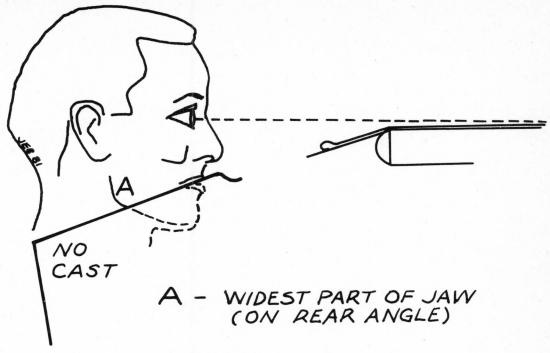

NO CAST

A - WIDEST PART OF JAW (ON REAR ANGLE)

Figure 45 Fit, Crooked Stock

below, and in line with, the eye on that side (Figure 44). If there is indeed a "natural" manner of gunmounting and a "natural" stock for it, then surely these are they, and it is not surprising to find them in use in the earliest days of true shotgunning.

The only point at which such a stock touches the shooter's face at all firmly is where the comb crosses his jaw. Forward of this the comb lies against the side of the jaw, passing well below the front of the cheekbone (Figure 45). Very minor movement of the head before gunmounting makes it quite easy for almost anyone to place their jaw on a comb of the dimensions given in such a way that the barrel comes in line with the eye in the lateral sense. Since the comb contacts a relatively narrow part of the face (rather than the widest part of the jaw, A in Figure 45) even for the widest-jawed of shooters no casting of the stock is required to allow the eye to be placed squarely above the breech. Nor does he need to cant his head sideways over the stock. Cast is unusual on crooked stocks of any period.

The crooked stock is one of only two kinds of stock that can be used when the shooter is wearing any kind of high, hard, or thick collar, coming well up under the ears and chin. Such collars, in fact, as our ancestors have affected at various times in history, even when shooting! Since in using them the shooter's head is erect, crooked stocks can be, and usually are, relatively short without the shooter's nose being in danger of being struck by his fingers during recoil. Lengths of 13 to 14 inches are usual.

Until about two hundred years ago, such "crooked" shotgun stocks were the norm virtually everywhere in Europe and North America. They remained the usual choice of the American hunter until about a hundred years ago. Such stocks are still in use. Modern American authors who mention this type of stock at all almost all do so only to poke fun at it, and to wonder out loud how anyone could have put up with such a thing at all, let alone used it habitually and all their lives. Though it is not long since such stocks were in fairly common use in Britain (a fact for which we have photographic evidence, though they were replaced as the majority choice much earlier) modern British authors never mention them at all! It is doubtful if the belittlers of the crooked stock have ever used a gun with such a stock, let alone for long enough to get used to the mounting style it needs, for had they done so it is unlikely that they would be so condemnatory. The fact is that for game shooting such a stock is perfectly usable if the other factors (specifically gun weight vs. shot load and velocity) are right.

When a crooked-stock gun is put to the shoulder and face in the way described above, its natural pointing elevation is, as noted, about horizontal or a little above this. Guns fitted with modern, American-style factory stocks ("field" types as well as those intended for trap and skeet) have combs, and more so, heels, much higher than those on crooked-stock guns, and hence point (as we shall see later in this chapter) well above the horizontal when mounted to the shoulder and an erect head as described above for the crooked stock. But this does not mean that the crooked stock is something tolerable only for shots at targets at low elevations and useless for anything else! It may be noted here in passing that the British styles of gunmounting described later in this chapter all result in a "natural" point which is horizontal or a trifle higher, yet are precisely those used with spectacular success on (among other things) driven birds at high to vertical angles. Despite what has been written by some modern authors, the same success can be attained with the crooked-stock gun in shooting at high-angle birds as at birds at head-height if care is taken to maintain the same dispositions of head to stock comb and stock to shoulder. This has to be done with any and every kind of stock, and is not perceptibly harder with the crooked stock than with any other. The proof of the efficiency of the crooked stock, if the shooter is used to it and the other factors are right, can be seen in its long use in America on muzzle and breechloading shotguns (right through the 19th century indeed). These included domestic and imported guns for the use of the market hunter of ducks and geese, most of whose shooting was at birds at angles well above the horizontal, and who was so successful at this that he had reduced the numbers of waterfowl to a tithe of their former abundance *before* the repeater became the common gun.

If the crooked stock was so satisfactory on these guns the obvious question is one that asks why so few guns are so stocked today: "What killed the crooked stock?". The answer can be given in two words: increased recoil.

As we saw in the first chapter, all else being equal, the more "crooked" the stock:
a) The more the gun rotates upward in the second phase of recoil, and
b) The more the shock applied to the shoulder by the rearward movement of the gun tends to jerk down the head against the rising comb.

We saw, too, that the combination of these effects is usually far more important than is the rearward movement itself in causing discomfort to the shooter, though if the gun is very light in relation to the load being shot, this rearward movement may also become objectionable.

The crooked-stock flintlock fowling pieces of the 17th and 18th centuries were mainly single-barrelled guns. They had barrels as long as 46 inches, but they balanced well between the hands and pointed quickly and easily. Nor were they heavy guns. Gauge for gauge they weighed about the same as modern British and European side-by-side double game guns, from about 5½ lbs for a 20-gauge to 6¾ lbs for a 12-gauge. Possibly most popular of all were guns of about 16-gauge and 6 lbs. Shot loads, too, were about what would be used in guns of these gauges in Britain and Europe today, ranging from a 20-gauge load of ¾ oz to 1¼ oz in 12 and 11-gauge guns. There were some heavier guns of larger gauges used mainly in shooting at flocks of waterfowl (*on* the water . . . .).

Later guns of such weights (flintlock and percussion-cap muzzleloaders, and breechloaders) matched with the shot loads mentioned and each loaded in the way normal for that type of gun, would, if fitted with crooked stocks, produce recoil in terms of face punishment quite unbearable after a few shots. Yet these earlier flintlock fowling pieces were comfortable to shoot, and it is interesting to see why.

The reason is that, until the development of various kinds of patent breeches in the final third of the 18th century (the most famous was Nock's) smoothbore guns in particular burned their black powder very inefficiently. The resulting shot-velocities were a good deal lower than those we are used to today, and recoil was proportionately less. There was another bonus: the low velocities resulted in shot scattering less widely from the choke-less barrels of the time (added velocity always tends to give a wider spread of shot, other things being equal). Few of these barrels were truly cylindrical internally. Owing to their mode of manufacture most were of slightly greater internal diameter at breech and muzzle than in the middle of their length. Incidentally, barrels continued to be made thus centrally-constricted (despite being manufactured differently) perhaps following tradition, perhaps responding to a feeling that some modification of internal diameters must be better than making the barrel truly cylindrical, until about 1870, at which time the knowledge and practice of choke-boring to control shot spread became general among gunmakers. At that time gun-makers began to take pains to ensure that as far as possible their barrels, excluding any choked section at the muzzle, were true cylinders from the chamber-cone forward.

The more efficient burning of powder in patent-breech flintlock guns raised the muzzle velocity of the shot charges, and with it the recoil of the gun. Thus was disturbed the equilibrium which had hitherto existed between shot charge, muzzle velocity, gun weight and stock shape. Nevertheless, since the patent breech virtually eliminated those occasional shots when the powder burned so slowly as to give the shot charge a quite uselessly low velocity, shooters adopted the device with enthusiasm.

Several means were available to reduce apparent recoil to its former, manageable, levels. The most obvious one: reducing the powder charge to bring down muzzle velocity, and with it recoil, was not the choice of most shooters. The rise in velocity, by cutting down required leads for the ''majority method'' leaders, made hitting birds noticeably easier for most shooters.

Another means: reducing the weight of the shot load hitherto regarded as normal for a certain weight and gauge of gun, was not something generally seriously contemplated either. Though increased velocity had made it easier to intercept the bird with the shot charge, at the same time it caused pellets to spread more widely at any range. Thus, at farther ranges particularly, it was easier to *hit* the bird, but some birds that formerly would have been killed were now being struck by too few pellets to bring them down. Things were helped to some extent by the general improvement in the last quarter of the 18th century in the quality of lead shot available to the shooter, but increased velocity resulted in means being sought of shooting *heavier* shot charges in comfort.

Two other means were left open to decrease recoil as felt by the shooter: to increase the weight of the gun firing a particular load of shot (thus decreasing its rearward and rotational velocities in recoil) and, still more effective, to reduce the heel-drop of the stock. This last reduces the punishment of the shooter's face, not only by decreasing the tendency of the gun to swing upward in recoil, but by requiring a style of gun-mounting at low birds in which the head and neck (and body) are already tilted forward, so that the head is less likely to be jerked downward against the comb by the recoil of the gun. I should make it clear here (for reasons which will become apparent later in this chapter) that I am not considering stocks with appreciable cast at this time, and neither did the gunmakers at the time we are discussing.

In Britain and Europe guns became heavier and heel-drops less, and in the twenty years before 1800 the heyday of the crooked stock came to an end in that part of the world, though the occasional new British gun made for a British shooter was fitted with such a stock until about 1900.

However, in America the fortunes of the crooked stock did not decline for another hundred years after they faded on the east side of the Atlantic. Perhaps because he was used to seeing and using crooked-stock rifles, the American hunter went on demanding similarly-stocked smoothbores. After the invention of the patent breech and its application to the flintlock gun, and right through the percussion-cap muzzleloading, and early breechloading, periods, American smoothbores continued to be crooked-stock guns. To be usable thus stocked they had to be relatively heavy overall (relative to the shot charge) as well as heavy forward, and they were. For the first 80 years of the 19th century 12-gauges of 9 lbs and 10-gauges of 10 lbs were the norm in America, the former shooting but 1 to 1⅛ oz of shot and the latter a maximum of 1¼ oz. Whereas today American loads for a particular gauge tend to be heavier than those usual in the rest of the world, the opposite was true in the 19th century. Not until after 1900, indeed, was the crooked stock quite supplanted on new American guns by stocks of the dimensions we are used to seeing on such guns today (as well as on other guns whose makers have copied American guns in this regard). The 19th century American hunter needed, and got, a robust gun which would stand up to the rough and tumble of the conditions in which it was used, a gun that would withstand hard knocks from the *outside*. In essence this means a gun with a stout barrel or barrels, these (always *relatively* thin-walled) tubes being the most vulnerable feature of any shotgun. The fashionable barrel-lengths were greater than those of today. The result was heavy guns with a lot of weight forward. Though the crooked stock on the American shotgun of the 19th century was mainly a matter of fashion, an imitation of the American rifle-stocks of the day, it was a sustainable fashion. The stock was in equilibrium with the weight and balance of the guns and the loads with which they were used.

In contrast to what happened in late-18th century Britain a hundred years earlier (when increased velocity was the factor that disturbed the equilibrium between the fowling piece and its load) the heavy, crooked-stock, American double-barrelled gun of the 19th century was simply removed from the scene, locks, stock and barrels, by two factors. One was the success and prominence of British guns in American live pigeon trapshooting, guns as much as 2 lbs lighter than their American-made counter-parts, and stocked with drops of about 1½ inches at the comb and as little as 2 inches at the heel (and still usually with little or no cast). The other factor was the develop-ment of successful repeating shotguns, again (and inherently) a good deal lighter in weight than the then current American crooked-stock doubles. We shall pick up this historical account again farther on in this chapter.

As for the crooked stock since then: its story is not yet finished and may never be. American manufacturers of replacement "semi-finished" shotgun stocks go on listing such stocks with heel-drops of as much as 3½ and 4 inches, for a wide variety of factory-built guns. There is a steady demand for such stocks from these sources, and

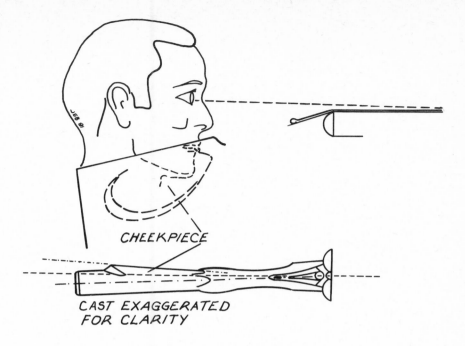

CHEEKPIECE

CAST EXAGGERATED
FOR CLARITY

Figure 46 East European Stock

from makers of custom stocks, particularly by upland game hunters and for heavier gun models, including gas-operated autoloaders.

As we saw above, the crooked stock gun is particularly appropriate when fashion calls for the shooter to wear a shirt or coat with a high collar (Figure 44) since mounting such a gun to face and shoulder raises the shoulders the minimum amount and the head remains erect. The coat collar does not get between face and stock, and the shirt collar doesn't threaten to cut off the shooter's head! Thus, the crooked-stock fowling piece and some of the recurrent fashions of its heyday went well together. By the same token, a stock that can be mounted thus (without either marked forward lean of the body on low targets, or shrugging up the shoulders, which actions are required with some other styles of stock as we shall see) is equally useful to today's cold-climate hunter, in thick, high-collared clothes, and possibly carrying a rucksack containing the necessities of existence (should he be forced to spend the night out) and perhaps with some already-shot game on the outside of it. Under such handicaps, the less the shooter has to incline his body or raise his shoulders to shoot a woodland grouse skimming away, or a hare bounding through the bog grasses, the less likely are his intentions to be frustrated by what he is wearing or carrying interfering with his accuracy. The crooked stock remains more than merely useful under such circumstances.

The standard field stock of eastern Europe provides another solution to the same problem. These stocks have somewhat less drop than the crooked stock (2¾ to 3½ inches of heel-drop is usual) but incorporate enough cast to allow the comb to cross the widest part of the shooter's jaw (the head being tilted neither much forward nor at all sideways over the comb) without the jaw pushing the comb sideways (and with it the breech end of the rib) out of the line from eye to bird. Thus the stock is mounted a little higher in the shoulder pocket than is the crooked stock, and its natural pointing elevation is about horizontal (Figure 46). The Monte Carlo comb featured on some of these stocks parallels the underside of the cheekbone, giving good facial contact while allowing the drop at the heel of the stock correct for a shoulder raised but little (and not at all voluntarily) to shoot. The usual cast on these stocks is about ⅜ inch where the jawbone crosses the comb, which takes care of all but the widest-jawed of shooters.

Most of these stocks have a cheekpiece, and though the cast is applied in a virtually straight line from the head of the gun to the heel of the stock, the cheekpiece thins forward (Figure 46). Thus, rearward recoil of the gun *decreases* pressure on the face of the shooter. But for the presence of a cheekpiece shaped like this, the side of the cast stock would tend to maintain or even *increase* its force on the shooter's cheek during recoil. This important subject is one we shall return to when discussing British game gun stocks with cast.

If the purchaser alters the surface contours of the cheekpiece to make it fit his face better, or to reduce its thickness by an amount needed to allow him to bring his eye in line with the rib when his face has a light, comfortable pressure on the stock, he should be careful to maintain the forward thinning of the cheekpiece and with this, the recoil attenuation produced by this feature. He can do all this with the stock remaining on the gun for repeated trial as the work progresses. It would be difficult to demonstrate that there exist better stocks than these for the 7 to 7¾ lb 12-gauge guns one finds them on, particularly for the hunting circumstances of their countries of origin, where the usual 12-gauge load is about 1⅛ oz, and it is unusual to fire a lot of shots in a day.

THE AMERICAN FIELD AND SKEET STOCK
(The Victorian British Game Gun Stock)

HISTORY

The history of the 20th century American field and skeet stock really begins on the *eastern* side of the Atlantic, where (as we have seen) in the closing years of the 18th century gun weights were increased, and stock-drops decreased, to maintain recoil as felt by the shooter at manageable levels. These developments were made necessary by the increased velocities that had resulted from the use of the patent breech and the desire of shooters to use heavier shot loads in each gauge to counteract the increased spreads of shot due to these increased velocities. In Britain, shot loads up to a third heavier than had been the norm in a particular gauge became usual. Further, better ignition allowed burning of all the powder in a shorter length of barrel, paving the way for the near-universal adoption of the double-barrelled gun (except in very large gauges intended for waterfowling). There had been double-barrelled fowling pieces in the mid-18th century, but they were few in number, and two barrels of over 40 inches meant they never could be so well balanced as the, then usual, single-barrelled gun. In 1750 the typical British shotgun was a single-barrelled 16-gauge weighing about 6 lbs, having a barrel about 42 inches long, a stock with drops of 2 inches at the comb and 3½ inches at the heel, and shooting an ounce of shot. By 1800 the normal British game gun was a double-barrelled 20 or 16-gauge of 7¼ lbs, with 30 or 32 inch barrels, shooting up to 1¼ or 1½ oz of shot respectively, and having a stock with drops of 1½ and 2½ inches at comb and heel.

These stocks greatly resemble the American-style "field and skeet stock" of the present day. Few of them incorporated more than a mere trifle of cast (if any), which means that as a class they were intended for mounting in the ways that today's American-style stock is mounted (see below) and *not* in the manner of the "Standard British" and "Churchill" styles described later in this chapter. Indeed, if the American shooter of today (and those shooters all over the world who now use the modern American-style stock) were to have put in his hands a series of the usual British game guns of the period from 1800 to 1880 (after which other developments began to take place in British gunmaking) he would find himself completely at home with them in weight, balance and stock dimensions! Hence the rather strange title for this section. As the century grew older and development went first through the percussion-cap muzzle loader and then to breech loaders, slightly larger gauges and somewhat lighter loads in each gauge became the norm. In Britain by 1870 the usual gun was a 12-gauge of 7 to 7½ lbs, shooting 1⅛ oz of shot for game and 1¼ oz for trapshooting.

In America, in response to the demand created by the presence of British double-barrelled guns (lighter than their American counterparts and particularly prominent in trapshooting) and to the appearance of successful repeaters (also lighter than most then-current American doubles) American made double guns began progressively to lose weight. Necessarily, to decrease apparent recoil and punishment of the shooter, the stocks of all kinds of American guns had to be built with less heel-drop than hitherto, and by about 1910 the field stock had reached the dimensions we are familiar with today: a length of about 14 inches, drops at comb and heel of 1½ to 1⅝ inches and 2¼ to 2⅝ inches respectively, and zero cast. All types of shotgun except the gas-operated autoloader were well developed by this time, though few over-and-under guns were seen in America until the 1930's.

GUNMOUNTING

Several styles of gunmounting are used successfully with the American field and skeet stock, and I propose to describe each of these in turn, beginning with the "classic" style in which the butt-end of the stock is mounted in the shooter's "shoulder pocket" (between chest and shoulder joint) and the comb runs *under* the rear angle of the jaw.

a) Classic style

Being determined to shoot from the same side as his master eye if (as is usual) he has one (or to take appropriate steps as described in Chapter 1 if he hasn't) the shooter should stand, gun in hand, with his toes on a line running precisely in the direction he wishes to shoot (Figure 47). The disposition of the feet shown in the figure, with the forward foot at about 40 degrees to the line and the rear one at about 70 degrees and a distance between the heels of about 8 inches, is typical but subject to modification by individual shooters in achieving a certain direction of pointing without lateral strain, as described below.

At this stage the shooter should stand quite upright, with his weight equally shared by his feet, and with his head and neck erect. His hold on the fore-end of the gun is one to be adjusted later when the gun is at the shoulder, so that the forward arm is not then unduly extended. As a preliminary: a hold about the middle of the fore-end of a self-loader is about right for the shooter with medium-length or long arms, and this can serve as a gauge for other lengths of arm and other types of guns. It translates into a

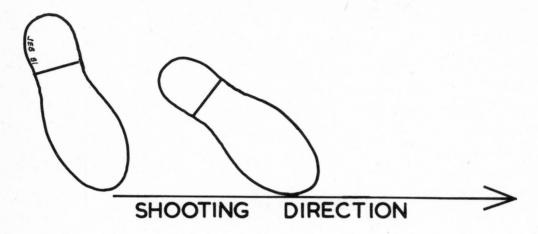

SHOOTING   DIRECTION

Figure 47   Position of Feet, American styles

hold on the forward half of the fore-end of an over-and-under gun for example. Shooters with shorter arms should hold correspondingly closer to the receiver of the gun. The disposition of the feet described and shown causes the upper part of the body to face about 45 degrees from the intended direction of fire.

In what immediately follows, it helps in avoiding faults of position (such as tilting the head forward to meet the comb of the stock instead of bringing the stock up to the face) if the shooter closes his eyes.

The head and body are kept still while the gun is raised in the line of fire but pointing upward at 15 to 20 degrees to the horizontal, the butt plate or recoil pad a little forward of the shoulder, until the comb of the stock contacts the face. In raising the gun to this position, the elbows are allowed to come up to an extent that is comfortable. While perhaps not consciously raised, they are certainly *not* kept down. When the gun is angled upward as described, the rear elbow will be a little below shoulder-height, the forward one at about shoulder-height. Allowing the rear elbow to rise thus creates a pocket of relaxed muscles between shoulder and chest and lower than the collar bone, a pocket in which the butt is about to be placed.

The hold on the gun with the hands should not be tight. That of the rear hand should be firm, that of the forward hand relatively light: ideally no tighter than is required to prevent the fore-end moving in the hand when the gun is fired.

The upward tilt of the gun is adjusted until the comb of the stock lies just below the rear angle of the jawbone (lightly contacting the side of the jaw where this begins to narrow below the rear angle) and below the cheekbone, but with a finger-thickness of clearance between the comb of the stock and the underside of the forward end of the cheekbone. Maintaining the upward tilt of the gun, which is the natural pointing

COMB OF STOCK UNDER
REAR ANGLE OF JAW

HEAD AND
BODY ERECT

FEET FLAT
ON GROUND

Figure 48   American "classic" style, "natural" pointing elevation

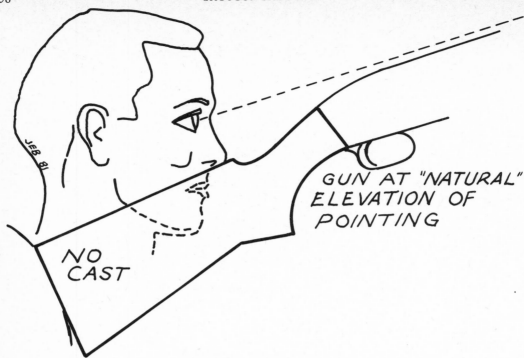

Figure 49   Fit, American "classic" style

elevation of this particular American-style field and skeet stock for this particular
shooter when the gun is mounted in the "classic" style being described, the gun is then
slid gently back so that the butt end contacts the relaxed musculature of the shoulder
"pocket" referred to above, the stock-heel below the collar bone. At this point the
shooter should open his eyes (Figure 48).

Unless the comb of the stock is too low for him, the shooter will find himself looking
along the top of the gun with his gun-side eye, the line of sight passing just above the
breech as in Figure 49. If the comb is too low for him the shooter will find himself
looking at the back of the receiver with his gun-side eye, this therefore hiding the rib
and frontsight from the view of that eye, and the comb of the stock will have to be built
up for him in achieving a proper "fit". Conversely, if the eye is well above the breech,
so that the whole length of the rib of the gun is easily seen by the shooter, the comb
of the stock may be cut down to an extent that later tests in actual shooting prove
advisable.

If the shooter finds himself looking down one side or other of the rib (generally the
left side for right-shouldering shooters, and vice versa) and thus not over the dead-
centre of the breech, then before any work is carried out in making the comb thinner
to adjust for this (rarely a thicker comb will seem to be indicated) the shooter should
attempt to bring the frontsight, the centre of the breech, and the eye he uses for gun-
pointing, into a straight line by turning the head slightly on the vertical axis of the
neck, towards or away from the stock as required. If the comb is the right height, often
this rather than removal (or rarely addition) of wood, is all that is needed to produce
the desired lateral alignment. It may be noted that *some* similar turning of the head is
required in all shotgun shooting, in any style, with any kind of stock (professionally
fitted to the shooter or not) and the right amount for a particular stock, fitted to the

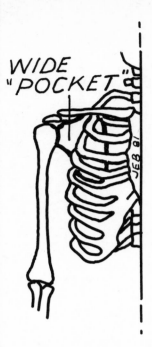

Figure 50   Shoulders wide relative to rib-cage

shooter for use in a certain style by him, is soon learned, and after some practice is assumed without conscious effort by the shooter when using that stock. However, when using this "classic" style there is no need to cant the head sideways over the comb to achieve the line-up of eye, breech-centre and frontsight. Any such necessity, like that for cast of the stock, has been removed by placing the comb of the stock *under* the widest part of the jaw, along a narrower part of the jawbone.

It is important to note, again, that though the face should be in definite, unvarying, contact with the stock, the comb must *not* be tightly pressed against the underside of the front end of the cheekbone or soreness will surely result, quickly followed by flinching. This may manifest itself as a hesitancy to pull the trigger at the right time (in order to avoid being hit again by the comb!) but in this instance the phenomenon will more usually take the form of an involuntary raising of the head just as the trigger is pulled (again, to prevent the sore spot being struck once more). The eye will still insist on putting the muzzle of the gun into its proper vertical relationship to the bird as if the head were still on the comb, but since the eye is now well above its proper position the shot will go over the bird (Figure 9). The muzzle faithfully "follows the eye" just as in the "majority method" of leading.

The next check to be carried out is to see that the butt-end of the stock is cut at the correct angle (pitch) to ensure that the butt plate or recoil pad is in proper contact with the shooter's shoulder. The upward tilt of the gun described above is maintained for this check. Contact should not be at the heel alone, or worse, at the toe of the stock only, but evenly over the upper half to two-thirds of the butt plate or recoil pad. The most important aspect of the shooter's anatomy to be considered at this point is the width of his or her shoulders *relative to the rib-cage*. If the shooter's shoulders are a good deal wider than his rib-cage (Figure 50) a state of affairs common among adult

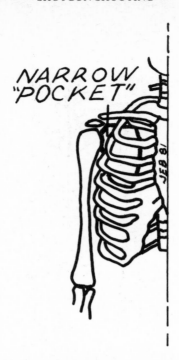

Figure 51   Shoulders narrow relative to rib-cage

males, then the lower end of the "shoulder pocket" when the arm has been allowed to rise as described above, will be found to lie outside or "outboard" of the rib-cage. When the butt of a stock is placed in a shoulder pocket of this type, the toe of the stock lies ahead of the armpit, touching nothing. In fact, no matter how prominent that stock-toe, there is no danger of flesh being sandwiched painfully between it and the ribs of the shooter. On the other hand, if the shooter's shoulders are relatively narrow in relation to the rib-cage as in Figure 51, a conformation most common among women and juveniles of both sexes (but far from uncommon among adult males) the lower end of the shoulder pocket runs downward *onto the rib-cage*, and mounting the butt of the gun in that pocket puts the toe of the stock *on the ribs*. Shooting with the gun placed thus (unless the stock is fitted with a soft-toed pad put on the stock at such an angle that the toe does not bear heavily on the chest in static tests) will sooner or later result in sore ribs, followed by flinching in the form of hesitancy to pull the trigger, or mounting the gun ahead of the shoulder (which makes matters worse).

However, for most shooters having this kind of "inboard" shoulder pocket, a solution other than the use of a soft-toed pad on a stock of more-than-usual down-pitch (or mounting the gun on the shoulder joint or the upper arm) is possible. This solution is the preferable one where it can be made to work by and for the individual shooter, not simply because it will allow him to use guns fitted with the usual American-style field stock "right out of the box", or with minor alterations (presuming he himself is not of extreme dimensions) but, more importantly, because extreme down-pitch can bring its own problems, as we shall see shortly.

Here, then, is the other solution: with the rear arm raised into shooting position as described above, most shooters will find that, with practice the shoulder joint on that side can be pushed *outward* and forward, away from the rib-cage, thus widening the

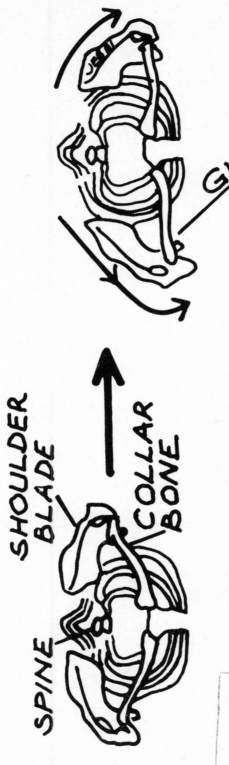

GUN

SHOULDER BLADE

COLLAR BONE

SPINE

TOP VIEW

Figure 52 Widening the Shoulder Pocket

shoulder pocket as shown in Figure 52 (where the contrast with the mere rotation of the other shoulder can be seen). Practice for this movement can be done without a gun and in front of a mirror. If the movement is hard to "get into" at first, do it with *both* arms and shoulders, pretending to put them around an imaginary tree trunk in front of the shooter.

How much movement, and consequent widening of the shoulder pocket, can be thus achieved varies from shooter to shooter, but the author's experience suggests that, with practice, enough can almost always be obtained to open the shoulder pocket far enough that the toe of the stock will be ahead of the armpit and free of contact with the ribs. The author has a naturally "inboard" shoulder pocket and learned to perform this movement in his late thirties, which shows that not having acquired it as a supple child is no bar to being able to do it later. Prior to that he had shot only in what is called in this book the "Standard British" style, in which (as we shall see) the form and disposition of the shooter's shoulder pocket are not a problem. No one showed him how to do it, incidentally. He wanted to be able to use American (and similar) factory stocks (field, skeet and trap) from the shoulder pocket rather than the shoulder joint or the upper arm, without resetting their butt plates or recoil pads to give vastly increased down-pitch, but without getting a sore patch of ribs from their toes, either, and one day it dawned on him how it could be done. Necessity is, after all, the mother of invention!

If an "outboard" shoulder pocket has been received from Nature, or has been achieved as described, there is some choice in fitting the butt to the shoulder. Note again that this fitting is carried out with the gun at its natural pointing elevation for the particular shooter, as described above.

One alternative is to make the whole butt-end of the stock (be this a butt plate, the end of the stock wood itself, or a suitably chosen recoil pad) the slope that fits the shoulder pocket, even though it is only the upper two-thirds of the butt that is in actual contact with the shooter. When a gun with this field-type stock has its butt shaped thus, to be mounted in the "classic" style we are discussing by people with "outboard" shoulder pockets, it will generally be found to have 2 to 4 inches of down-pitch (Figure 53) measured by the American method (Figure 3). I assume a 28 inch barrelled double gun or a 26 inch barrelled repeater.

The alternative in shaping the butt end for those with "outboard" shoulder pockets is to have a more prominent toe on the stock (since for these people the stock-toe lies ahead of the armpit, free of contact with the body) and to shape the butt-end as a whole in a slightly concave curve with just the upper two-thirds or so sloped to fit the shoulder pocket (Figure 54). When the butt, butt plate, or recoil pad is shaped like this (and I do not refer here to the highly concave, "trap-style" recoil pads with their prominent, sometimes horn-like, heels and toes) the prominence of the toe of the stock very much affects the pitch of the stock as measured in Figure 3. So measured it is generally 1 to 2 inches on guns with butts shaped like this. A prominent toe on the stock does seem to help some shooters in mounting the gun consistently, always providing that such a toe mounts in the armpit, free of contact with the shooter. On some stocks such a toe is angled outward a little, away from the shooter's body, to help make certain it will never come into painful contact with the ribs when the gun is fired.

For the other conformation, that in which the shooter's shoulders are narrow relative to his or her rib-cage (the "inboard" shoulder pocket) the usual solution tried by shooters has *not* been the one of trying to widen the shoulder pocket and thereby get it out of line with the ribs as suggested above. Rather has it lain in the use of greater-

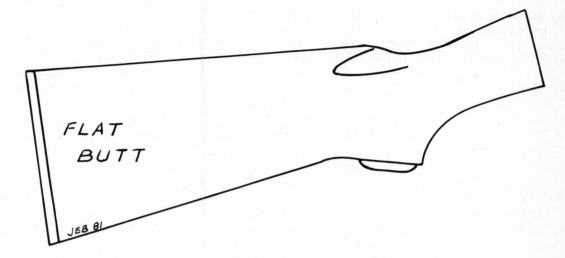

Figure 53   Stock with Flat Butt-end

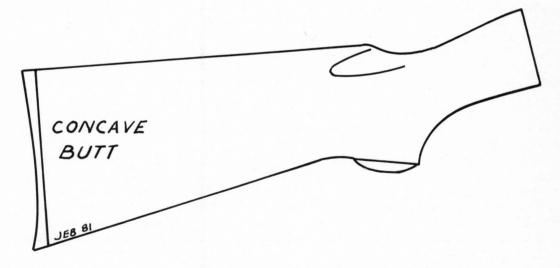

Figure 54   Stock with Concave Butt-end

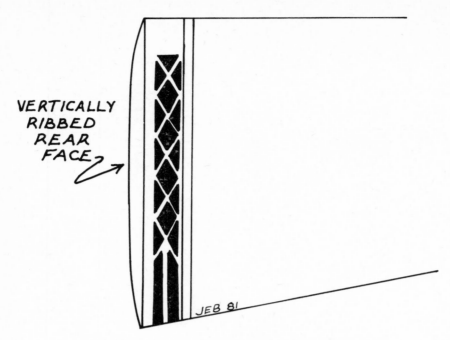

Figure 55   Soft-toed Ithaca Recoil Pad

than-usual down-pitch on stocks which are flat, or even convex ended. When this is done, the usual amount of down-pitch needed by such shooters when the stock is mounted in the "classic" style we are discussing here is 4 or 5 inches. But as much as 6 to 8 inches *may* be needed to ensure that it is the upper two-thirds of the butt, and not the toe over the ribs, which is transferring the rearward force of recoil to the shooter. Figure 55 is a sketch of the soft-toed Ithaca recoil pad on a Remington 20-gauge autoloader used by the author in early teaching sessions with juniors and ladies (early for them, that is). A majority of these have naturally "inboard" shoulder pockets, and hence mount the gun with the toe of the stock on the rib-cage. In later sessions they are taught (where possible) how to put the shoulder pocket farther out, and thus to be able to use guns of normal pitch. The toes of these pads are slotted parallel to the rear surface of the pad for extra softness. I do not know if these Ithaca pads are still made. Pachmayrs make an excellent soft-toed (and soft-heeled) pad, the Triple Magnum. Note that among men "inboard" shoulder pockets are not confined to "barrel-chested" or "heavy-chested" individuals. Both barrel-chested and flat-chested men may have shoulders that are narrow relative to the width of their chests. Nor among ladies has the problem of where the stock toe goes anything to do with what a wise Nature has seen fit to place on the front of their rib-cage (to a varying degree) for men can't stand to be hit by the stock toe there either, but it has everything to do with their shoulders being often narrow in relation to their rib-cages (much more often than among men). To put it another way, they are often "well filled up under the arms". The pad shown in Figure 55 is so fitted that the gun has 4½ inches of down-pitch on the end of its 26 inch barrel, the gun resting on the middle of the pad of course. It suits many ladies and slips of youths (male) who are anything but barrel-chested, until, if

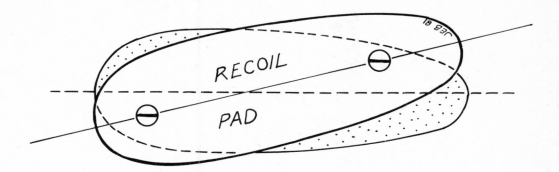

Figure 56 Recoil Pad set on at an angle

possible, they are taught to "hook" the shoulder-joint out sideways and forwards as part of gunmounting. Be it noted here for future reference that this action is nothing like the forward thrust of the tensed shoulder musculature that is part of all named British styles of gunmounting described later in this chapter, and which is carried out with a low elbow and results in there being, effectively, no shoulder pocket. All will be made clear shortly.

Not knowing the trick of widening the shoulder pocket and bringing it "outboard" of the rib-cage, and shying away from altering stocks so as to give much more down-pitch than is usual on factory stocks, some people with shoulders narrow in relation to their rib-cage have sought a solution to their problem in recoil-pads fixed on the stock twisted over at angles as much as 25 degrees (Figure 56) the idea being that the heel of the pad would be in the shoulder pocket and the toe under the armpit. Actually the inner side of virtually all shoulder pockets (where they join the chest) slopes outward when followed from top to bottom, but this slope is not followed by the butt in fitting any kind of stock to the shoulder. Pads and buttplates at wide lateral angles have been tried many times by people with "inboard" shoulder pockets, but eventually they are discarded, generally either for the solution of much more down-pitch, or that of mounting the butt on the shoulder joint or even the upper arm as described later in this chapter. Surprisingly few people know the trick of moving the shoulder pocket outward as described above, though some of those who carry it out do not realize they do.

We left our shooter some time ago with the gun at his shoulder, pointing upward at its (for him) natural angle of elevation. Fitting of the butt to the shooter for pitch angle is carried out with the gun thus raised, and is carried out by packing out the toe

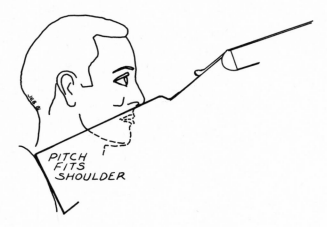

PITCH
FITS
SHOULDER

Figure 57   Correct Pitch to fit Shoulder, American "classic" style

or heel of the butt plate or recoil pad, if and as required, with washers on the top or bottom screw between the plate or pad and the wood of the stock. The angle thus found is later made permanent by refitting the plate or pad (or another plate or pad if necessary) to the stock, at the same time adjusting the stock to the right length (found as described below) if required, by removal of wood or the addition of one or more spacers.

A reduction in down-pitch is often cited in American literature as a means of making a gun shoot higher. It must be said at once that in making this recommendation (presuming they have tried in practice the remedy they propose) its advocates prove they belong to that group of shooters who mount the gun with the stock toe ahead of the armpit. If they belonged to the other, "inboard" shoulder pocket group, they would have found that whatever *else* a down-pitch reduced from the right amount for them produced, it certainly resulted in a patch of ribs so painful from violent contact with the toe of the stock that such reduced down-pitch could not be tolerated.

For those who mount the stock with the toe ahead of the armpit reduced down-pitch may not result in noticeable discomfort (at least from the butt end of the stock). And for such shooters decreased down-pitch can result in the gun shooting higher due to one or both of two effects. However, the operation of either of these results in there being a price to pay for attaining higher shooting thus. Dealing with each in turn: As we saw in Chapter 1 the first action of a gun in recoil is to rotate around its centre of gravity while beginning to move rearwards as a whole as in Figure 30. Thus, these initial movements tend to lower the stock and raise the barrel. A normal conformation of shoulder and a butt end sloped to fit this result in such rotation being hindered (Figure 57). Too little down-pitch gives the result shown in Figure 58, the buttplate sliding down the shoulder during this initial period of recoil while the charge is still

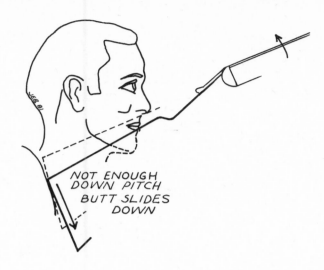

Figure 58 Too little Down Pitch

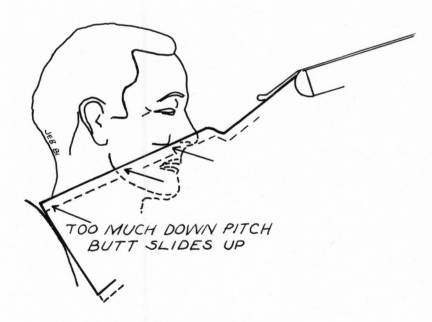

Figure 59 Too much Down Pitch

travelling up the barrel, resulting in high shooting. Extra down-bending (down-flip) of the barrel or barrels may compensate in part for this high shooting tendency, or even more than compensate in some thin-barrelled side-by-side double guns. However, supposing that the gun does shoot higher and that this effect is desired, the price to be paid is that the stock has to be remounted to the proper position for the subsequent shot (and a slippery buttplate of too little down-pitch may be completely off the shoulder after the shot). A butt that stays in place at the shoulder when the gun is fired is a big advantage when more than one shot is to be fired in sequence. This is true even for the "Churchill" style (in which the gun is deliberately demounted and remounted for each shot).

The other way in which decreased down-pitch can result in the gun shooting higher is by the now more prominent toe of the stock coming into contact with the front edge of the armpit as the gun is mounted and thus preventing the stock rising as fully to the face as it did before. This particularly applies to shooting at birds at no great angle above eye level, the gun actually pointing higher than hitherto for a similar muzzle/ target "picture". The price to be paid for the use of this somewhat makeshift device is in loose and variable contact between stock and face, and hence variable (if on the whole higher) elevation of shooting. Facial bruising may also result when the shooter, unmindful of the new "fit"(!) of the gun, cocks his head forward and down to meet the lower-mounted stock, and thus gets his cheekbone alone on the comb (of course, he then shoots as low as he used to!).

The right way to produce higher shooting is, of course, by raising the comb of the stock. This places the eye higher above the breech, resulting in greater, and constant, elevation of the barrel.

On guns of more than slight recoil (the 20-gauge autoloader mentioned earlier is not one of these!) marked down-pitch combined with a slippery butt or buttplate can result in the comb of the stock being brought into painful contact with the face as the stock rides back and *up* in recoil (Figure 59) especially so since this movement is added to the upward rotation of the gun in the later stage of recoil. By contrast, concentration of the rearward force on the stock heel by too little down-pitch may produce no noticeable discomfort to the shoulder.

Returning again to our shooter for whom we are checking gun-fit for the American "classic" style: with the gun again at the shoulder, pointing upward at the "natural" angle of elevation (Figure 48) a check should now be made for the right length of stock. This is correct for the shooter when not less than one finger-width (¾ inch) for guns of light to normal recoil, and not less than two finger-widths (1½ inches) for guns of heavy recoil, can be placed between the end of the nose and the ends of the fingers on the stock-grip (Figure 60) and not more than three finger-widths (2¼ inches) can be so placed for any gun. Note that this rule does not apply to stocks for what are termed in this book "Standard British" and "Churchill" styles, where other criteria apply, nor to the American-style field and skeet stock used in what I have called the "Modern British" style, but it does apply to all other combinations of stocks and styles mentioned in this book. In all these last the length of stock a shooter needs is dictated principally by the length of his neck and the width of his shoulders. If clearance between nose and fingers is as described, the nose will not be hit during recoil, but even the shorter-armed shooter will be able to push the stock out so that the butt clears the shoulder during gunmounting.

With the gun mounted as described the shooter may find that his natural direction of pointing deviates laterally somewhat from the line he toed when beginning this

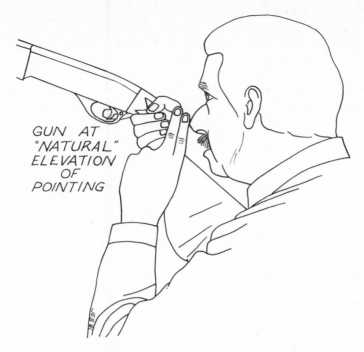

GUN AT
"NATURAL"
ELEVATION
OF
POINTING

Figure 60   Fitting for Length, American style

exercise. This is quite immaterial. He now knows more about how to place *his* feet to achieve a certain direction of shooting without tension or torsion in body or lower limbs. He may find foot positions and angles varying a little from those in Figure 47 more comfortable, and if so he should adopt them. However, for reasons detailed below, he should hesitate about adopting a stance with feet wider apart than shown in that figure.

Assuming that the shooter has now achieved a position and gun-fit as described above: erect stance, weight balanced on both feet, stock comb beneath the rear angle of the jaw and comfortably (with clearance) below the cheekbone and the gun pointing up at the angle that results, the butt against the shoulder and fitting same, elbows raised to a comfortable height, suitable clearance between the nose and the tips of the fingers, the forward hand on the fore-end at a point which leaves a comfortable bend in the elbow, frontsight and breech-centre in line with the eye which takes charge in pointing the gun, and the line of sight passing ¼ to ⅓ inch above the breech — the next thing the shooter has to learn is that in this (as in all other styles of shotgun shooting) the relationship of head, shoulders, arms, hands, stock-comb, butt, face and eyes, thereby established **is maintained for shooting in every direction at every elevation** (Figures 61 to 64). Directions of pointing other than the one in the basic stance just described are achieved by bending the *body* forward or backward as required (principally at the waist) and by swivelling right or left (again, principally at the waist) leaving the relationship of gun and gunner *undisturbed*. The movements are accompanied by weight transfer from foot to foot as required (the feet then no longer carrying an equal share of the weight above them) and by some forward or rearward inclination of the body, as well as the bending referred to above.

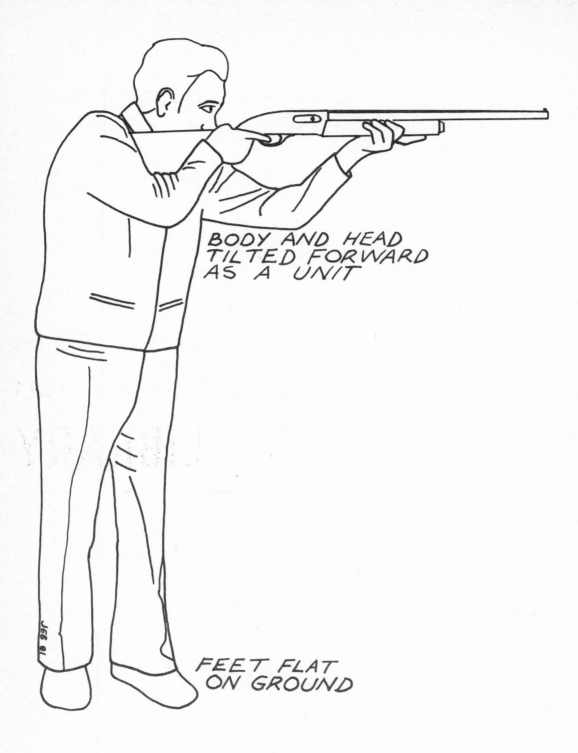

Figure 61   Horizontal shot, American "classic" style

FEET FLAT
ON GROUND

Figure 62 Swing to left, American ''classic'' style

Where shooting is carried out with a pre-mounted gun (as in all kinds of trap-shooting and in skeet under American and English national rules) maintenance of a constant, correct relationship of gun and gunner presents few problems to the shooter in this "classic" American style, particularly if the gun is always first mounted (by the new shooter at least) as shown in Figure 48 and then whatever elevation and direction of pointing required before calling for the target or targets achieved by bending and twisting the body as needed. Specialist textbooks on trapshooting and American-rules skeetshooting are full of instructions as to where the shooter should face when putting up the gun (this dictating his "natural", straight-ahead, direction of shooting) as well as to where he should actually point the gun before actually calling for the target or targets (these two directions being often considerably separated) and parallel instructions exist for International-rules skeet (though in this the shooter may not mount his gun until the target or targets appear). To devote a large part of this book to the relatively specialised techniques of trap and skeet shooting would be to unbalance it, and for these the reader is referred to whatever are the favoured, relevant, modern texts at the time his interest is aroused. However, he will find a general account of these games (and of Sporting clay target shooting) in these pages, as well as some advice on guns and ammunition for them.

When the gun has to be mounted to face and shoulder *after* the bird or target is seen (as in ordinary field shooting and in International skeet) the right inclinations of body and head to receive the gun, pointing in the right direction and at the right elevation as it contacts these, have to be learned. They have to be learned for *any* kind of gunstock of course, but the American-style field and skeet stock mounted in the "classic" style being described here differs from other kinds of "field" stocks (the crooked stock, and laterally cast East European stocks and stocks for the "Standard British" and "Churchill" styles) in that for a horizontal shot *the shooter must tilt the whole "gun turret" of body and head forward some 15 to 20 degrees before he puts the gun up to face and shoulder.* If he doesn't do this, or tries to do it by merely tilting the head, or head and neck, forward, to allow the stock comb to come under the rear corner of the jawbone as well as under the cheekbone (Figure 65) then not only is this likely to result in pain (since it is probable that the underside of the cheekbone will be struck by the comb during recoil) but the action has to be carried out to a different extent for each elevation of shooting from the "natural" 15 to 20 degrees above the horizontal, to somewhere below the horizontal in shooting at low birds and ground game. This results in disturbance of the relation between gun and gunner: the constancy of the arrangement is gone. And it is this constancy, if adhered to, which gives this method of gunstocking and gunmounting the potential of any other as regards accuracy, and it is a method, note, that allows amateurs to fit themselves with suitable stocks, and to help each other to do so. This is not to say that those people in America profession-ally fitting for this style, and those professionals in Britain fitting for this style, and the closely allied style termed "Modern British" in this book, cannot fit a shooter with a stock more quickly and with less effort than he can himself, or with the help of another amateur, and thereby earn their fee. But by following instructions such as those given above, the amateur can obtain a good fit of stock for this style, whereas he would be likely to run into great difficulties in trying to fit himself with a stock for the "Standard British" or "Churchill" styles unless he was already familiar with the specialised kinds of gunmounting which are part of these styles — which he cannot be in practice unless he already has a gun stocked to pretty well fit him when mounted in these styles!

Figure 63 Swing to right, American "classic" style

However (and here's the rub) leaning well forward to shoot at a low bird seems not to be one of those actions that "come naturally" to most people, so that tilting merely the head, or the head and neck, forward to do this when shooting in this "American classic" style is a common manifestation of the only pitfall associated with shooting with the American-style field stock (in any style *except* what is called in this book "Modern British" — see below) as well as with most stocks nowadays used in clay target competition.

All these stocks are short when compared with the stocks used in the "Standard British" and "Churchill" styles. They are not used, either, from the relatively rigid framework of bones and muscles common to these and the "Modern British" style. The result is that when using these shorter stocks (mounted in ways that involve little muscle tension in the arms and elsewhere, i.e. relatively "loosely") shooters with long flexible necks (in particular) are apt to fall into the habit of making use of the *flexibility of the neck* when they shoot, bending *it* down to shoot at low targets, and twisting *it* right and left in shooting at birds at either side, rather than bending and twisting from the waist and hips. There is often an allied tendency to move the gun with the arms alone rather than with the body, and even to mount the gun variably farther in toward the chest, or farther out on the shoulder, or even the upper arm, to facilitate shooting on either side, rather than turning the body at the waist, or as a whole, in the required direction. Tilting the head down apart, these actions are more difficult for those with a shorter or less flexible neck (our model of Figure 65 has a short neck, notice) but even these people often show the same kind of tendency. It is, at best, a doubtful habit, for every variation of shooting direction achieved like this results in the face being at a different place on the comb of the stock, and with a varying firmness. Shooters who put the gun to the right shoulder and who have fallen into this habit usually soon begin to miss birds that have to be shot to the right of their "straight ahead" position (and vice versa for left-shouldering shooters) by the face coming off the stock as the arms swing the gun farther than the face can follow it. The shooter sometimes finds a "remedy" in the shortest-possible stock he can use, which expedient he then recommends to all and sundry. A scenario like this is common in skeet. In fact a stock a good deal *longer* might force the shooter into swinging with his whole torso and thus result in his face staying on the stock.

Learning to use the American-style field stock, fitted to the shooter as described above, in the "classic" style being discussed, so that it has a constant relationship to face and shoulder on targets and birds at any elevation and over a fair arc to either side of the shooter is easy if it is tackled in two stages.

The first stage is carried out with the gun **at the shoulder**, first mounting it against an erect head on an erect body as described above and shown in Figure 48. Being careful to maintain the relationships of head to stock-comb and butt to shoulder **exactly** as they are with the gun thus mounted, the shooter then practises pointing high and low, left and right, as in Figures 61 to 64. This should be done as an exercise by novice shooters, for a minute or two at a time, whenever time can be spared, certainly once or twice a day, returning often to the initial position to check that no "components" have moved relative to each other. Imaginary targets, lower and higher, and to each side of the initial direction of pointing, from an imaginary rabbit 15 yards in front of the shooter to a ghostly duck straight overhead) should be covered by a combination of inclination of the whole body and bending of the upper part of it. It will be found that both targets mentioned can be covered while both feet remain flat on the ground, though it is easier to point at targets below the horizontal by allowing the knees to bend

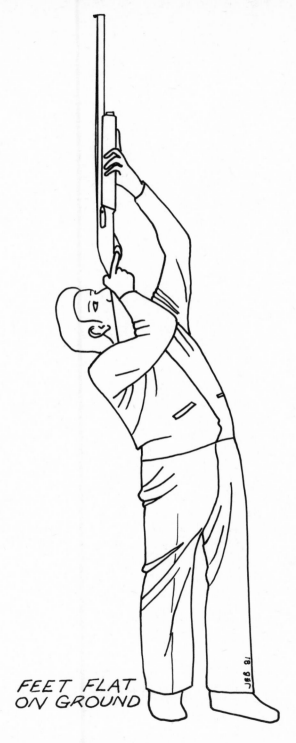

FEET FLAT
ON GROUND

Figure 64 Overhead shot, American "classic" style

Figure 65   Head alone tilted forward to meet Stock-comb

a little, and this should be done (Figure 116). Also, it is easier to cover overhead targets by allowing the heel of the forward foot to rise, **or,** conversely, by keeping most of the weight on that forward foot and allowing the heel of the rear foot to rise as the rear knee bends forward (a feature of the "Standard British" style, Figures 93 and 100).

In swinging onto targets well to one side or other of the shooter, if the feet are kept flat on the ground it will be found that the shooter who puts the gun to his right shoulder can swing farther to the right than to the left for the same degree of tension in the body and legs (the reverse of what is usually written: but just try it). Allowing the right heel to rise when swinging to the left (and vice versa) allows a greater arc to be covered, but also produces a tendency to allow the muzzle-end of the gun to droop at the end of the swing (what the shooting coach calls, somewhat poetically perhaps, "rainbowing"). There is less tendency for this when a stance with the feet closer together is adopted (as in the Churchill style of Figure 105) **or,** if the feet are placed as in Figure 47, when most of the shooter's weight is kept on the forward foot *at all times,* unnatural as this may at first feel. The heel of the rear foot is slightly raised. Such a distribution of the shooter's weight is a feature of the "Standard British" style (Figures 96 to 100). There is no reason why it, or the narrow "Churchill style" stance, should not be eventually adopted by the shooter to give greater flexibility in where the gun can be pointed without strain. In shooting at birds on the right, particularly those at fair elevations, shooters who put the gun to the right shoulder should take care not to drop that shoulder as they swing to the right from the "straight ahead" position (vice versa for the left-shouldering shooter). Not keeping the shoulders level usually means a miss, the charge passing below and behind the target.

The second stage in the familiarisation with the American-style field stock used in

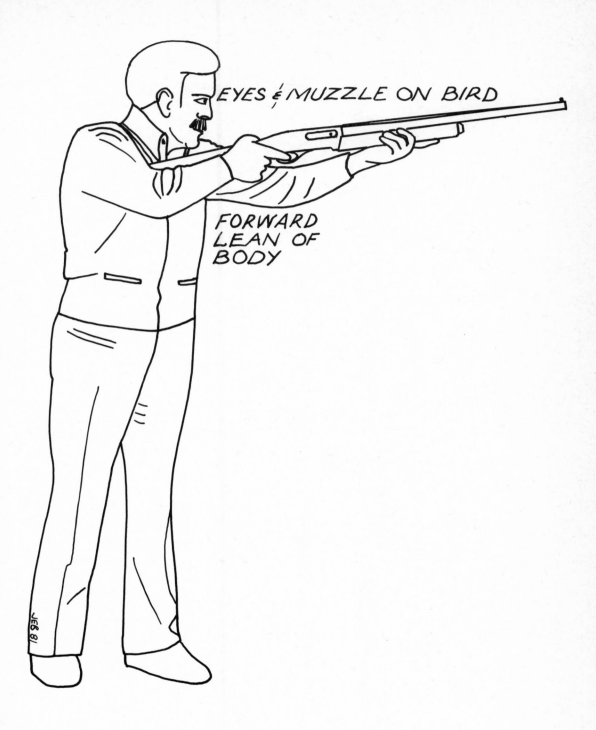

Figure 66 Ready to mount at Head-height Bird, American "classic" style

Figure 67 "Port Arms"

the "classic" style being described is designed to give the shooter practice in mounting the gun at a target anywhere within the area that can be covered from a certain placement of the feet. Since it is mounting the gun at low birds that presents the main difficulty to the novice in using this combination of stock and gunmounting style, he should take the bull by the horns and tackle this first. He should first make, or fix, an easily-visible mark on a wall, or other vertical surface, about five feet from the ground, and then place himself, gun in hand, a few yards from this mark, so that the mark is in his natural lateral direction of shooting. Next, he should mount the gun as described above, against an erect head and with an erect body, so that it points upward at the "natural" elevation, above the mark, as in Figure 48. He should then incline forward as already described, maintaining the relationship of gun to face and shoulder undisturbed, until the gun is pointing at the mark (Figure 61). This accomplished, he should push the butt forward from the shoulder an inch or so and then lower it so that the heel of the stock is at a level an inch or two below the armpit (Figure 66), the muzzle remaining on the line from eye to mark. The shooter is now in the exact position he must assume at the commencement of gunmounting proper on a head-height bird (outgoing, incoming or crossing) if this is to be done correctly.

The gun is mounted by raising the stock comb to the face and bringing the butt into the shoulder pocket whence it was lowered, thus restoring the exact relationship of gun and gunner that existed (Figure 61) before the stock was pushed forward a little and lowered. The butt should not be jerked into, or thumped into, the shoulder pocket, but placed therein smoothly and gently. Having been turned to the position that experience has shown to be correct with the gun mounted, the head is kept **quite still** relative to the body during gunmounting. Any deviation from this rule is liable to result in mismounting of the gun as regards direction, or elevation, or both.

Deliberate practice should be undertaken in achieving the right degree of forward bend and inclination required to shoot at low birds, and in mounting the gun at them, at first at the fixed mark as described, and later at outgoing, incoming and crossing clay targets at head-height. When he graduates to clay targets, the shooter should place his feet so as to give himself, so far as possible, a "straight ahead" view of the targets where these first become visible, and stand upright with the gun at "port arms" (Figure 67) when calling for his targets (which is the position he would often be in on first seeing a bird in the field). When the target is seen he should incline forward the requisite amount, bringing the gun into a position where the muzzle is visually on the target (and moving with it as the body turns as necessary), the heel of the stock being an inch or so ahead of the shoulder and a couple of inches below the armpit. This is shown in Figures 68 and 69 for birds crossing left and right of the shooter's front and a little above eye level. He should then bring the stock up and back against the face and into the shoulder pocket, and having obtained the requisite amount of lead (if any) by looking ahead of the bird, pull the trigger while keeping the gun moving. The whole sequence should be carried out with whatever speed is necessary, but never with hurry. The turning of the body prior to the final stage in gunmounting closely parallels that in the "Standard British" method shown in Figures 96 and 98.

Similar gunmounting practice can be taken for birds at other elevations, first at fixed marks and then at appropriately thrown clay targets. Only a small fraction of such clay-target practice can be obtained on skeet and trap fields. Even on the former the highest-angle shot is only some 25 degrees above eye-level. The highest International trap targets are but 10 degrees above eye-level. Thus, unless the shooter is

Figure 68 Swing to left, Gun not yet at Shoulder, American "classic" style

Figure 69   Swing to right, Gun not yet at Shoulder, American ''classic'' style

lucky enough to reside near a clay target ground or club which includes a fairly full selection of "sporting" targets in its layouts (which is quite likely in Britain, but still very unlikely in North America at the time of writing) he will have to fix himself up with his own trap or traps, suitably disposed, if he wishes to have clay target shooting which will be really useful to him as practice for the field.

Though Figures 62 and 63 show the shooter in action at targets well to either side of him (and Figures 68 and 69 on his way to such action) it is desirable in any kind of shotgun shooting that whenever possible shooting shall be from the shooter's "straight ahead" position at the point where the trigger is pulled (Figures 48 and 61). This does lead to greater accuracy. Later practice for the shooter, then, should involve the appearance of targets at angles to right and left of the shooter not known to him prior to the appearance, requiring him to move his feet to give himself, as best he can, a "straight ahead" shot as he pulls the trigger. Various odd ways of moving the feet to achieve this have been suggested in literature, but the best and simplest way is always to swing the body towards the bird or target by taking a step in that direction with the foot on the *opposite* side of the body (Figure 70) then restoring the correct sharing of weight between the feet. This applies to *all* styles of shotgun shooting, and will not be repeated in describing other styles farther on in this book. The importance of the action may be gauged from its prominence in the terse advice on shooting given by the 2nd Marquess of Ripon, probably the greatest game shot who ever lived.

Note that in the style of shooting we are discussing the stock is brought up *and back* to the shoulder in gunmounting, and this is true of all the styles of using this kind of stock described in this book (even that termed "Modern British", which remark will become clear later!). In this "classic" style the butt is clear of contact with the shoulder (though not by much: an inch or so perhaps) until it is at the right height to be brought rearward to its resting place inside the shoulder. This allows the use of a rubber recoil-pad on the butt of the gun without this becoming a nuisance by its rear face catching on the jacket or shirt during gunmounting (this is usually not true of the "Standard British" and "Churchill" styles as we shall see). Strange as it may seem, in the style we are discussing in this section, the *sides* and *top* of the recoil pad may still catch on the clothes as the stock is on its way to the shoulder. For this reason it is a good idea to give these lateral surfaces of the pad a coat or two of varnish. Most kinds of "exterior" varnish are durable in this situation, as well as being unobtrusive and easily renewed. Smooth, plastic, electrician's tape is an excellent, quickly applied, substitute.

When the butt is mounted in the shoulder pocket, most recoil pads, despite their name, serve only to anchor the butt better at the shoulder than does any kind of hard butt-plate, or checkering of the end of the butt. This is useful when more than one shot has to be fired in a sequence (a very usual situation!). The recoil pad as usually constructed is only ideal when shooting is off the shoulder joint or the upper arm, and we shall examine this shortly. However, when the heel of the stock contacts the shooter, as it does in the style of gunmounting we are discussing, only a pad with a soft heel (as well as a similarly soft centre-section) can be of use in cushioning recoil. Few pads are constructed with a soft heel, among them being Pachmayr's Triple Magnum model, which is actually soft over its full length including the toe. A soft-toed pad mounted at a suitable pitch-angle is the only kind useful to a shooter with an "inboard" shoulder pocket and who mounts the gun with the stock-toe on the ribs as discussed above. In fact, a pad with cushioning over its full length is the best kind for every purpose, and the Triple Magnum pad is made with modifications for all kinds of shooting in which a recoil pad is useful.

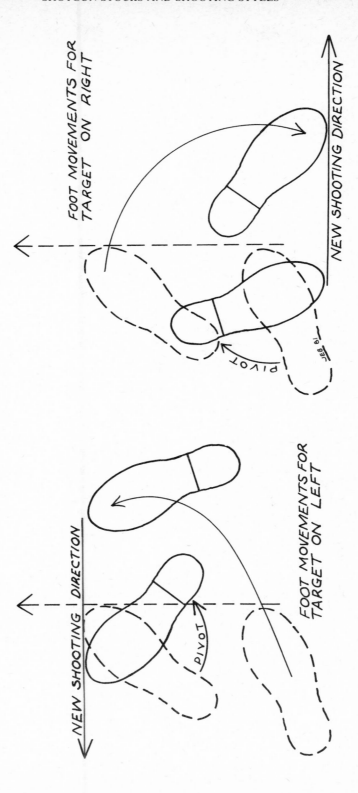

Figure 70 Moving the Feet

With regard to this American "classic" style applied to targets at higher elevations, it may be noted again that the standard American style field stock, mounted in this style, has a natural elevation of pointing some 15 to 20 degrees above the horizontal (Figure 48). Thus in shooting at targets at high elevations it may be said to have 15 to 20 degrees "start" on guns fitted with stocks having a lower "natural point" (or mounted so as to have a lower "natural point" with this same stock) and requires this many degrees less backward inclination and bending by the shooter than do these others (which include the crooked stock, the East European stock, stocks fitted for the "Standard British" and "Churchill" styles, and this same standard American-style field stock mounted in the "Modern British" style, or with a canted or much-turned head). The correct preliminary "classic"-style point for birds at high angles is shown in Figure 71.

The American-style field stock is often referred to in literature as a "field *and skeet*" stock (my italics) and it is not hard to see why. The maximum elevation of the gun above the horizontal at skeet is about 25 degrees, the least about eight degrees. The average is about 12 degrees (there being more shots nearer the minimum than the maximum elevation) but the mean is 16 to 17 degrees. Thus, this kind of stock, mounted in this "classic" style, would seem to be ideal for skeet, and in fact such stocks (or slight modifications of them) are the commonest type on guns intended for International-rules skeet. Only slight forward or backward tipping of the "gun-platform" of trunk, shoulders, arms and head from the position shown in Figure 48 is needed on any shot, and virtually none on many. International skeet may be the one common shooting situation wherein the "natural" pointing elevation of the gun is important, since very quick gunmounting is required from an initial position with the stock far below the level of the shoulder (Figures 121, 122), this preliminary position being called for in the rules. Gunmounting must be fractionally quicker when the only body movements required are turning with the target and minor inclinations from a preliminary position which is comfortable for the shooter.

The 15 to 20 degrees that a shooter must lean forward in maintaining a fixed relationship to the gun in shooting at low birds when using the American-style field stock mounted in "classic" fashion, once learned, is no handicap to hitting. Stocks of this kind were the norm in Britain for 100 years, and the majority of Victorians seem to have used these stocks in this style, rather than canting or turning the head to get the eye over the breech. Stocks with a "natural" pointing elevation still higher than this (i.e. having higher heels) not only necessitate more forward lean by the shooter when using the "classic" style on low birds, they also give rise to inherently high shooting due to the raising of the shooter's eye relative to the breech (unless the drop at the front end of the comb is correspondingly and markedly increased, which in practice it rarely is). However, most people who have used a high-shooting gun (within the practical upper limits for field shooting, Figure 12) and have got used to it are loth indeed to give it up for one which requires them to cover up rising birds with the muzzle in order to hit them. It must be said that the majority of people find the modern trap stock too high for any kind of field shooting (Figure 9). The methods described in the next two sections, incidentally, allow the use of high-heeled stocks without the necessity of the shooter leaning well forward in tackling low birds.

b) Canted-head styles

By no means all users of castless, American-style stocks mount these to face and shoulder in the "classic" fashion" described above. Many shooters cant the head sideways over the comb as shown in Figure 72. This enables them to get the eye into the line breech-muzzle-bird, while mounting the stock on the side of, rather than under,

EYES AND
MUZZLE
ON BIRD

Figure 71 Preliminary position for Overhead Birds, American "classic" style

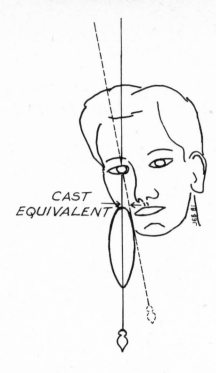

CAST
EQUIVALENT

Figure 72   Head canted sideways over Comb

the rear angle of the jaw. The head is rotated about an approximately horizontal, fore-and-aft axis, sufficiently to allow the jawbone to run along the side of the stock when the eye is directly above the breech. The pad of muscle which covers the rear angle of the lower jaw rests on the comb. It forms an effective cushion, and is a major factor in the comfort of shooting in this style. The natural pointing elevation of a gun fitted with an American-style field stock, mounted thus, with the butt in the shoulder pocket and the head fairly erect in a fore-and-aft sense, is about horizontal (Figure 73). The head is canted the requisite degree sideways, and a trifle forward, before gunmounting proper is commenced.

Some writers have opined that such a cant of the head is fatal to good shooting. However, although it may not be a pretty style, these writers cannot have seen any of those excellent shooters who consistently cant the head over the stock. For cant angles up to 15 degrees or so, each eye rotates in the counter direction in its socket and thus remains level. For normal, slight, angles of cant therefore, the eyes are scarcely impaired in their function. It should be noted that if the stock crosses the jaw 2 inches below the line of sight (a quite representative figure) a head-cant of 15 degrees produces the equivalent of a cast on the stock at that point of $\frac{9}{16}$ inch (Figure 72). Few people need so much, and a cant of half this allows most people to align the gun properly mounted as described.

A broad, rounded stock-comb helps to spread the force of the upwardly-rotating gun against the jaw-muscle during the later stages of recoil. A thick, rounded comb is useful in this way only to those shooters who cant the head sideways over the comb, or the gun towards the head, and vociferous advocacy by some shooters of such a

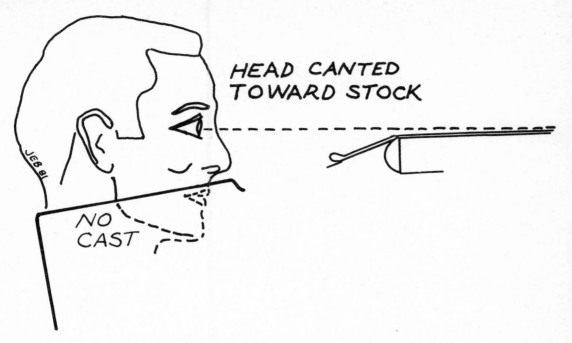

Figure 73   Fit, side-view, Canted-Head style

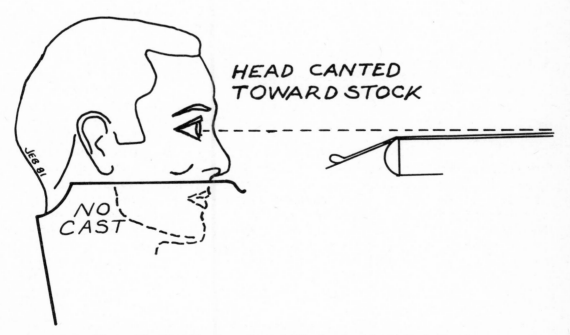

Figure 74   Fit, side-view, Canted-Head style, Monte Carlo Stock

Figure 75   Canted-Head style

comb on a castless (or virtually castless) stock is almost a guarantee that they do one, or other, or both (unless they are narrow indeed in the jaw). If the shooter mounts the butt in the shoulder pocket, the case we are considering at the moment, then a thick, rounded, Monte Carlo comb (Figure 74) level (or even sloping downward towards the front) fits better against the canted head (or when canted against the face) than does the rearward sloping comb of the standard field stock. The Monte Carlo comb endangers the forward part of the cheekbone less than does a comb sloping upward from rear to front, and the drop at heel can be made low enough to come into the pocket of the shooter's relaxed shoulder. A Monte Carlo comb on a field stock (except for those shooters preferring a high-shooting gun) will usually be appreciably lower than that found on trap stocks of a similar type, a drop of 1¾ inches being an average figure.

Some head-canters accommodate themselves to the castless stock by mounting it with the buttplate or recoil pad on the shoulder-joint or even the upper arm, rather than inside the shoulder-joint in the "pocket". Most such shooters raise the rear elbow to provide a resting place for a high-heeled, level-combed stock (no Monte Carlo notch) giving a roughly horizontal "natural elevation" of pointing with such a stock (Figure 75).

Mounting the stock on the upper arm brings the receiver of the gun rearward 1½ to 2 inches nearer the face of the shooter (mounting on the shoulder-joint somewhat less). The shooter therefore needs this much extra length added to the stock correct for him when shot from the shoulder pocket, to bring his face to the same place relative to the nose of the comb, and his nose a safe distance from the tips of his fingers. The resulting 15 to 16 inch stock length, correct for the shooter of average physique who mounts his gun like this, is more often seen among off-arm trapshooters than else-

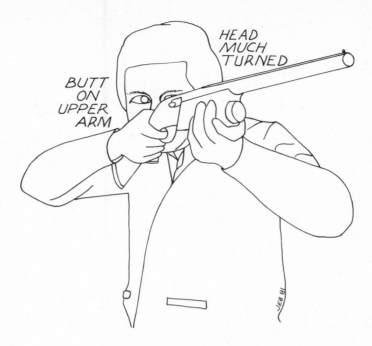

Figure 76   Turned-Head style

where. Adding length to a stock is a simple matter, but if a stock is intended for this style of mounting outside the shoulder pocket, the final length should include a recoil pad quite soft in its centre-section (at least). Some concavity in the rear face is also desirable, but this should not be exaggerated unless intended solely for trapshooting, when this is no disadvantage. It will not be lost on the reader that most recoil pads are constructed as if they were intended to be mounted precisely as we are discussing here, with their soft centre-section on shoulder-joint or upper arm, and the hard heels and toes thus free of contact with the shooter. The fact is that they *are* so used by an increasing proportion of American shooters, on stocks with drops differing but little (if at all) from comb-nose to heel, with the head either canted somewhat over the comb or else (as we shall see in the next section) turned towards the stock on the vertical axis. The canted head style we are discussing here has a greater recoil resistance than the latter. Before we discuss this style, it may be noted here that few people cant the *gun* noticeably except certain trapshooters and a few skeetshooters. We shall return to them eventually.

c) Turned-head style
Rather than canting the head sideways over the comb, some users of castless American style stocks bring the eye over the breech by turning the head towards the stock on a vertical axis, thus turning the wide jawbone away from the stock. To allow this to be done the butt has to be mounted on shoulder-joint or upper arm (Figure 76) and the desirable features noted above for a stock to be thus mounted with a canted head apply here too. However, it will be noted that the stock crosses the shooter's face at a sharp inward angle, the comb contacting the face deep under the forward end of the cheek-

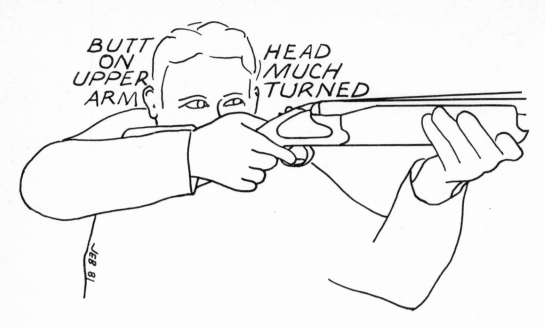

Figure 77 Turned-Head style

bone. Depending on the conformation of the shooter, a thick well-rounded comb may
not be thus accommodated without an element of head-canting as well as turning. This
area of the cheekbone, next to the nose, is extremely sensitive and particularly liable
to be hurt by upward rotation of the comb in recoil. Guns used in this style should be
relatively heavy for the loads being used, and the gas-operated autoloader with its
decreased apparent recoil has obvious advantages. The style is in common use by
American-rules trapshooters (Figure 77) including certain champions, some of them
using gas-operated autoloaders, but more with level-combed fixed-breech guns incorporating added weights to bring them to 10 or 11 lbs.

The turned-head style is not one for the shooter who needs prescription spectacles
to shoot. Such a shooter is forced by the style to look out of the extreme sides or
corners of the lenses. Not only is this far from the optical centres of the lenses (unless
the optician has put them near the appropriate edge in response to the shooter's special
requirements) but the frames in any case interfere with the shooter's view.

Concerning gun-fit for the canted-head and turned-head styles, it should be noted
that, despite the canting or turning of the head, some combs will be found too thick
or too thin to result in the shooter's eye being laterally in line with the rib when the face
is at its most comfortable on the comb, and adjustments have to be made accordingly.
The right stock-length and comb-height still have to be sought of course, and the right
pitch for head-canters who mount the butt in the shoulder-pocket. Those who shoot
off the shoulder-joint or upper arm, canters or turners, are generally best suited by a
soft-middled (at least) recoil pad set on the butt so that the middle section of the rear
face (where it contacts the shooter) results in between zero and a couple of inches down
pitch (Figure 3).

d) Modern British style

The versatile, castless, American-style field stock is now a feature of the majority of guns intended for game shooting (and International-rules skeet shooting) no matter where in the world the guns are made. Exceptions to this are those Italian guns turned out by their makers with a variety of stocks as regards length, drop and cast on each model, so that the shooter (or his retailer) can sort out (or order) a stock to suit his style of shooting usually without this having to be specially made (and waited for). In the dear, dead days beyond recall, British gunmakers did the same thing. Nowadays the small number of high-grade guns they continue to turn out each year (a few hundred in all in 1983) are fitted with high-combed cast stocks carefully fitted to the intended user in ways that will concern us later in this chapter. The third exception are those East European cast stocks we have looked at already.

Year by year, more and more European and Japanese over-and-under guns are being used for game shooting in Britain. These for the most part are 12-gauge guns, usually weighing between 7¼ and 7¾ lbs, and fitted with stocks 14 to 14½ inches long, having drops at comb and heel of about 1½ and 2½ inches, and usually virtually no cast: in short the standard American-style field stock. New recruits to shotgun shooting in Britain often enter the sport via clay target shooting with such guns. Naturally, those who go on to become game as well as clay target shooters prefer these same stocks on the guns they choose to shoot game. Often, indeed, these are the same guns they use at skeet and on Sporting clays. In a sense these shooters have returned to the customs of their grandfathers in gun weight and stock dimensions, the difference being that they prefer their barrels one above the other, rather than side-by-side. They have been joined in their choice of a game gun by those British shooters who have decided to allow their British guns by famous makers to accrue in value while safely stored, rather than risk such valuable items in actual shooting.

These factory-built over-and-under guns (and the smaller number of similarly-stocked side-by-side doubles, mostly Japanese) are used by British shooters in an adaptation of what we have called the "classic" American style of gunmounting: the comb running under the rear corner of the jaw as well as under the cheekbone, and therefore having no need for cast. However, inevitably someone, somewhere in Britain (perhaps more than one person, indeed, and in different places) developed a method of ending the act of gunmounting by bringing a tensed shoulder musculature *forward, towards the butt of the gun* as the butt is brought back to meet the shoulder. This is not at all surprising since such a bringing forward of the shoulder to the butt in gunmounting is an action typical of the other, peculiarly British, styles of gun-mounting in general use today. In performing it, it helps if the elbows are kept down.

This style is now so common in Britain that if there is a "Modern British" style, this is it (Figure 78). The shooter's neck muscles are deliberately tensed, and he does not tilt his head forward to the comb, or cant it sideways over the comb at all. Due to the forward thrust of the shoulder the head is relatively far back on the comb. In combination with the raised shoulder, this results in a "natural" pointing elevation about horizontal. The upward shrugging of the shoulders, and the forward thrust of the rear one, are described fully in the next sections of this chapter.

Since the butt is placed on the tensed musculature at the front of the shoulder, rather than in any kind of "pocket", it matters less whether the shooter belongs to the class with "outboard" or those with "inboard" shoulder pockets. However, the down-pitch angle on the butts of most of these American-style field stocks is such that rather more pressure may come on the toe of the stock so mounted than on the heel. If this

SHOULDER
THRUST
FORWARD
AND
UP

Figure 78   ''Modern British'' style

is so, it is a simple matter to alter the pitch to suit. These details of gunfitting and gunmounting apart, everything else about this style is the same as for the "Standard British" style discussed below, and so will not be repeated here.

The typical factory-built, 12-gauge over-and-under gun weighs some 7½ lbs (more or less) and with typical loads of 1⅛ oz of shot doesn't *need* such a style of gunmounting to decrease felt-recoil (or not for the average shooter at least). The tensing of the shoulder musculature (which inevitably brings with it some tension in the neck muscles) merely makes such a combination of gun and load very comfortable to shoot (though it is doubtful if the clay target competition shooter should dabble with it as we shall see). However, the style actually makes *possible* the use in sustained shooting with 12-gauge loads of 1 to 1⅛ oz of those light (6 to 6½ lb) side-by-side European doubles which have begun to appear on the market with American-style castless (or virtually castless) stocks with drops at comb and heel of 1½ and 2½ inches. If these guns, so loaded, were to be used in any of the "pure" American styles (which would seem to be indicated by the manner of their stocking) from a relaxed shoulder, or off the shoulder-joint or upper arm, recoil would be quite punishing. The restriction to rearward travel of the gun provided by the firm shoulder helps to keep the jawbone from the painful contact with the rearward sloping comb that would result from such rearward movement, but a firm grasp with the forward hand also helps by reducing the upward rotation of the gun about the shoulder in the later stages of recoil. Churchill found these things to be true with the very light guns he advocated so single-mindedly, even though these were especially stocked to decrease apparent recoil.

BRITISH GAME-SHOOTING STOCKS

HISTORY

It is somewhat ironic that while the developments in American guns in the latter years of the 19th century were taking place as outlined in the previous section (developments which resulted from the prominence of British guns in competitive shooting in America at that time) British game guns were themselves undergoing a new spurt of development.

The typical British game guns of the 1860 to 1880 period differed little from the British trapshooting ("pigeon") guns, as popular for their avowed purpose in Britain as they were in America. The usual British game gun at this time was a 12-gauge side-by-side double with 30 inch barrels and weighing about 7 lbs (rather than the 7¼ or 7½ lbs of the more stoutly-built competition gun). Its stock, usually virtually without cast, typically was a little lower in the heel than that of the trap gun (by 1880 perhaps averaging 2¼ inches or a little more, as opposed to about 2 inches for the pigeon gun) but was otherwise similar, having a drop at the nose of the comb of about 1½ inches and a length of 14 to 14½ inches (all these measurements to be understood as averages liable to modification for the individual customer). The barrels of the game gun were chambered for the 2½ inch (actually $2\frac{9}{16}$ inch) case, rather than the 2¾ inch ammunition popular for trapshooting, and the gun was intended for use with 1⅛ oz of shot as standard, rather than the 1¼ oz "pigeon" loads.

The average British game gun was still physically thus after the transition from outside-hammer to successful "hammerless" actions, the development of choke-boring (and its adoption in whatever degree suited the task in hand) and the replacement of black powder by various kinds of "nitro" smokeless propellants. The British gun trade was again in the kind of position it had been in during the 1830 to 1850 period, when it seemed to have supplied its clientele with everlasting guns, with no further technical advances in sight. Then the impasse had been ended by the development of successful, viable, breech-loading actions and ammunition. No such fundamental development was on the horizon in 1880.

Refusing to countenance such stagnation after their glorious third quarter of the 19th century, British gunmakers cast about for innovations, or even old ideas for revitalization, in their efforts to sell new guns. Such efforts resulted in due course in successful British designs for single-triggers and for over-and-under guns. But neither of these was the main thrust. This, and it was one that until recently succeeded mightily, was something quite subtle.

Perhaps in part responding to customer demand, certainly augmenting that demand by promoting such guns by word of mouth and in their advertising, British gunmakers began to produce ever-lighter, side-by-side double-barrelled game guns with shorter barrels, in a trend that reached its zenith in the 1930's as regards the *average* weight of new British game guns, and in the 1970's as regards the length of their barrels. British shooters and shooting commentators who branded British (and other) models of over-and-under guns, and all single-trigger actions, as mere gunmakers' ploys aimed at selling new guns to people who needed no such thing, for the most part swallowed the development of ultra-light, ultra-short-barrelled guns, hook, line and sinker (or barrels, action and stock perhaps) as worthwhile and legitimate, even egging on gunmakers to greater excesses in these directions, to the eventual embarrassment of some of the latter: it being not difficult to make a durable gun *or* a very light gun, but difficult to make a durable, very light, gun at any price or of traditional materials.

Certain well known, and able, British shooting coaches stood out as opposed to this trend, but were generally regarded by most shooters and commentators, especially after about the middle 1930's, as being hopelessly biased by having done too much clay target shooting, even to the extent of having had their brains addled by this. But, however they deceived themselves in regard to the views of these coaches, these shooters and their scribes should have regarded it as significant that the famous names who shot driven game in such incredible quantities in Britain and Europe at the very zenith of such shooting in the years from 1880 to the outbreak of World War II, and whose game-shooting prowess with the side-by-side double gun has not been surpassed, took little or no part in this movement to lighter and shorter-barrelled guns, except that some of them took advantage of a new style of fitting the gun to the shooter, and the gunmounting that went with it, which decreased apparent recoil still further. Prior to this they had been shooting stocks very like the American field stock dealt with in the previous section, mounted in what we called there the "classic" style. But it must not be forgotten that many of the biggest names of all went on shooting such stocks in that fashion to the end of their careers, well inside the 20th century.

For those shooters who had adopted the new-style, lighter British game guns (a sizeable proportion, indeed the majority of British shooters who began their careers between the Wars) measures to reduce apparent recoil were quite necessary, since, again the balance which had existed between gun-weight and stock-shape on one hand, and the weight and velocity of the shot-load on the other, was disturbed. The necessity was sharpened for those many British shooters whose chosen sport was driven game shooting, the best of which may involve the firing of many scores of shots in a fifth,

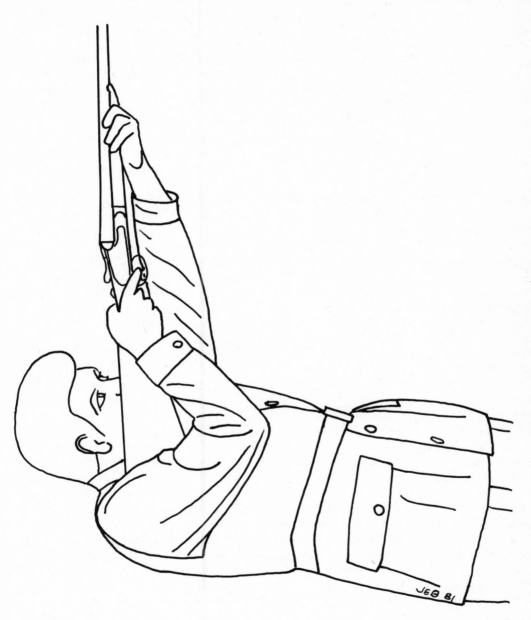

Figure 79 "Standard British" style

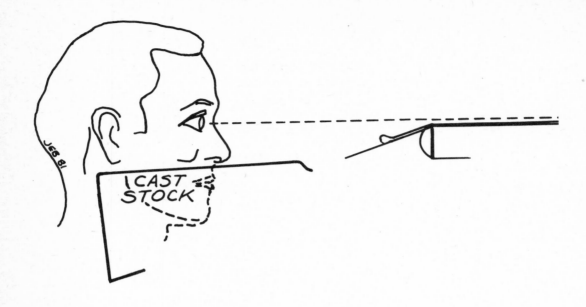

Figure 80   Fit, "Standard British" and "Churchill" styles

or even a tenth, as many minutes, at each drive, and repeating this six to twelve times in the course of an autumn or winter day.

Of course, it would have been possible to restore equilibrium by cutting back the shot-loads used, but this measure, as a general thing, did not come until years later. In a nutshell: the British game gun stock had to be straightened still further, its heel raised yet again, to decrease upward rotation of the gun in the later stages of recoil (this, as ever, being the greatest single source of discomfort during recoil). Yet, as we have seen above, to do this and to continue to mount the gun to face and shoulder-pocket in the way described for the American "classic" (equals Victorian British!) style, results in a tendency to very high shooting, as well as a requirement for the shooter to lean far forward before mounting the gun at low birds. There is a practical limit to the extent of required forward lean which can be tolerated in the field, a limit set by overall success (as those present-day shooters who try to use a modern, high-combed trap gun with a castless stock mounted thus, for long-range walked-up birds, find every season).

Nor was it possible to avoid the requirement for a marked forward inclination of the body in shooting at low birds by mounting the butt on the shoulder-joint or upper arm, and turning and lowering the head to meet the comb of the stock. The discomfort to shoulder-joint or upper arm from the punishment of repeated sharp recoil resulting from the combination of light guns and normally-loaded ammunition would have been exceeded only by the pain inflicted by the comb on the cheekbone! To adopt such actions would have been to replace half the problem with a new one: flinching, while leaving the unwanted tendency to high-shooting unaffected.

The problem was solved (or things much ameliorated to say the least) by the bold, wholehearted use of cast in stocking this new generation of British game guns. In simple terms: stocks were so shaped as to have a lateral bend, to suit the user, so that they could cross the rear part of the face high up on the closed jaw (on the widest part of the latter, just under the ear in fact) without the jawbone and its covering muscle pushing the eye out of alignment with the line bird-muzzle-breech, and this with the head not canted sideways towards the comb, nor turned markedly towards the stock, and with the butt mounted inside the shoulder joint (Figure 79). I have written "closed" jaw above quite deliberately, and will explain why shortly.

The British game gun stock is fitted to the shooter so that the "natural" pointing elevation of the gun is about horizontal when the shooter's head and body are erect and the line from the frontsight to the centre of the pupil of the eye in line with the breech passes about ⅓ of an inch, or so, above the latter (Figure 80). There is no difficulty in tilting the whole "gun turret" of head, shoulders, arms and gun backwards to align the gun on birds at higher angles (typical of driven game shooting) without disturbing the relationship of gun and shooter (Figure 81).

Are there then no drawbacks to this style? From the game shooter's viewpoint there is, I think, just one. If a gun is mounted in the manner shown in Figures 79 to 81, the stock has to have the *exact* amount of cast required by *that shooter* if success is to be forthcoming in consistently accurate shooting. If the proper cast is not present, and the shooter brings the butt and comb into unvarying contact with shoulder and face for each shot (the jaw closed and the head neither canted over the comb nor turned sharply towards it) the gun will faithfully and consistently shoot to one side of the mark, and there is little the shooter can do about it, the more so because, as we shall see, in the style as fully developed there is a rigid consistency in the relationship between gun and gunner. Having to bias one's shooting *laterally* to hit, that is to say, having to shoot to one side or the other of straightaway targets for example, or to have to give crossing birds flying in one direction more lead than those flying in the opposite direction) is fatal to good shooting. The case is quite different from the one in which the eye is *higher* or *lower* than is ideal, for the shooter can become accustomed to seeing a lot of vertical space between muzzle and bird, or to covering the bird with the muzzle, should either of these be what is required to hit consistently. But a stock mounted as in Figures 79 to 81, assuming the head to be neither canted sideways over the comb nor turned markedly towards the stock, *has* to have a cast exactly suited to the shooter (even if he is narrow-jawed and the correct cast is zero) if he is to shoot up to his full potential.

Thus, if a factory decides to turn out guns intended for this style of gunmounting, it has to produce guns with cast-off and cast-on, in varying amounts to do the job properly, and this some Italian factories, for example, do. Factories seeking a "standard" amount of cast do well to remember that too much cast is better than too little. The latter leaves a proportion of shooters necessarily missing pretty consistently to one side of the mark, while the former can be compensated for (with some success) by cheeking the stock less firmly. The "average" of required amounts (say $\frac{3}{16}$ inch where the jaw contacts the stock) would leave about half the users shooting to one side of the mark. Twice this is a logical amount for a "standard" cast and enough for almost everyone. Where most guns are factory products, turned out in large numbers, rather than the individual creations of the custom gunmaker each stocked to fit a particular client, there would appear to be a good deal to be said for the factories fitting their guns with castless, American-style stocks, allowing the customers to find

Figure 81 ''Standard British'' style

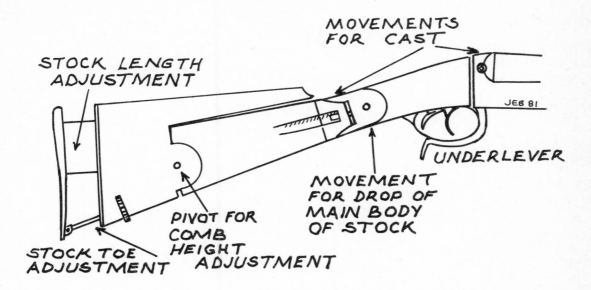

Figure 82 Try Gun

means of shooting straight with these, often with slight modifications carried out by the purchaser. Nevertheless, many East European factories, and some others, turn out guns with cast stocks as standard, the cast averaging about ⅜ inch where the face contacts the stock, but often varying from ¼ inch to ½ inch at that point on individual guns of the same model, to the obvious satisfaction of their customers at home and abroad. We examined the use of these stocks earlier in this chapter.

With the advent of a new style of gunfitting in Britain there arose an instant desire by gunmakers for a gun with a stock that could be adjusted for cast (and preferably for all other dimensions) and shot for trial of these dimensions by the customer being fitted for a gun. And there was such a thing already in existence: the "try-gun" (Figure 82), an American invention. The try-gun was (and largely is) a flop in America, since America has never adopted the cast stock as a general thing, and it is in arriving at this dimension, as dictated by the gunmounting styles ("Standard British" and "Churchill") described in this section, that the try-gun is at its most useful in gun-fitting. The British gunmakers seized the try-gun with cries of delight, and they have never let go of it since.

A stock with a high heel designed to decrease apparent recoil can only fail in its avowed purpose unless that stock is properly supported by the shoulder behind it. Rather than bending forward to accomplish this (thus raising the level of the shoulder relative to the head) the British shooting school pupil is taught to raise his shoulder behind his high-mounted, high-combed, stock as he mounts the gun. Actually, he raises both shoulders and keeps his elbows down to facilitate this (just as if he were seated at dinner between two stout ladies). In a later development, which seems to have originated with Robert Churchill, the raised rear shoulder is also brought *forward*, the musculature on its forward face tensed, onto the butt of the gun. This further, and noticeably, increases the recoil resistance of the shooter. These actions, which are assumed in Figures 79 to 81, are now part and parcel of all current peculiarly British (and so labelled in this book) shotgun shooting styles, as are a deliberate tensing of neck and jaw muscles for the same reason of increased recoil resistance, and all undertaken in a tiny interval of time just before the trigger releases the shot. It should be noted that though the muscles of the neck can be stiffened when the head is turned (as is necessary in all styles of shooting) they cannot be so stiffened when the head is canted even slightly.

Tensing of the muscles of the closed jaw effectively widens the jaw on the lower, rear, angle (arrowed in Figure 13). The shooter can prove this for himself by putting his fingers on the muscle at the angle of the jaw while clenching and unclenching his teeth. The hardening, and bulging, of that musculature *increases the correct cast measurement* for the shooter from what it would otherwise be. Obviously this does not apply to the "Modern British" method, wherein the comb runs *under* the angle of the jaw. In all these British styles the shooter's jaw is positively closed at discharge. In describing the variety of American styles of gunmounting I deliberately made no mention of the state of the jaw muscles. In practice, in these styles, the jaw is neither consciously shut nor left sagging open, for the most part. Trap shooting, and American and English-rules skeet shooting, are something else again in this regard as we shall see.

The Langs were prominent among the earlier makers of the new generation of light British game guns, but it seems to have been H. A. A. Thorn of the Charles Lancaster firm who first made extensive use of the try-gun on his clients (together with his ability to see the shot-cloud in the air). Among those clients was the famous (and attractive) Annie Oakley. Robert Churchill probably made the lightest of all 20th century British game guns, some of his 12-gauge side-by-side doubles being only a little over 5 lbs in weight. He adopted 25 inches as the standard barrel-length for guns of his make. It should be noted that there were some British 12-gauge doubles *under* 5 lbs built before 1900. Perhaps it is not surprising that a surviving specimen is hard to find. Since World War II British game guns have tended to be a little heavier than was typical in the 1930's (which has resulted in a chorus of deprecatory comment from the same British writers who cannot even yet abide, for example, the over-and-under gun). However, average barrel-lengths have continued to decrease. The current norms for a 12-gauge gun chambered for $2\frac{9}{16}$, $2\frac{5}{8}$ or $2\frac{3}{4}$ inch ammunition, but intended for the lighter loads in any of these, are a weight of about 6 lbs 6 oz and a barrel-length of 27 inches.

Even with a high-combed (laterally cast) stock mounted against deliberately stiffened shoulder muscles, a head carried on an equally deliberately stiffened neck, and a tightly closed jaw, not all shooters can use even 1 oz, normal-velocity, loads in sustained shooting from such a gun, and loads of $\frac{15}{16}$ oz and even $\frac{7}{8}$ oz are now used by many British driven-game shooters from their light guns, particularly when they expect to fire many (perhaps several hundred) shots in a day. Perhaps all of them don't always remember to carry out all the muscular moves necessary to cut down apparent recoil. These will all be recapitulated with details in this section.

It must be said that some stocks fitted to British and European guns of the first three-quarters of the 19th century had some cast. This is sometimes so slight that it is difficult to be sure whether or not it is accidental. In other examples the main body of the stock is cast enough to make room for a padded cheekpiece for the face of the shooter. Hardly ever is enough cast present to take care of the shooter with a wide jawbone who mounts the gun with the comb high on the face (on the angle of a closed

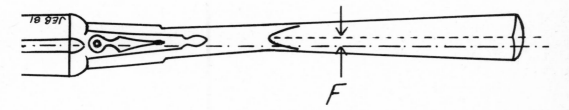

Figure 83 "Dog-Leg" Cast

jaw) and with the butt in the shoulder pocket, inside the shoulder joint. This indicates that in general these stocks were intended to be mounted in one of the ways described above for the castless American-style stock (not the "Modern British" style). Probably most shooters used what we have called the "classic" American-style (which was, as has been implied above, a British style before it was an American one!). Often these stocks are cast only in the area of the comb-nose and where the face contacts the stock, but not at all at the heel or toe of the stock. Cutting away of the face of the modern, thick-combed trap stock to make it fit the shooter who wants to use it mounted over the angle of the jaw of an uncanted head (page 179) is a parallel practice today.

In shaping cast stocks to fit the individual shooter, the amount of cast at the comb-nose, and at the heel of the stock, should be regarded as almost independent measurements, the former (and the combination of the two) being influenced by the requirement to put the shooter's eye in line with, and slightly above, a prolongation of the line of the rib, the latter by the desirability of keeping the butt on the musculature inside the shoulder-joint. Stocks custom-fitted to the individual shooter by Italian gunmakers will often be found to exhibit casts exactly similar at comb-nose and heel, the so-called "dog-leg" cast (Figure 83) the comb viewed from above being then offset from, but parallel to, the line of the rib. There is a laudable tendency apparent nowadays to shape British game gun stocks in like fashion as regards cast, perhaps due to there being more try-guns around with two movements for cast (Figure 82), one right behind the head of the gun and the other at the rear end of the grip. Many earlier try-guns had a pivot at only one of these points, meaning that only a "straight-line" cast (Figure 84) could be put on the try-gun, and often this was faithfully followed in the

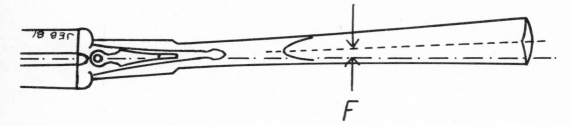

Figure 84   "Straight-Line" Cast

stock made for the customer. Note that the cast at F (where the face touches the stock) is the same in Figures 83 and 84. Figure 82 shows one possible configuration for a try-gun. There are almost as many "models" of try-gun as there are individual try-guns, hardly any two being alike in their detailed construction. In some, for example, the desired alteration of dimensions is achieved wholly by substitution of pieces rather than by use of hinged and sliding parts.

A stock with the same cast along the full length of the comb as suggested above (that cast being the amount dictated by the facial structure of the shooter) will be found to suit the vast majority of people for the shooting styles to be described in this section. Such a stock, as we shall see, has very real advantages over the stock with straight-line cast in terms of recoil-effect, and most people can, with no effort, find a position in which its butt rests on the musculature inside the joint of the raised shoulder. In fact, narrow-shouldered shooters are not able to use even a relatively long stock with straight-line cast without the butt coming onto the shoulder-joint (which is certainly not where the shooter would prefer it to be when he has gone to the trouble of trying to obtain a cast stock to fit him!). When the shooter elects to use a relatively short cast stock in any style of shooting (as many trapshooters do) or is forced to do so by other factors (short arms, for example, or the necessity to keep the weight of a heavy gun well between the hands and close to the body for ease of manipulation) "dog-leg" cast is a must, or willy-nilly the butt will end up on the shoulder joint or upper arm (note that we are not discussing canted-head or turned-head styles). Though both stocks have the same cast where contacted by the face, the shorter stock in Figure 85 has a much greater cast at heel. For the purposes of demonstration the cast dimensions in this figure are exaggerated beyond those which are normal, but the principle is un-

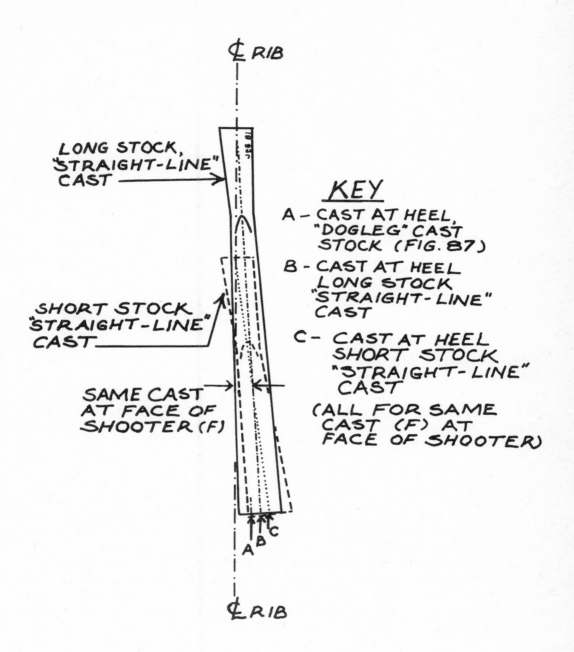

Figure 85 Cast comparisons

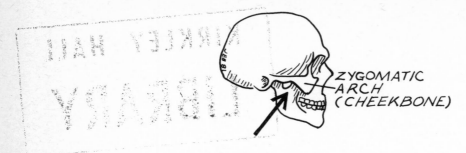

Figure 86   Site of Comb-fit under Zygomatic Arch

affected. Even for the wide-shouldered shooter it is doubtful if a prescription for cast at the heel of a stock should ever so exceed that at the comb-nose as to bring the face of the stock (on the shooter's side of it of course) farther away than parallel to the rib as viewed from above (Figure 5).

At this point it is necessary to reiterate that the idea and the force behind the development of these British game gun stocks was the reduction of apparent recoil, and hence of recoil effect on the shooter. In fitting a certain shooter, then, such a stock is made the longest he can get comfortably to the shoulder, with the highest heel he can use when taught to push his shoulder forward and upward behind it, and with the comb from nose to heel so shaped in drop and cast as to put hs eye in the right place, vertically and laterally, behind the rib. Such a relatively long stock ensures the maximum involuntary tension in the arms of the shooter when the gun is mounted, ensuring that the stock is held firmly to the shoulder. The high heel of the stock results in the minimum upward rotation of the gun at the shoulder in the second phase of recoil. In fact, as the stock of the gun is taken a little downward and rearward by the rotational (about the centre of gravity) and bodily movements of the gun in the first phase of recoil, the comb of the stock may never again touch the face of the shooter during recoil. This is particularly likely if the upward slope of the comb from heel to nose is slight (drop measurements at these points varying by ½ inch or less) and more so if, in addition, the cast is of the dog-leg type with measurements at comb-nose and heel differing but little, or perhaps not at all. Note that most stocks taper in thickness from the butt to the area just behind the grip. Slight downward and rearward movements of the stock in the first phase of recoil therefore tend to take the stock away from the face if cast at comb and heel are the same or similar.

Note that straight-line cast gives deceptive comfort in non-shooting trial against a wide-jawed face, as it nicely fits the rearward widening of such a face. But rearward travel of such a stock in recoil brings its face into ever-firmer contact with the shooter's face. A cast stock should fit against the widest part of the face, under the zygomatic arch (arrowed on Figure 86) and thence taper forward into *less-firm* contact. In particular, a relatively short stock having a lot of straight-line cast crosses the face at a noticeably sharp angle (Figure 85) making the face liable to suffer from forcible contact with the side of the stock during recoil. This is made worse by the freer rearward movement of the short-stocked (as compared with a longer-stocked) gun, the shorter stock being in looser contact with the shoulder. Contrast this with the dog-leg cast stock of Figure 87, which has the same cast at the face as the straight-line cast stocks of Figure 85, yet is so shaped that recoil does not bring it into firmer contact

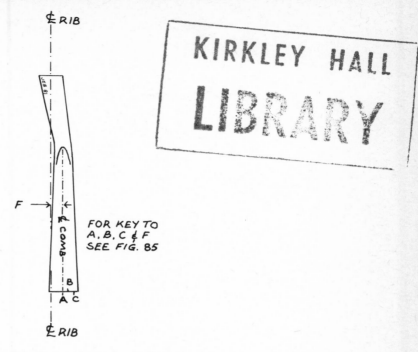

Figure 87 Short "Dog-Leg" Cast Stock

with the shooter's face. We have seen already how the problem of recoil of the short, straight-line cast stock is handled by means of a forwardly-thinning cheekpiece on East European stocks (Figure 46).

Over 80 years ago, G. T. Teasdale-Buckell wrote in *Experts on Guns and Shooting:* ". . . . . any stock that in its back recoil or kick does not automatically relieve the pressure on the cheek is entirely bad. That is, it does not fit the shooter, and it will sooner or later make him afraid of his gun with consequent bad shooting and want of confidence." He was writing in particular of British game guns to be used in driven game shooting where many shots are fired in a day (or even an hour) but what he wrote has general application in some degree to all shotgun (and rifle) shooting, and is as true now as when it was written. Unfortunately it is not a principle that has been followed by all gunfitters, in Britain or elsewhere, though there is never any excuse not to do so when a stock is being designed from scratch for a client. Nor is it always necessary to start with an unshaped piece of wood in obtaining a stock embodying this principle and fitting a certain shooter. The high-combed, castless or slightly-cast, stocks fitted to most trap guns, and to an increasing number of guns intended for American-rules skeet, can be reshaped into stocks hewing to this principle and suited to a variety of uses. The commonest application of such reshaping is of trap stocks to allow them to be mounted higher on the face, and this is discussed later in this chapter.

As every measurement in stocks for these British styles is a matter subject to careful adjustment for the individual shooter, averages are meaningless as such. Nevertheless, the reader, particularly the novice and the reader outside Britain, is due an idea of what is typical. For adult males, stocks are generally between 14½ and 16 inches long. This is about an inch longer than the usual range of correct lengths for stocks for the American "classic" style discussed earlier, but the principal factor dictating the right

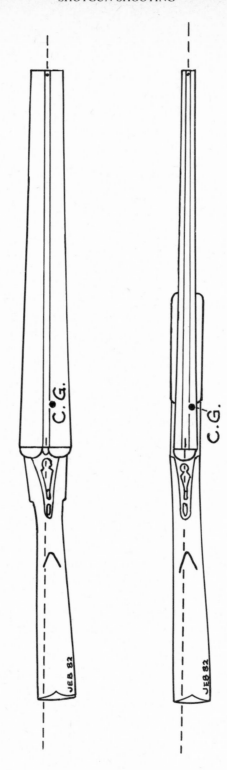

Figure 88 Centres of Gravity, Cast Stock Guns

length for these British styles is the length of the shooter's arms, not the length of his neck. Typical drops at comb and heel are 1½ and 2 inches, respectively. A typical cast measurement halfway back on the comb (where the upright part of the shooter's jawbone contacts it) is probably about $\frac{3}{16}$ inch. But this measurement at that point may be zero and it may equally be ½ inch or more (and this for a man with a definite master eye) i.e. it is made whatever is right to suit the shooter. And that is true of all these measurements. Average ''stand'' (down-pitch) is 2 inches off the vertical.

A bit of extra cast is often specified on the toe of a stock, as compared to the heel, by the British gunfitter who wishes to be certain that the toe will always be in the space ahead of the armpit (and never touching the ribs) when his client puts the butt of the gun, properly, on the musculature inside the shoulder-joint (or even on those occasions when he plants it a little *too* far inside the shoulder-joint).

Casting the stock of a gun moves the centre of gravity of the whole gun laterally (Figure 88). Since the stock with its fittings is commonly one-quarter the total weight of the gun, when the cast is substantial the shift in the centre of gravity becomes a factor of importance in the behaviour of the gun when fired, especially during the first phase of recoil. Since the centre of gravity is no longer symmetrically between the barrels, it might be thought that side-by-side doubles with a well-cast stock would have a noticeable tendency to shoot to a point to one side of a prolongation of the rib (to the left in the case of a gun with a cast-off stock). However, in the case of the usual British and European side-by-side doubles (which have no stock-bolt through the grip) ''buckling'' of the grip may be sufficient to counteract this tendency, and may in fact over-compensate for it. We shall return to this subject below.

The barrels of the over-and-under gun are not so resistant to lateral bending as are those of the side-by-side double. Even unaided by buckling of the stock-grip (which often has a stock-bolt through it) the barrels of an over-and-under gun whose stock has a lot of cast *may* undergo sufficient ''side-flip'' to partially compensate for lateral swinging of the whole gun in the first phase of recoil (Figure 89). But, again, correct stocking for a particular gun and user can only be refined through trial and error.

It may be noted that lateral rotation of the gun in the first phase of recoil tends to take the stock away from the face. However, this is a minor movement compared with the downward rotation of the stock and the rearward movement of the gun as a whole.

Having tested trap guns with cast stocks by shooting them with their ribs carefully aligned on the stationary mark, and having found that tested thus they shot laterally wide of a point on the prolongation of the rib (even over-and-under and single-barrel trap guns generally producing no compensatory ''side-flip'' due to their relatively massive barrels) certain trapshooters have condemned all cast stocks as something unusable by the trapshooter (who universally needs to be able to place his small patterns very exactly). It seems quite certain that they interpret the sideways swing of the gun towards the face in the second stage of recoil (after the charge has left the barrel) as responsible for the lateral ''off-shooting'' they observe. The fact is that, due to the lateral shift of the gun's centre of gravity caused by the stock cast, a gun having a cast stock *cannot* be shot thus and be on the mark laterally, except by a lucky accidental balance of lateral rotation and barrel-flip. The trapshooter who needs a stock with a lot of cast (and many are best suited by a well-cast stock) and who uses an intermediate bead on the rib for checking preliminary alignment, will have to find where that small bead should appear relative to the frontsight, both vertically *and* *laterally* when the gun shoots where he wishes it to. Since the ammunition that will be used in a particular trap gun will all be virtually identical in energy, variations in lateral

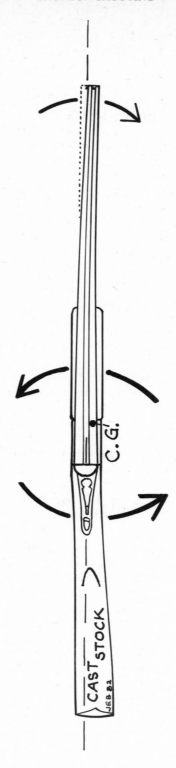

Figure 89 Sideways flexing ("side-flip") of Barrels, Cast Stock Over-and-Under or Single-Barrel Gun

movement of the gun from this cause are not a factor. Usually the correct fitting for a cast stock for over-and-under and single-barrelled trap guns is one which places the eye slightly out of alignment with the breech-centre (to the right in the case of cast-off stocks).

All this presumes straight barrels!

It may be well to reiterate here that in practice the shotgunner uses the muzzle-end of the barrel/s, alone, in pointing the gun. The eye does not mind not looking over the very centre of the breech (if this is what is required for correct fitting with a cast stock) any more than it does when there is a gross lack of fit and the line of sight passes well to one side of the breech-centre.

GUNMOUNTING

a) Standard British style

What is called in this book the "Standard British" style of gunmounting and shooting, I have so named because, despite the prominence in British print of "Churchill-style" advocates, the former is the more commonly used in Britain of the two methods developed in the United Kingdom earlier this century (between the two World Wars). These methods were developed to enable the shooting of a relatively great number of shotshells in a comparatively short time (certainly as many as a thousand, usually 12-gauge, a day, with loads of 1 to 1⅛ oz of shot) from relatively light guns (generally between 6 and 6¾ lbs) in driven game shooting, without the shooter suffering particularly or noticeably from the effects of recoil. As the reader will have already gathered, I have termed the other style the "Churchill" style from its progenitor and greatest advocate.

The keys, and features common, to these styles are their use of cast stocks with the minimum drop at heel and the maximum length the shooter can be taught to use, thus decreasing the upward rotation of the gun in the second phase of recoil and helping to ensure that the butt is tight to the shoulder when the gun is fired, together with the careful coaching of the shooter in the method of using such guns from a rigid framework of bones and muscles deliberately tensed as the gun is fired. The styles depend heavily on careful shaping of the gunstock in all its dimensions for the individual shooter, so that the eye is correctly placed relative to the line of the rib when the shooter is thus braced to shoot.

The initial steps in the development of these methods, both "Standard British" and "Churchill", lay in the deliberate raising of the shoulders as the gun was mounted (attained by keeping the elbows low and shrugging the shoulders upward) and in a definite "thrust" of the gun at the bird in gunmounting. Actions of this kind enable most people to put their shoulder fully behind a stock with a heel drop of 2 inches or somewhat less (the actual measurement depending more on their flexibility in thus raising the shoulder than on its natural "unshrugged" height) and an inch or more longer than would suit them for gunmounting not involving such an outward thrust. The length of the stock for these styles of gunmounting is governed by what the shooter can get to the shoulder, without the heel catching under the armpit, using such an outward thrust. Obviously such a stock keeps the fingers on the grip well clear of the nose of most shooters. The comb drop is such that, in conjunction with the heel drop, it allows the comb to run with comfortable clearance under the cheekbone of an erect head. The resulting "natural" pointing elevation is about horizontal (Figures 79, 80). As will be seen from the figures, the comb of the stock mounted thus passes across the

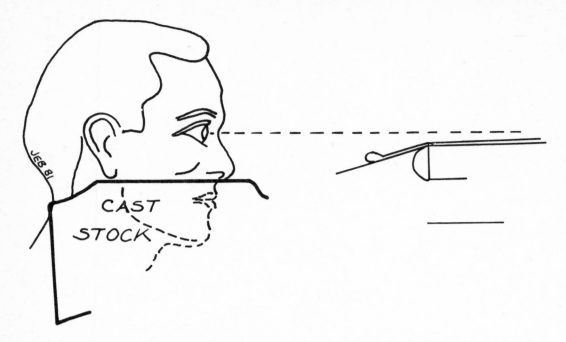

Figure 90   Fit, "Standard British" and "Churchill" styles, Monte Carlo Stock

shooter's face on the widest part of the lower jaw. Thus most people will require a cast stock, the comb and the face of the stock being offset laterally the correct amount to allow the eye to be placed in the proper relationship to the breech end of the rib.

A long-necked shooter, particularly if his shoulders are sloping and/or somewhat inflexible, may be best fitted with a stock with a lower-than-average heel and a Monte Carlo comb (the latter running over the angle of the jaw when the stock is mounted as in Figure 90). The head is not canted and there is the same requirement for exact fitting for cast. The Monte Carlo comb in this instance is simply the mark of a stock of reasonable fore-and-aft comb-slope, stepped down at the heel to fit a lower than usual shoulder. Without the Monte Carlo feature, the resulting steeply-sloped stock comb would contact the face positively only under the front edge of the cheekbone and result in soreness after only a few shots. A short neck is actually an advantage to the shot-gunner.

The relatively long stocks suited to the "Standard British" and "Churchill" styles result in the top of the shoulder being pulled forward somewhat by tension in the arm, and the face of the musculature on which the butt is placed being nearer the vertical when the gun is mounted at a head-height target than it would otherwise be. Despite the forward inclination of the body being more apparent in the "Standard British" than in the "Churchill" style, average down-pitches for these styles do not differ noticeably, being about 2 inches for either measured in the American way of Figure 3. Measured in the British way of Figure 4, a similar pitch would result from a length to toe measurement some ⅜ inch greater than the length of the stock to the centre of the butt (this on the usual side-by-side double gun). For those shooters for whom the stock toe is over the ribs this toe has to be reduced to give comfort, and a stand of 4 or 6 inches off the vertical (Figure 3) may be necessary.

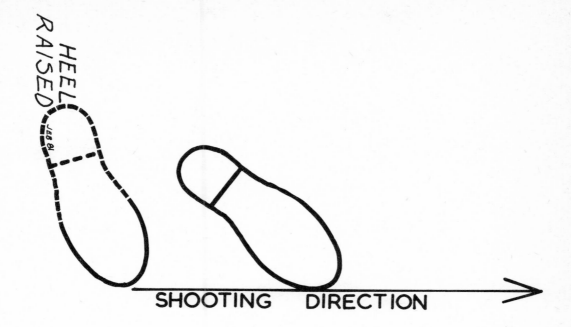

Figure 91 Position of Feet, "Standard British" style

The "Churchill" style had its origins later than the style I have termed "Standard British". Churchill further developed gunmounting to decrease apparent recoil, thus enabling the use of still-lighter guns with standard 12-gauge loads. He did this by adding two further actions, both of them carried out at the exact moment the gun is fired. These are:

a) Deliberately tensing the shoulder musculature behind the butt.

b) Grasping the gun with the forward hand.

Coaches of the "Standard British" style, having observed the success of the first of these actions (which had no counterpart at that time in their own style) forthwith adopted it. They have never been enthusiastic about the second one. The main differences in the two styles today are in the placing of the feet relative to each other and the line of fire, in weight distribution on the feet, the necessity for shorter-barrelled guns for the "Churchill" style (these are also traditionally, and unnecessarily, lighter) and, most importantly, in the methods advocated by each school for obtaining the requisite lead on quartering and crossing birds (requiring a marked difference in the disposition of the gun prior to the final act of mounting it to face and shoulder).

The basic method of leading used by the shooter of the "Standard British" style is the "majority method" of Chapter 1, but he doesn't totally restrict himself to this method any more than does, say, the American hunter. By contrast, the "Churchill" method incorporates a single, distinct way of getting the lead, as an integral part of the method. And it may be noted here that experience has shown that, for most people, the double gun for the "Standard British" style should have barrels not shorter than 28 inches, and that many people shoot their best with a 30 inch barrelled gun of about 7 lbs weight.

Figure 92   Ready position, Low Bird, "Standard British" style

In the placing and spread of the feet (Figure 91) the "Standard British" style resembles the American styles described earlier in this chapter. However, there is a difference in that in the "Standard British" style there is never at any time any substantial part of the shooter's weight on the rear foot. Prior to gunmounting proper, the muzzles of the gun are placed so as to be visible to the shooter in the line from eye to bird (Figure 92). As a preliminary to shooting at birds at elevations above the horizontal the body is tipped backward the requisite amount before gunmounting (Figure 93): the gun is *not* simply mounted at a higher angle against head and shoulder for these shots. Rather is a single relationship of gun and gunner preserved intact. Prior to gunmounting proper the head is turned slightly towards the stock and then kept still relative to the body.

In gunmounting, the gun is pushed outward toward the bird, the muzzle keeping pace with the latter as discussed in Chapter 1 for the "majority method" of leading (and its variants) as the stock is raised. Simultaneously, as the butt is coming up into place on the shoulder, the shoulders are shrugged upward (the elbows being kept down) and the neck muscles deliberately stiffened. The jaw is in the closed position throughout gunmounting and the firing of the gun. The raised rear shoulder is brought forward onto the butt, the musculature on its front surface deliberately hardened, just before, and as, the trigger is pressed. The position that results, in shooting at a head-height bird, is shown in Figure 94.

The gun is held by the forward hand at a point which leaves no more than a slight, comfortable bend in the elbow when the gun is at the shoulder. Thus, typically, the elbow is less bent than in any American style we have looked at. The grasp with the rear hand at the moment of firing is firm, that of the forward hand, light. Some shooters slide the gun out toward the bird *through* the loose grip of the forward hand in mounting the gun, then pull the gun back with the rear hand a short distance as the shoulder comes forward to meet the butt. The argument for this action is that it enables the shooter to use the long stock right for the style, yet without risk of pulling the gun off the line of the bird with the forward hand during gunmounting, due to tension in the forward arm. However, the "Churchill-style" shooter keeps his forward hand in a fixed position throughout gunmounting and seems to manage very well thus. Perhaps sliding the gun through the forward hand in gunmounting for the "Standard British" style helps some people, while others don't need it.

The usual kind of gun used in the "Standard British" and "Churchill" styles is, of course, a side-by-side double with a slim fore-end. Care has therefore to be taken to keep the ends of the fingers and thumb off the top surface of the barrels, and in particular off the rib. A forward hand hold typical of "Standard British" style shooters is shown in Figure 95. Many shooters do not extend the index finger forward, and it should only be placed thus if this is comfortable to the shooter.

The gun ends up almost "locked" in place, pulled firmly against the tensed shoulder muscles by the slight stretch in the extended arms, and in contact with the closed jaw of a head on a stiff neck. The comb crosses the face at about the same level as the mouth and that of the meeting-line of the teeth inside the cheek, usually descending slightly to the rear.

A note on the effects of styles of gunmounting ("Standard British", "Modern British", "Churchill") in which the butt is held firmly against a pad of stiff muscles, on *where* the gun shoots seems appropriate here.

When a gun relatively light for the loads being used (a circumstance not at all unusual in Britain where a 12-gauge gun under 7 lbs may be used with loads of 1⅛ oz

Figure 93   Ready position, High Bird, "Standard British" style

or more, and guns of 6 lbs or under with loads of 1 oz) is thus mounted, the gun *may* enter the *second* phase of recoil (Figure 31) in which the gun as a whole rotates upward about the shoulder, *before* the charge leaves the muzzle. If this were the sole, simple, effect, then the charge would tend to be thrown high. However, modifying factors are often present. For example:

    a) A gun with a thin grip (hand) lacking internal reinforcement in the shape of a stock bolt, and being possibly ill-supported by weak tangs into the bargain, may buckle at the grip when fired. If the charge is still in the barrel when this takes place, the overall effect will be *low* shooting (since the butt is supported below the line of the barrels). If the stock is also cast, buckling can result in lateral off-shooting (to the right of a prolongation of the rib if the stock has cast-off).

    b) Variations in the manner in which a gun is held can cause variations in where it shoots. Light guns with relatively heavy shot loads are particularly sensitive. As we saw in Chapter 1, when the left barrel of a side-by-side double gun is fired, the gun pivots to the left around the centre of gravity (and to the right when the right barrel is fired). When such a gun is mounted to the right shoulder (for example) then ahead of the C. of G. it is supported from the left side, behind the C. of G. from the right side. When gunmounting is such that there is a minimum of tension in the arms, and the butt is placed relatively gently against the shoulder, the charge leaves the muzzle while the gun is still in the *first* phase of recoil. In these circumstances the asymmetry of the support by the arms noted above has little effect (though it is American shooters, note, who mount the gun thus, who also remark on the sideways swing of the side-by-side double when fired). However, when the arms are rigid, the butt tight against the hardened shoulder muscles, and the charges leave the barrels of the relatively light gun during the *second* phase of recoil, the gun (having been prevented from pivoting laterally as far to the left when the left barrel is fired as it does to the right when the right barrel is fired) may tend to shoot to a point to the right of a prolongation of its rib (with both its barrels if they have been properly converged to superimpose their charges when the gun is shot like this). If, in addition (as is often true of the light side-by-side doubles used by many or most British game shooters) the grip of the gun is small and relatively flexible, and the stock is cast at heel and toe, there may be buckling at the grip during recoil, *also* tending to cause off-shooting to the right (for the cast-off stock). Note that if a gun correctly fitted for tight gun-mounting is occasionally mounted by the same shooter in a looser fashion, it will then tend to shoot *left*, and high, relative to the mark! Note, too, that most try-guns are *quite rigid* in the grip area (this being full of "hardware" to give the required pivoting actions). Thus, the cast and drop arrived at with the try-gun are not likely to be right for unmodified transference to a slim-gripped, light, game gun, the stock of which is held in place by two short tangs. The reader may consider the difficulties of the gunmaker in arriving at the correct cast dimensions for a cross-eyed stock on a light side-by-side double gun, and come once more to the correct conclusion that cast and drop dimensions on all guns for a certain shooter can really only be arrived at with confidence by trial and error in real action by that shooter with each gun.

    c) Since the over-and-under gun rotates more around the C.G. when the upper barrel is fired than it does when the lower one is fired, and since tight mounting of the butt against the shoulder results in less than usual downward rotation of

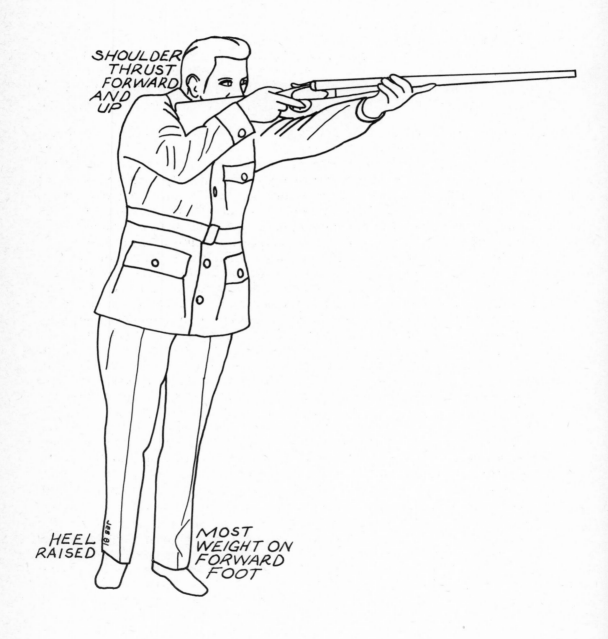

Figure 94   Gun mounted, Low Bird, "Standard British" style

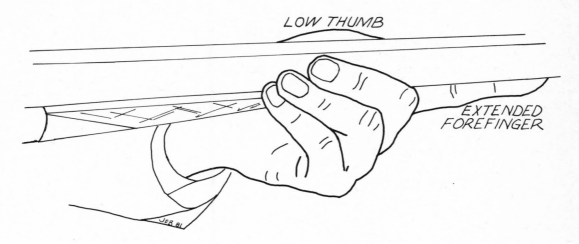

Figure 95 Grip of Forward Hand, "Standard British" style

the stock in the first phase of recoil, in these circumstances the upper barrel shoots lower than it does with a looser mount.

Returning to the general discussion of the "Standard British" style: recoil pads on the relatively long stocks which are suited to this and to the "Churchill" style, unless covered in leather or some similar substance, are a nuisance, persistently catching on the clothing in the last stage of gunmounting when the butt is "skidded" up into place, already in light contact with the shoulder. In these, and the "Modern British", styles of shooting, the shooter's own, deliberately tensed, shoulder musculature forms the "recoil pad". The pad is on the gunner rather than the gun. And there *is* great recoil resistance inherent in these styles when the actions that go into them are carried out correctly.

In the "Standard British" style the weight is kept on the forward foot at all times, both when swinging on birds well to either side of the shooter as well as on overhead birds (Figures 96 to 100). This gives great flexibility in where the gun can be pointed with relative ease. Note that in Figures 96 and 98, a good deal of swing takes place before the gun is fully mounted to face and shoulder to shoot. There is no difficulty in shooting at birds directly overhead (or even at those which have passed over and are now a little behind the shooter). Even with the relatively long stock suited to the style of gunmounting described above, the head can be kept on the comb without difficulty while the gun is swung over wide lateral arcs.

b) Churchill style

Our Mr. Average Competent Shotgunner of Chapter 1 is one day in a hide (blind) with a spread of duck decoys in front of him. He glances down at his watch and as he looks

Figure 96 Swing to left, Gun not yet mounted, "Standard British" style

Figure 97 Swing to left, Gun mounted, ''Standard British'' style

Figure 98 Swing to right, Gun not yet mounted, "Standard British" style

HEEL
RAISED

Figure 99   Swing to right, Gun mounted, "Standard British" style

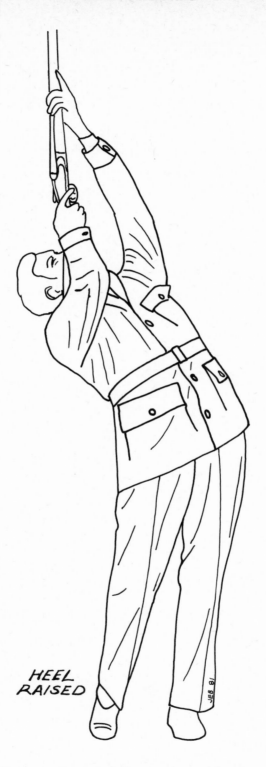

HEEL
RAISED

Figure 100 Overhead Bird, "Standard British" style

up again he sees a duck crossing his front, fast and close. He swings the gun after it, pulling the trigger as the muzzle passes the bird. The duck is killed dead in the air.

The following day as he is walking through the woods he disturbs a woodcock which flashes across an open space to one side of him. He quickly gets the gun after it, and, as he did with the duck, kills it cleanly with no lead apparent to himself.

The next day is Sunday. On the skeet field our hero breaks all his Station 8 targets (please see page 150 if you are not familiar with skeet) by (it seems to him) shooting straight at them. Though he breaks them oncoming, near mid-field, his preliminary point of the gun was always at the house from which the target was to come.

What these three situations have in common (in addition to successful hitting of a crossing or quartering target with no lead apparent to the shooter) is that in each the gun begins its movement from a point relatively far behind the speeding bird or target. When the muzzle catches up with either of the latter, the gun is moving very fast. The reaction-time of many people is such that if, in these circumstances, they decide to fire as the muzzle passes the bird, the slight delay before the trigger is *actually pulled* (combined with some other tiny mechanical delays in the system for firing the gun) will ensure that a crossing bird not too far away will get enough actual lead to be hit by the shot charge. The shooter is conscious of neither delay nor lead.

In any method of shooting at crossing birds in which the shooter can, it seems to him, shoot straight at the bird and yet hit it, there is an early stage in which the gun is pointing quite far behind the bird. So far behind it, indeed, that the gun *must* be swung very quickly thence to catch up with the bird. Such a stage is a necessary and integral part of the method of shotgun shooting taught by an English gunmaker, the late Robert Churchill, and more closely associated with his name than that of any other person. This is the method mislabelled the ''English method'' in so much of present-day American writing on shotgun shooting, as if it were the method of the majority, rather than a minority, of Britons. When carried out properly it results in no lead apparent to the shooter being necessary to hit any crossing or quartering bird.

When a shot is expected the strict ''Churchill-style'' shooter tucks the butt of the gun high up under his armpit. For birds at low elevations the position is pretty erect as shown in Figure 101, and the gun about horizontal. In gunmounting, the butt is slid up the front of the shoulder as the gun is thrust out at the bird. As in the ''Standard British'' style, the shoulders are shrugged upward, and the musculature on the face of the rear one tensed. The neck muscles are also deliberately stiffened. The head, jaws closed, is turned slightly towards the stock and is kept still during gunmounting. These actions are eventually performed quite subconsciously. Gunmounting culminates with the shoulder on the gun side being deliberately brought forward onto the butt of the gun (Figure 102). When the gun is mounted in true ''Churchill'' style it is not brought back to the shoulder at all in gunmounting, and the length of the stock has to be carefully adjusted (even more so than for the ''Standard British'' style) to ensure that there is no need for any pulling back of the gun to the shoulder: forward movement of the shoulder in the last stage of gunmounting being itself sufficient to give firm support to the butt. The elbows are kept low, and the gun ends supported in the same rigid, recoil-resistant framework of bones and tensed muscles as in the ''Standard British'' style. The gun that fits the shooter for one style will be found to suit him pretty well for the other.

Further to decrease recoil taken by face and shoulder, Churchill advocated grasping the gun firmly with the forward hand at the moment of discharge: this being timed to be exactly as gunmounting is complete. Churchill's own grip featured a high thumb

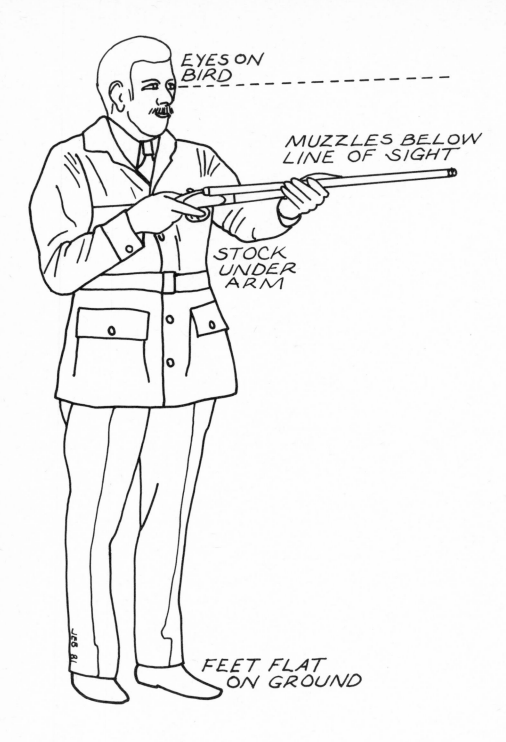

EYES ON
BIRD

MUZZLES BELOW
LINE OF SIGHT

STOCK
UNDER
ARM

FEET FLAT
ON GROUND

Figure 101   Ready position, Low Bird, "Churchill" style

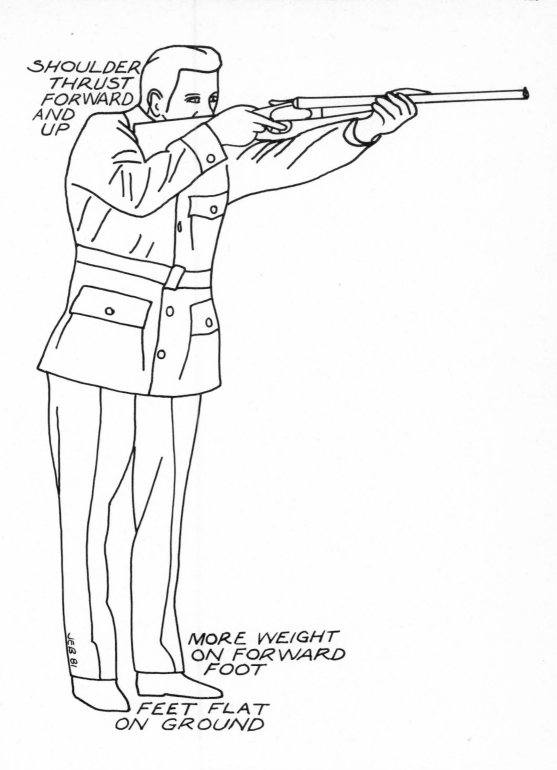

Figure 102   Gun mounted, Low Bird, "Churchill" style

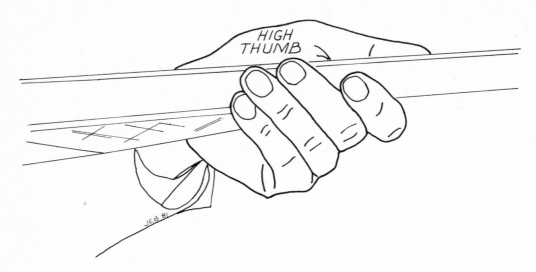

Figure 103   Grip of Forward Hand, "Churchill" style

(Figure 103) which blocked the front end of the barrels from the view of the eye not behind the breech. This was useful to Churchill, whose eye-dominance was apparently slight and inconstant after an accident during World War I.

In the first stage of shooting at quartering and crossing birds (including those at high angles above the horizontal) the shooter turns with the bird. On high-angle birds (such as the overhead incomer) he tips back his body also, but the stock stays under the armpit, and the approximate right-angle between body and barrels as viewed from the side is maintained (Figure 104). If at this stage the gun points higher than horizontal it is because the body has been tipped back ready to shoot at a high-angle bird, not because the gun has been raised to a higher angle independent of the attitude of the body.

The stout, stocky Churchill had a narrow stance (Figure 105) and transferred his weight to the side towards which he was swinging (Figures 106 and 109), lifting the opposite heel, golf-swing fashion. He transferred his weight to the forward foot for low incomers and outgoers (Figure 102) and to the rear foot in shooting at overhead birds (Figures 110, 111). However, the "Standard British" practice of a wider stance with the weight kept on the forward foot at all times (Figure 91) is also perfectly satisfactory for what would be in all other aspects a "Churchill" style.

Gunmounting begins with the shooter's gaze fixed on the bird and with the gun pointing where he is looking. However, as the shooter continues to follow the flight of the crossing bird with his eyes, the gun lags in its direction of pointing *behind the eye* (its stock under the shooter's armpit, still, remember) and hence *behind the bird also* (Figures 106, 108, 110). The proof of this is devastatingly simple: Churchill and all his followers emphasize that the swing of the gun must be accelerated in the last part of gunmounting as the stock comes right up to face and shoulder. This can only mean that prior to this the gun was pointing behind the bird if accelerating its swing brings

Figure 104 Ready position, High Bird, "Churchill" style

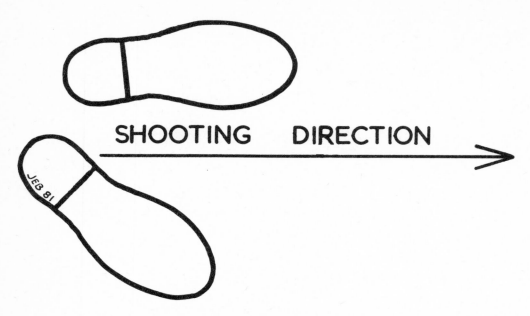

Figure 105   Position of Feet, ''Churchill'' style

the muzzles onto (and beyond) the bird as the trigger is pulled. It also means that the Churchill school are in error in maintaining, as they do, that the gun is pointing at the bird throughout the whole of the gunmounting process: beginning, middle and end.

The ''lagging'' of the swing of the gun, the fact that until the very last stage of the gunmounting process it points some distance behind the bird (on which the eye is fixed, as in Figures 106, 108 and 110) is quite apparent in a number of action photographs in Churchill's books. *It is absolutely necessary to the method.* It is not apparent to the shooter, and cannot be allowed to become so to *his* eyes or he will at once (at a stage premature for this method) attempt to *catch up to the bird* with the muzzles of the gun. In short, the ''Churchill method'' of obtaining lead would become the ''majority method''! To make sure that the actual direction the gun is pointing is NOT apparent to the shooter until the very last stage of gunmounting, the muzzles in particular must be kept low and out of the centre of the shooter's field of vision (Figures 106, 108, 110) out of the line of sight from bird to eye, until the last split second when the swing is accelerated as the gun is fully mounted and the trigger pressed as the muzzles pass the bird. If, in this *late* stage, the gunner sees the rapidly accelerating muzzles a fraction of a second too early, he will often, conversely, *slow down (and indeed stop) the gun* because it is apparent to him that the muzzles are indeed going far faster than the bird. From the stationary gun the charge flies harmlessly behind the bird. To execute the ''Churchill'' style properly is to tread a narrow path indeed in regard to when the gun is seen in the gunmounting process, but it is one followed with success by many game shooters.

The tucking of the stock well under the armpit has two effects. First, it ''ties'' the gun to the body. The body has more inertia than do the eyeballs, it takes more ''getting going'' in the early part of the swing on crossing birds. This is what produces the ''lag''

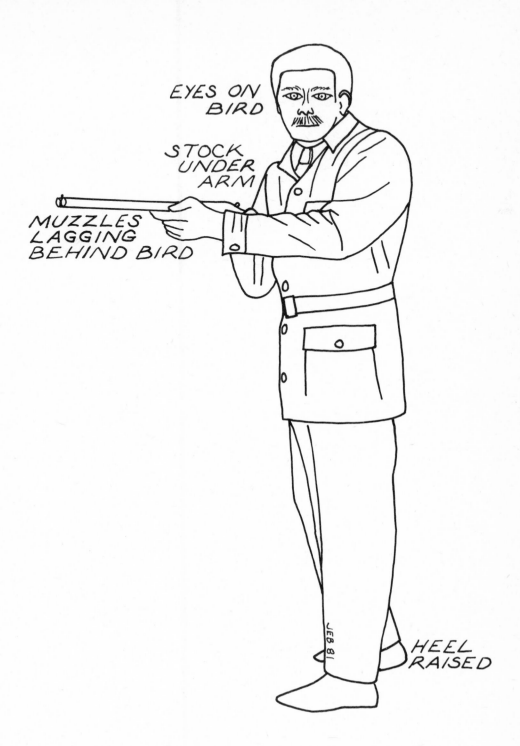

Figure 106   Swing to left, Gun not yet mounted, "Churchill" style

of the gun behind the eyes in the swing before the gun is mounted, referred to above. Second, it shortens the amount of barrel sticking forward into the lower part of the shooter's field of view, and in the "Churchill" method the less the gun thus sticks forward the better, as being less likely to have its actual pointing direction in the middle and later stages of swinging with a crossing bird noticed by the shooter and "corrected" (the essence of the "Churchill" method being a single, swift, correction of gunpoint at the very end of the process (Figures 107, 109, 111)). Matters are helped by choosing a type of gun itself inherently short, its breech as short a distance as possible ahead of its trigger or triggers, and fitting this with short barrels. This means the use of a double-barrelled (rather than a repeating) gun, but so important is this factor that even the minor difference in this distance from breech to triggers between boxlock and sidelock guns puts the former in a slight but discernible advantage for the method.

Further to ensure that the gun points behind the bird except in the final moment when the muzzles are accelerated "through" it, Churchill and his disciples lay great emphasis on being in no great hurry to mount the gun (no matter how fast the body is turning, stiff-necked, after the bird). Whether they know it or not, what they are doing is giving time for the "lag" to develop. Also, a long stock takes longer to mount than does a short one, and in the "Churchill" style the long stock serves to delay the completion of the final stage of gunmounting (making certain that the final acceleration is fully developed before the trigger is pulled) as well as to reduce recoil effect, the latter being an important factor with the very light guns affected by many "Churchill-style" shooters.

Such especially-light guns, of low inertia, are not necessary to most people in reaching the necessary acceleration of swing in the last stage of gunmounting. In building, and vehemently advocating, the light, side-by-side double-barrelled guns, with the short (25 inch) barrels associated with his name, Churchill was simply going to an extreme to take advantage of a fashionable trend for light guns he perceived among British driven game shooters. He backed up their manufacture with continuous advertising, never beaten for its mixture of cajolery and carefully selected facts. As a live pigeon trapshooter he knew, contrary to his advertising, how very quickly guns much longer and heavier than his XXV game guns could be brought to bear on birds travelling quite as fast as the average game bird, and carrying money on their backs.

Strange to say, there is no evidence in Churchill's books, nor in those of any of his followers, that he or they understood or understand why the method he advocated works if it is carried out properly. Specifically, there is no hint of a realisation that the vital factors are:

1. The adoption of a way of holding the gun that causes its swing to lag behind the movement of the eyes as they follow the bird, until the very final stage of gun-mounting.
2. Keeping the gun low, out of the centre of the shooter's field of vision, so that his eyes do not register this lag.
3. The cultivation of a leisurely attitude to beginning the final stage of gunmounting.
4. The combination of factors 1, 2 and 3 to produce a gap so large between the lagging muzzles and the speeding bird that the acceleration needed to reach the bird with the muzzles (as these become apparent to the eye in the last stage of gunmounting) carries them well beyond the bird in the interval between the decision to press the trigger (as the muzzles pass the bird) and the actual release of the shot, the shooter having the impression that he gave the bird no lead at all.

HEEL
RAISED

Figure 107 Swing to left, Gun mounted, "Churchill" style

Weight is lent in the books of Churchill and others of his school to all kinds of minor details of the style, and there are a good many errors of interpretation. Already mentioned has been their belief, continually reiterated without a shred of evidence, that the hands are pointing the gun at the bird throughout the whole process of gun-mounting from beginning to end. If this were so, no final acceleration would be required to bring the muzzles onto the bird, and every crossing bird fired on would be missed by shooting behind it (at best, or at worst be caught by a few pellets of shot sufficient to wound).

Also reiterated in the misleading half-truth that the eye and the brain judge the speed of the bird and can be left to do their job in producing a speed of swing allowing the shooter to shoot right at crossing birds and yet succeed in hitting them. In the ''Churchill'' method such unconscious judgement is only part of the story, and the lesser part. We have seen above how the method depends for its success on the adoption of a rather specialised technique in holding and mounting the gun. That is not the end of the story as regards the learning and use of specialised techniques by the successful ''Churchill-style'' shooter, and here it is necessary to dig a little deeper into the general experience of shooters trying to use it.

Many people have great success and few difficulties in applying the ''Churchill'' method on crossing birds at relatively close ranges, say 15 to 25 yards. This, it is true, covers the shooter's needs in a lot of game shooting, and duck shooting over decoys. In order to succeed at farther ranges, however, many of these same shooters find they have to adopt a different style of leading: the ''majority method'' of Chapter 1 in fact. This even applies to many of Churchill's avowed disciples, who, when shooting at more distant crossing birds, start talking about ''seeing a bit of lead''. The ''transition zone'' between the ranges at which a certain individual among these shooters can use the ''Churchill'' style, and those at which he has to begin ''seeing some lead'' if he is to hit crossing birds, is relatively narrow: just a few yards in fact. Often such a shooter will consistently hit crossing birds at 25 yards using a pure ''Churchill'' technique, but will miss 30 yard birds just as consistently, unless he gives them some lead visible to himself as he pulls the trigger. The general experience, then, in trying to use the ''Churchill'' style at relatively distant crossing birds is one of consistently shooting behind them. *This is due to allowing the low apparent speed of such birds (their angular velocity — and the farther away they are the slower this becomes) to affect the velocity of the swing of the gun in all stages of gunmounting, including the final acceleration of the gun to and beyond the bird.* Churchill's books offer no further guidance on, or differentiation of, such situations, and doubts have often been expressed by unbelievers as to whether or not he himself could use the method he advocated, pure and unadulterated, on distant crossing birds, since he offers no explanation of how such birds receive greater angular lead than the method would seem naturally geared to give them.

However, the point to be grasped is that it doesn't matter whether or not Churchill himself could use the pure ''Churchill'' method with success on crossing birds near *and far*, because lots of other people *can!* Here is how:

The *apparent* speed of the bird governs the speed with which the eyes follow it: they being fixed on it. The body and the gun (the stock tucked under the armpit) lag somewhat behind the eyes, but a fast, close, crossing bird produces a quicker rotation of the body-plus-gun than does an equally fast, distant, crossing bird. Thus, the movement of the gun *before* the final act of mounting it to face and shoulder is governed by whether it is following a close bird (which flashes by) or a more distant one, which,

Figure 108 Swing to right, Gun not yet mounted, "Churchill" style

because it takes longer to cover the same angle in front of the shooter, seems slower. But, *and this is the crux of the matter*, the final acceleration of the gun as it is mounted fully to face and shoulder is NOT governed by these differences in apparent speeds of near and distant birds (actually flying at similar speeds) when the Churchill method is used successfully at distant, as well as near, quartering and crossing birds. In fact, all other things being equal (principally the species of bird and the angle at which it is crossing) **about the same acceleration** (as felt by the hands, arms and body, and stored in "muscle memory") is used on ALL birds, regardless of the fact that the more distant a bird is, the slower it seems to be. Thus, the kind of unconscious message governing the speed of the final acceleration of the gun by the successful "Churchill-style" shooter is not "This bird looks fast" and "This one looks slow", but perhaps something like "Crossing mallard . . . . . needs a good strong swing like this . . . . .", or "Quartering partridge . . . . . gently does it . . . . .". Naturally, variations are neces-sary for different kinds of birds, and to meet the difference in conditions when they are flying in still air, or going with, or battling against, a strong wind. Sooner or later all the required actions, and modifications, become unconscious decisions.

The "Churchill" method of leading as it is applied to relatively distant birds (which is what allows it to become one of universal application for some people) is not an easy thing to learn. Though its use by the successful "Churchill-style" shooter eventually becomes for him an unconscious matter, there is nothing "natural" about it, and it has to be learned. Nor is the idea an easy one to get hold of. My only consolation for its having taken me a long time in observation of the occasional, excellent "Churchill-style" shooters I encountered before I was able to discern exactly what they were doing, *particularly on distant birds*, is that if the explanation ever dawned on Churchill, or on any of his disciples, they certainly never explained the matter in anything they have written. None of the shooters referred to was of any more help to me in analysing his own actions than the books of Churchill or any of his followers had been.

Living in North America, I will try to give a good North American analogy to drive home what I have been talking about. Readers from other parts of the world will be able to translate it into their own terms I'm sure. Suppose you are batting at softball practice (the very amateur inter-office league, say) and are facing a pitcher who is putting balls all around you, not just (properly) in front of you over the plate. Perhaps it's that nice brunette from Accounts, and you don't really give a darn where she pitches the ball, she's such a pleasure to have around. O.K.: *where* she pitches the ball and *how fast* determine *where* and *how fast* you have to turn to hit it. That is the part analogous to the early part of the "Churchill" swing, stock under armpit, before the gun is started on its way to face and shoulder. Returning to the softball practice: being now shaped-up to hit the ball (the bat in the right place to do so — which corresponds to the placing of the gun by its lagging behind the bird which I keep harping on) you can now *choose* how hard to hit the ball. Getting back to the shotgun: The "Churchill-style" shooter "hits" at quartering birds more gently than at those which cross at a near or full right-angle. But all true crossers at normal speeds of bird flight need a good, smooth, solid "hit", *particularly the distant ones that seem so slow*. At first, as I have said, this has to be done consciously, later it becomes a subconscious matter. Note, however, that nowhere are there "subconscious allowances" in any of this.

At this point some words of caution are necessary. People with quick and very quick reflexes find the "Churchill" method hard to use successfully. Their decision to fire is followed so quickly by the discharge of the gun that, despite the speed of the final

HEEL
RAISED

Figure 109 Swing to right, Gun mounted, ''Churchill'' style

accelerating part of the swing, if they decide to pull the trigger as the muzzles pass the bird, often sufficient time does not elapse before the gun fires to build up enough lead to hit the bird.

The minor factors in building up this time are such things as the time the hammer takes to fall after its release, and the time taken for the primer to ignite the propellant. These amount to only a few thousandths of a second. Because those people who have their finger on the trigger at all during the early part of the swing (by far the majority) always put some pressure on it then, pulling the trigger with the little extra force needed to release the sear seems to take very little actual time (unless the pull is quite heavy) perhaps effectively less than 1/100th of a second if the trigger is in contact with the bony part of the hinge nearest the tip of the finger. If the trigger is in contact with the fleshy pad of the finger tip, more time will elapse until this "cushion" is squashed flat. If the finger is kept off the trigger altogether until the decision to shoot is made, and then brought into forcible contact with it ("slapping" the trigger, as is the custom of some "Churchill-style" shooters as well as some trapshooters who pull the trigger on every clay target just as the muzzle passes it) then still more time will elapse, since the finger has to be moved some distance to contact the trigger. But, with any of these methods, the time-lapse in actually pulling the trigger (including any preliminary finger-movement) seems still to be only a few hundredths of a second (though every little time-lapse between the decision to fire and the shot beginning its travel is a help to most people in trying to use the "Churchill" method, and hence a step in the right direction!).

The biggest time-lapse of all, and the governing one in the situation, is that resulting from the reaction-time of the shooter: the time between his decision to fire and the application by the finger of the final increment of pressure which releases the sear and fires the gun.

There are two important things to be grasped about reaction-times. One is the point just made: that for most people and their trigger-pulling style, the reaction-time is several times greater than any other factor causing lapse of time between the decision to shoot and the shot-load actually starting on its way up the barrel. The other thing is that reaction-times vary very much from person to person. In a group of people it is common to find that the longest reaction-time in the group is several times that of the shortest, perhaps five or six times as long indeed.

Suppose we have two shooters with reaction-times of 2/100ths and 6/100ths of a second respectively, times quite typical of "fast" and "medium" reflexes. Each will try to shoot crossing birds "Churchill-style". Let us suppose, too, that during acceleration of the muzzles past the bird in the final stage of gunmounting each has a speed of swing such that the muzzles pass a 40 mph bird at 20 yards range, 50 mph faster than the bird is travelling (i.e. the muzzles would keep pace with a 90 mph bird at the same 20 yard range). Fifty miles per hour is about 73 feet per second. If our friend with the short reaction-time presses the trigger just as the muzzles pass the bird he will get (due to his reaction-time, and neglecting the other slighter factors mentioned above) only $2/100 \times 73 = 1\frac{1}{2}$ feet of lead. His slower-reacting colleague gets *three times* this ($6/100 \times 73 = 4\frac{1}{2}$ feet) which, incidentally, is about the right order of actual lead to hit the bird.

Note:−

1) The completely different order of lead given by a mere 4/100 second difference in reaction-time.

Figure 110 Swing on Overhead Bird, Gun not yet mounted, "Churchill" style

2) That one is an effective lead, the other quite useless. This accounts for the lack of agreement (and even of understanding) between shooters on any kind of lead (''Churchill'' *or* ''majority-method'') resulting in whole or in part from an accelerating swing, from behind the bird or from the bird itself. Persons of fast and slow reflexes find it impossible to imagine each other's physiology, and difficult indeed to reconcile the results accruing in this instance from the difference. Obviously no shooter of either class gets much added, unconscious, lead from the other, slighter, delays of lock-time and ignition-time. These give a couple of inches (or so) added lead for everyone. Time taken in pulling the trigger varies, but whatever method takes the longest time (and so gives the greatest delay) probably adds not more than a foot and a half to the lead. However, this much can make the difference in allowing some people to use the ''Churchill'' method successfully. A heavy trigger, too, takes longer to pull than does a light one. It may be noted here that while a relatively long-barrelled gun of full weight, with a light trigger-pull gives good, steady shooting using the ''majority'' leading-method, a short-barrelled, possibly lighter gun with a relatively heavy trigger-pull (it must be constant and without creep!) helps the ''Churchill-style'' shooter to get the necessary (to him, unseen) lead. The requirements in the two styles are, in a sense, poles apart (though a *light* gun cannot be classed as a real requirement for the ''Churchill'' style). Thus, despite what appears in some writing on the shotgun, a heavy trigger-pull can be part and parcel of someone's shooting success. It isn't always bad. Note how dependent is the success of the ''Churchill'' style on the balance of trigger-pull weight against gun-weight and inertia. A change in this balance can leave the ''Churchill-style'' exponent missing *every* crossing and quartering bird until he finds the new ''formula''.

3) If the shooter with the 6/100ths of a second reaction-time used the same speed of swing on a 40 mph bird at 40 yards in his final acceleration, then that part of his lead resulting from his reaction-time alone would amount to 9 feet. Again, this is the right order of actual lead needed to hit the bird. In practice he would again get a bit more lead from the effects of those other, minor, delays built into the system catalogued above. His final swing (the same pace as before) would keep pace with an imaginary bird 40 yards away travelling at 180 mph; 140 mph faster than the bird being shot at. ''Ridiculous''? No, indeed. This speed of swing, useful to the person of medium reaction-time in using the ''Churchill'' method (and to those of slightly shorter reaction-times if they can speed up their final swing without it becoming uncontrollable, and/or find a method of pulling the trigger which takes them a relatively long, constant, time) is a bit *slower* than the swing needed to keep up with the ordinary American and British rules skeet target from Station 8 (page 153) as it nears the shooter's position. It is not, therefore, some outrageous, impossible, speed. Note that the skeet shooter of medium reaction-time who wishes to be able to pull the trigger with success just as his muzzle passes the targets must use about this *same* final speed of swing on his *more distant crossing targets also* (shot from the middle Stations, 3, 4 and 5). Just as the ''Churchill-style'' game shooter uses about the same speed of swing on birds travelling at a certain speed, be they near or far. Some skeet shooters (including the author's elder son) shoot skeet thus by preference.

4) A person with really slow reflexes can swing much more slowly past the bird, pull the trigger as the muzzles pass it, and still hit it. For example, if his reaction-time is 12/100ths of a second, then in the example above he would need a speed

HEEL
RAISED

Figure 111   Swing on Overhead Bird, Gun mounted, "Churchill" style

of swing only an apparent 25 mph faster than the 40 mph, 20 yard bird. However, the person of really slow reflexes is often not capable of anything more than a pretty slow swing anyway, so gains no particular advantage in using the Churchill method.

5) Conversely, people with really short reaction-times (fast reflexes) usually stop trying to use a "Churchill" type of method (if they ever try it) and, since they have to look (and hence point) ahead of the bird anyway in order to hit it, use the "majority method" of Chapter 1 as a general thing, and the "sustained lead" under some circumstances (e.g. on skeet targets). If their eyesight is good, these are people who have all the time in the world, almost, to point a gun anywhere they choose in relation to the bird (or most clay targets) though it is sometimes hard to convince them of this. Of course, they can try to use the "Churchill" style by deliberately using more force in the swing in the final stage of gunmounting. However, for the person of really short reaction-time, this has to be so fast that it inevitably lacks control, and hence accuracy. And if a shooter *can't* pull the trigger as the muzzles pass the bird, there is for him no point in the "Churchill" method. Far better that he should stick to other methods of leading, chosen to fit the circumstances. He should shut his ears to talk about the "Churchill" method, refrain from pointing out that it is suited to those who are innately slower in their reactions than he himself is, and rejoice inwardly that corrections of pointing and trigger-timing are possible for him in the last split-second. These are much more difficult (and often impossible) for the "Churchill-style" shooter, who is already deeply committed to direction of pointing and timing of discharge at an earlier stage in his gunmounting, despite the fact that at that stage the gun has not started on its travel to face and shoulder.

As was mentioned in Chapter 1, on birds which are either rising straight towards 12 o'clock in front of the shooter (or say between 11 and 1), or oncoming straight overhead (which in terms of angle amounts to the same thing if you think about it) or are diving steeply down towards some point between 5 and 7 o'clock, few people can successfully use a method of shooting in which the gun is triggered immediately it comes fully to shoulder and face. The attempt to get the right lead, or the right velocity of muzzle to remove the need for apparent lead, simultaneous with mounting the gun, usually results in mounting the latter too high or too low at the shoulder, giving rise to frequent misses from shooting over or under the bird. The most consistently successful approach to such shots is first to mount the gun fully to shoulder and face pointing at, and keeping pace with, the bird, and *then* to seek the proper lead by the "majority method", looking (and hence accelerating the muzzle) a suitable distance ahead of the bird before the trigger is pulled. That Churchill himself had difficulties with such shots is made obvious by his advice on how to shoot high, incoming, driven pheasants. This advice amounts to holding the head high, off the comb of the stock, putting the eye far above the rib to give "automatic" (his term) lead on such birds. Leads given by the normal "Churchill" method we have been discussing above depend on the speed of movement of the gun from behind the bird. In sharp contrast, most of the lead in this other method advocated by Churchill results from the eye being far above the breech! It seems not to have occurred to Churchill, incidentally (any more than it does today to a high proportion of British or American coaches of any style of shotgun shooting) to tell the student to turn through 90 degrees right or left (presuming there is time to do this) to convert such birds into pure "crossers" to be shot by any method of lead the shooter favours.

As we have seen, when mounted in the true "Churchill" fashion, the gun is not brought back to the shoulder at all, nor are the elbows raised. There is the same thrusting point at the bird as in the "Standard British" style. A stock that suits a person for one style will suit him equally well for the other. But, whereas he may well like a 30 inch barrelled gun for shooting in the "Standard British" style, shooting well in the "Churchill" style may require him to use a gun with barrels four or five inches shorter in order to keep the muzzles out of the central area of the field of view until the last part of gunmounting.

Churchill himself, and those instructors who still teach his methods to all comers, taught, and teach, everything that Churchill found suitable for himself to everyone, any variations being regarded as little short of heresy. This extends beyond gunfitting and gunmounting even to such details as Churchill's personal manner of holding the barrels with his forward hand. This phenomenon will bear looking into, since these instructors do advocate these things as universal prescriptions, and one is forced to wonder if they would do so had they considered the matter at all deeply, instead of accepting things almost as a matter of faith.

Churchill began managing his late uncle's gunmaking business in 1911, and his biographer, Hastings, says that, though at first his main work was the building of the relatively heavy, relatively long-barrelled guns for live-pigeon trapshooting for which his uncle, E. J. Churchill, had been so justly renowned, Robert Churchill quickly perceived the well-to-do British game shooter as a potentially richer market. By 1912 he had built what is described as the "prototype" of the 25 inch barrelled ("XXV") game guns with which his name was to be so closely associated. With all respect, I submit that this is of minor importance. There had been numerous previous excursions into the building of light, short-barrelled guns in Britain and Europe. There was nothing new in that in 1892, let alone 1912, and the earlier guns may also be said to have claims as the "prototype" of the "XXV" gun.

Of far greater importance in this saga was the severe injury Churchill's right eye received when he was testing experimental tracer ammunition for the Royal Flying Corps in 1917 or 1918. Blowback from the breech of a self-loading rifle using this ammunition almost cost Churchill the sight of his right, master, eye. Subsequently, it appears that his left eye would at times take over mastery in gun-pointing from the right one. In solving this problem. Churchill continued to shoot from the right shoulder (after all, his right eye was master most of the time) but he made a particular point of grasping the gun with his left hand so that the barrels were cradled well down in all four fingers and the thumb stood high by the side of the left barrel (Figure 103). The base of the thumb blocked the left eye's view of the muzzle-end of the barrels (Figure 112) preventing cross-firing at those times when his left eye assumed mastery. After World War I, Churchill was effectively a one-eyed gun-pointer. Using his left thumb he achieved a remedy for his personal eyesight troubles, without the need of "gadgets". He was still able to keep his left eye open, thus retaining full visual acuity in his right eye, and not subjecting himself to the tension of having to close the left eye, or the possibility of forgetting to do so.

But, like all one-eyed (or effectively one-eyed) gun-pointers, he could not see under the barrels of his gun (or "through the gun" as the shooting coach says). This is what the open eye which is not directly above the barrels allows the shooter who keeps both eyes open to do (Figure 113) unless its view is blocked by some kind of gadget, or in some other way (as by Churchill's left thumb, Figure 112). It is true that when keeping both eyes open, the user of a side-by-side double-barrelled gun does not see as deep a

Figure 112   High left thumb, Eye cannot see under Gun

field under it as he would if using an over-and-under or a repeater. These are narrower, and the lower position of the forward hand frees a greater field of view, particularly in the foreground. But, keeping both eyes open, the user of the side-by-side double gun can certainly see birds behind (or beneath) his barrels, even if these are high, fast incomers, and he the kind of shooter whose leading method requires substantial apparent lead on such birds, so that they are well behind the barrels and beneath the muzzles when shot at.

Churchill had been an effectively (and effective) two-eyed gun pointer, but could be so no longer. If you are one of the majority who have a master eye and who shoot with two eyes open, go out sometime and shoot incoming clay targets taking care to keep that eye not over the gun closed. Without further demonstration you will know why Churchill had to try to develop a method of gunmounting and leading that allowed him to pull the trigger on *all* birds while they were still in view, including those that using any other method would be "blotted out" by the barrels for the one-eyed gun pointer. It is ironical that, while the method he developed was successful for Churchill on other birds, as we have seen it didn't give him enough lead on the very archetypal bird that gave him the impetus to develop the method in the first place: the oncoming, high, driven pheasant. However, the success of the technique in his hands and that of a proportion of his driven game shooter clients on other birds is unquestioned. It must not be lost sight of that the average range at which such driven game is shot is under 20 yards, lots of birds being hit at 15 yards from the shooter, and few being shot at more than 25 yards away. The really high driven pheasants shown at a handful of British and European localities are an exception to this.

Figure 113   Low left thumb, Eye can see under Gun

The key features in equipment for success in the "Churchill" style are short barrels and a long, suitably cast, stock. The light weight of the typical Churchill game gun is not necessary to the speed of swing required in the final stage of gunmounting in the "Churchill" style. It is impossible for Churchill not to have known this, accustomed as he was to live pigeon trapshooting with guns 2lbs heavier, the "secret" of this game (if it has one) being to get off the first shot so fast (but accurately!) that the pigeon is hit within a few yards of the trap. It is equally impossible for him not to have known that there remained in existence a method of leading other than the one he advocated, which did not, either, involve mental calculation, and which was in use with complete success by most of the best shots of the day (as it still is). Nevertheless, Churchill prescribed his short-barrelled, long-stocked (and extra-light) game guns for all his clients: short and tall, stiff and supple, young and old, slow as molasses or quick as lightning. All were assured that these guns were right for them. The argument was that if the stocky, stiffly-built Churchill could shoot well with them, how much better, then, for example, a slim, supple, naturally-fast 6 footer with constant, complete eye-mastery on his gun side! Churchill turned a blind eye to the fact that such a shooter can afford to see all his oncoming birds "through the gun" by taking the usual grip with the forward hand on a double gun (i.e. with a low thumb as in Figure 113) and can therefore use the "majority method" of leading on these, and all other, birds, swinging more slowly (and therefore more controllably and accurately) in relation to the bird.

Such a shooter, indeed anyone who shoots in other than the "Churchill" style, is better suited by longer barrels. He doesn't have to keep them out of his field of view in all but the very last stage of gunmounting (indeed the reverse is the case, as we have seen, for the muzzles should be in the line from bird to eye from the very beginning of the process). Too, the longer barrels are by their very nature suited to the slower swing of the "majority method" lead, since if they are accelerated too fast in relation to the bird, the muzzles, being relatively far from the eye, tend to become a blur, which being unsatisfactory to the brain, the latter insists that they be moved more slowly! There is no midway compromise possible between the "Churchill" method and various forms of the "majority method" (or the "sustained lead" method of course) in technique or in ideal equipment as regards barrel-length, and this is an important point.

Churchill insisted that less apparent lead was needed when using short as opposed to longer barrelled guns when methods involving a visible lead were used, all other things being equal. For any variant of the "majority method" lead he was correct (though not for the "sustained lead" method). The reason is that the shorter the barrels, the greater the angular velocity with which the gun can be moved and still have the muzzles (though not being looked at, remember) clear to the eye. For this reason shorter-barrelled guns tend to be swung quicker than longer-barrelled ones and the weight and inertia of the guns is but a modifier to this tendency. It must not be lost sight of that added speed usually means decreased control, and that it is easy to swing so fast that timing the pulling of the trigger becomes difficult.

As well as recommending his short-barrelled guns, and his method of gunmounting and leading, to everyone, Churchill himself, totally without perceptible logic, went so far as to recommend that everyone grip the barrels of the side-by-side gun (the virtually universal choice of his customers) exactly as he himself did, thus quite unnecessarily converting those people with eye-mastery on their gun side (the usual case) effectively into one-eyed gun-pointers (as he himself was by then) and depriving them, quite without cause or any compensatory advantage, of the useful faculty of being able to "see through" (actually around) the forward end of the gun barrels. Perhaps he hoped by this means to force everyone into swinging fast enough in the final stage of gun-mounting to be able to hit most oncoming and rising birds if the trigger were pulled with the bird still clearly in sight over the muzzles, and to gain mastery of his method of leading via this route. Coaches of the pure "Churchill" school continue to recommend this forward hand grip to all their clients today, and again one wonders if it has ever occurred to them to analyse the characteristics that go together to make up the "Churchill" style, or if they are simply repeating "the doctrine as received" as articles of faith. Because, no matter how he obtains his lead, and in what style he shoots, the sole virtue of holding the barrels in Churchillian fashion for a shooter with eye-dominance on his gun side is that it is easier to grasp the barrels firmly at the moment of discharge if they are held thus, than it is if the grip is the lighter one of the "Standard British" style (Figure 95) and this facilitates the taking of some of the recoil of the gun down the forward arm (if the shooter wishes to do this, and it *is* taught as part of the Churchill "package" to decrease recoil-effect). However, if a "Churchill-style" grip on the barrels is taken for this reason alone, it should be modified by lowering the base of the thumb (Figure 114) until the eye not over the gun can see what is going on under the barrels.

Fashion certainly played an important part, but the greatest help Churchill had in selling his very light guns was his discovery (or was it his further development of someone else's discovery?) of a way to use such featherweight weapons with impunity loaded with charges that most people would have found (and still find) too heavy in recoil in such guns even for a few shots, let alone for sustained shooting. This was, as

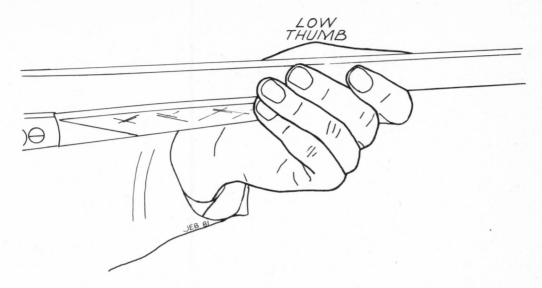

Figure 114 Grip of Forward Hand, modified "Churchill" style

already mentioned, the putting of the braced shoulder forward to the butt of the gun in the final stage of gunmounting: to "grasp the nettle" as he put it. And this action is indeed highly successful in decreasing apparent recoil when carried out positively and purposefully. As Churchill's earlier book reveals, he had been already shooting with a deliberately braced neck and a closed jaw in the manner of most British driven game shooters.

However, in gaining recoil-resistance for such shooting by these means one loses something too, and that is relative accuracy over a short series of shots (while *gaining* it over a series that proves to be long, when using guns of low weight relative to the load being used, due to less "wear and tear" on the shooter by recoil!). For, when timing of the trigger-release is partly due to the trigger being thrust *forward* against the trigger-finger, it is not so exact as when in the sole charge of that finger. I believe that the forward thrust of the shoulder onto the butt of the gun has its effect on the accuracy of gun-pointing as such, also, though this may be slight.

In fact, it really does seem that for birds having a high, angular velocity relative to the shooter in particular (typified by the fast, close, crossing bird) one shoots better with an absence of tension about the shoulders, neck and jaw. And such an absence of tension is an axiom for success in all kinds of competition shooting as we shall see later in this chapter. However, in game shooting, unless guns a good deal heavier than is the usual British game gun for a particular load are used, the neck should certainly be braced, the jaw closed, and the shoulder put forward and upward to the butt. I am convinced that heavier guns, requiring none of this, and in fact stocked for and shot in the style referred to earlier in this chapter as American "classic" (the style of our Victorian forebears!) would help the performance of most people in shooting driven game. Some British shooters will regard this as the heresy of a clay pigeon addict, but there it is.

The increased resistance to recoil when the butt is resting firmly against deliberately tensed, rather than naturally slack, shoulder muscles (aided or not by a firm grip of the barrels at the moment of discharge) is very real. Churchill advocated 12-gauge game guns of a *maximum* weight of 6 lbs for the usual British game charge of $1\frac{1}{16}$ oz. of shot. He made some 12-gauge, boxlock, side-by-side doubles chambered for the $2\frac{1}{2}$ inch cartridge as light as 5 lbs, and many of $5\frac{1}{2}$ lbs. He himself could use these with loads of 1 oz and $1\frac{1}{16}$ oz with apparent impunity. Until the instructors at shooting schools other than his own learned Churchill's "trick" of putting the shoulder, hard-muscled, forward onto the butt of the gun, these guns were the subject of vitriolic criticism by these other instructors on account of their insupportable recoil. Once the other instructors learned the "trick" they grafted it onto their "proto-Standard-British" methods for use with the heavier, longer-barrelled guns they continued to advocate (rightly so for their methods) making these still more comfortable to shoot!

Early XXV guns, made in the early 1920's, had concave, swamped ribs of normal width, set on the barrels with normal pitch: level with the tops of the barrels at the breech and just below the tops of the barrels at the muzzles. Because of the decreased down-flip (Figure 37) of 25 inch as compared to longer barrels, producing an inherently higher-shooting gun, these early XXV guns must have been fitted to the shooter so as to put his eye lower in relation to the breech than was customary with longer barrelled guns. When the gun is at the shoulder, no part of the barrels or rib of such a gun except the very muzzle-ends is then visible to the shooter. Perhaps it was Churchill himself, perhaps one or more of his clients, who found this psychologically unsatisfying, thus paving the way for his development of the narrow, flat, level, file-cut rib for side-by-side double guns, the rib now universally identified with his name. Churchill put this on his XXV guns with a pitch that brought it higher at the muzzle-end, thus putting the frontsight higher. This required that the eye be correspondingly raised above the breech, thus restoring the eye's view of the barrels normal with longer-barrelled guns. The narrowing of the rib further decreased the inertia of the barrels of Churchill's XXV guns (albeit very slightly) but perhaps its most important effect was that it gave the customer looking at the gun in the London shop a narrow, black line he felt he could point with accuracy at anything that moved. It would be hard to demonstrate that the narrowness made, or makes, any difference to performance in the field.

Certain well-known writers on shotgun shooting (not all of them Americans) have tried the "Churchill" method (or, usually, as much of the method as they could interpret from the books of Churchill and possibly from some of those of his spiritual successors) generally in the absence of a coach descended directly or indirectly from Churchill's old establishment, and have found that they couldn't make it work in any universally applicable way, and in particular not on crossing birds at medium to full ranges. Some, no doubt, have been people of fast reflexes who, inherently, would find the method difficult. However, the general reaction of virtually all these writers has been to dismiss the method out of hand as something no one can do. This is as ridiculous as if a non-swimmer had tried several times to swim (having some idea from the written and spoken word of how it was supposed to be done) and found that he couldn't do it, and had then gone into print saying that swimming was impossible for human beings. We have millions of human swimmers in the world, and goodness knows how many thousands of pretty pure "Churchill-style" shotgunners!

Some of the latter, in their turn, have been so ill-advised as to express themselves in print to the effect that no one who shoots the shotgun in a style in which he has to look ahead of crossing birds (let alone is conscious of his gun pointing ahead of them) will ever be any good at all at shotgun shooting. This despite the fact that what I have called the "majority method" of leading suits people of every variation of reaction-time, and is used by the majority of competent shotgunners everywhere. Its success has much to do with the conscious tracking of the muzzle of the gun along the bird's line of flight, which makes for accuracy in elevation. It is also easier to adjust a visible space than a speed of swing, to take care of variations (particularly sudden variations) in the speed of a bird. To say: "I mount my gun and swing like this, and *I* don't need to lead crossing birds to hit them. You'll hit them, too, if you just do the same thing", is really saying: "When we, you and I, shoot at the same kind of crossing bird, the combination of your speed of swing and your reaction-time will produce the same actual lead as does the combination of the speed of swing that I use on it together with my reaction-time". In fact, it usually isn't true and success may not be attained until the listener receives proper tuition in the "Churchill" method (which he may not want to use after he *has* mastered it).

People get very emotionally attached to a shooting style that has worked well for them in their circumstances, and quite unreasonable in their condemnation of others, particularly when a short trial leads to failure, even if the trial is uncoached. However, using any method of leading, be certain that when you saw what you well know was the right lead and elevation on a crosser, and your head was properly on the stock, yet missed it, the chances of this being due to a stopped gun are very, very high.

"Churchill-style" shooters (even at skeet) lower the butt of the gun from the shoulder and go through the last part of the process of gunmounting again for each shot they fire. This applies to shots at the same bird (if missed with the first shot) or at another one, and is for the purpose of allowing the lead-giving delay we have discussed to build up for each shot. Virtually all shooters in the other styles we have discussed keep the gun to the shoulder for repeat shots at the same bird, or at one near the first, lowering the butt a little and then remounting it only for subsequent shots at a different bird widely separated from the first one.

After this chapter was written, news of the business difficulties and eventual demise, of the Churchill firm was released. The Churchill episode in British shooting and gunmaking may have drawn to a close, but Churchill's influence will never be quite gone. He never could be, and never will be, ignored.

Before leaving this discussion of British shotgun shooting styles, a further comment on the use of the try-gun is necessary. The fitter has ever to be on his guard against using the try-gun to nullify the effects of faults in gunmounting, or those of habitual flinching. These things have to be corrected before any exactness in gunfitting is attempted. With the more experienced shooter with no blatant "bad habits", the fitter has to be vigilant in discerning slight accommodations of the shooter to the stock when the measurements of this are not quite ideal. This needs a keen eye so as to be able to alter the stock to allow the shooter to adopt a position of least strain (modified only by deliberate dispositions to decrease recoil effect where these are advisable and agreed on). In short, *experience* is necessary to the use of the try-gun (as is it in interpretation of the measures arrived at in its use when these are to be transferred to certain types of game guns, as we saw earlier). Used properly, the try-gun does result in a perfect fitting of gun to gunner for a given style of shooting and a certain purpose.

THE AMERICAN FIELD AND SKEET STOCK REVISITED

A LITTLE MORE HISTORY

While the process of building ever-lighter game guns, and the development of gun-mounting to suit them, were going on in Britain, a quite different trend began in America after World War I. This was the development of heavier loads for every gauge of gun. This was intended to appeal (and did, and does) to those shooters who feel that the answer to their problems lies in throwing more shot for each pull of the trigger (occasionally they are right). This trend has seen the development of such loads as 1 oz in the 28-gauge (since discontinued), 1¼ oz in the 3 inch 20-gauge, 1½ oz in the 2¾ inch 12-gauge, 1⅞ oz in the 3 inch 12-gauge, and 2¼ oz in the 3½ inch 10-gauge. Whether any of these are advisable developments, or invariably give greater effective range than lighter loads, is not the issue here. What is important is that the general tendency to shoot more shot from every gauge and shotshell disturbed an existing equilibrium with gun weight which gave withstandable recoil.

The response of American gunmakers (often the same firms putting the new, heavier loads on the market) has been in the manufacture of guns heavier, in general, than those made in America in the 1900 to 1920 period, and in the development of various models of autoloading shotgun, all of which (but the gas-operated type most of all) decrease apparent recoil by spreading it out over a longer time. In connection with this, it may be noted that their usefulness in trap and skeet has done not a little to legitimize the heavyweight shotgun in America. Field stocks have changed little, if at all, in this period. Stocks for American-rules trap and skeet have tended to ever-higher combs, as we shall see later in this chapter.

GROUND GAME

Before leaving game shooting styles and beginning our discussion of clay target shooting, something specific has to be said on the subject of shooting ground game: rabbits and hares. The signal that this may be something different from the shooting of game birds is given by the numbers of shooters who are highly successful at one, and but a poor performer at the other. Instances are legion of "gentleman gunners" from whom no bird is safe but who constitute little danger to a rabbit at any range, and of farmers who rarely miss any rabbit within 40 yards (jink around bushes and rush-clumps though it may) but who put up a poor show indeed at feathered game.

The writer spent some of his youth in a British countryside seething with rabbits, and was privileged to see many of the latter kind of shooter in action. The best rabbit shots had (and have) a style in common, different from anything that is described above (Figures 115 and 116).

Regardless of the placement of the feet relative to each other (which varies from shooter to shooter, and may resemble the American style (Figure 47) or the "Churchill" stance (Figure 105) the feet should be *flat* on the ground (the ground permitting!), *the knees relaxed*, and the forward lean of the body towards the target marked. The relaxation of the knees allows a good deal of flexibility in shooting to

Figure 115 Ready position, Ground Game

either side of the straight-ahead position, but any chance to "face the shot" (Figure 70) should be taken. One might think that (following the principles of the "Standard British" *or* "Churchill" styles) putting virtually all the weight on the forward foot, and raising of the heel of the rear one, would be an appropriate balance and stance for this kind of shooting. In practice such an arrangement has insufficient stability for good shooting when the body has the forward lean of the expert rabbit shooter. In Figures 115 and 116 about 60 per cent of the weight is on the front foot.

CLAY TARGET STOCKS

Clay target shooting is so important a part of shotgunning today that direct reference must be made to it.

THE GAMES

Skeet

Skeet began in the 1920's as practice shooting for the New England ruffed grouse and woodcock hunter. It is rarely thought of as game shooting practice by today's skeet shooters. Figure 117 is a sketch of a skeet field. The High House targets begin their flight 10 feet above the ground, the Low House targets 3½ feet above it. All targets are 15 feet above the ground at the midfield crossing point, six yards out from Station 8. A round consists of 25 targets.

Skeet has three branches today. In the American-rules game the targets are thrown 55 to 60 yards. They appear at once to call, and it is permitted to put the gun to the shoulder before calling for targets. Singles from both houses are shot from all stations, and doubles (a target being released simultaneously from each house) from Stations 1, 2, 6 and 7. The 25th target is a repeat of the first miss, or another Low 8 if the shooter has hit all 24 targets to that point. Since 1981 doubles shot from all stations except 8 (twice from Stations 2 to 6, the shooters coming back around the field from 6 to 2 after shooting at Station 7) has been a regular, registered event in 12-gauge competition. The 25th target in this instance is another High 2. There are separate competitions in American skeet for 12, 20, 28 and .410 gauge guns. Shoot-offs in all gauges often consist of doubles at all stations (except 8 of course) or sometimes doubles from Stations 3, 4 and 5 only.

English skeet replaces the two Station 8 singles by a double from Station 4. The 25th target is a Low or High target from Station 7 if the shooter has hit all 24 targets to that point. The targets are thrown 55 yards. Shoot-offs consist of regular rounds.

In International (I.S.U. = International Shooting Union) skeet the targets are much faster, being thrown 71 to 73 yards. They appear after a randomly-timed delay of up to three seconds after the call. It is not permitted to bring up the gun to face and shoulder from a deeply-dropped preliminary position (the butt must touch the body at the waistline) until the target or targets are in the air. The High House target is the sole single shot from Station 1, and no singles are shot from Station 7. Singles from each house are shot from all other stations, and doubles from Stations 1, 2, 3, 5, 6 and 7. Shoot-offs consist of regular rounds.

Except for Low 7 (which needs no lead) and the two Station 8 targets, many skeet shooters use what is called in this book the "majority method" of lead. That is to say, they bring the muzzle to bear on the target, move with it momentarily, and then look

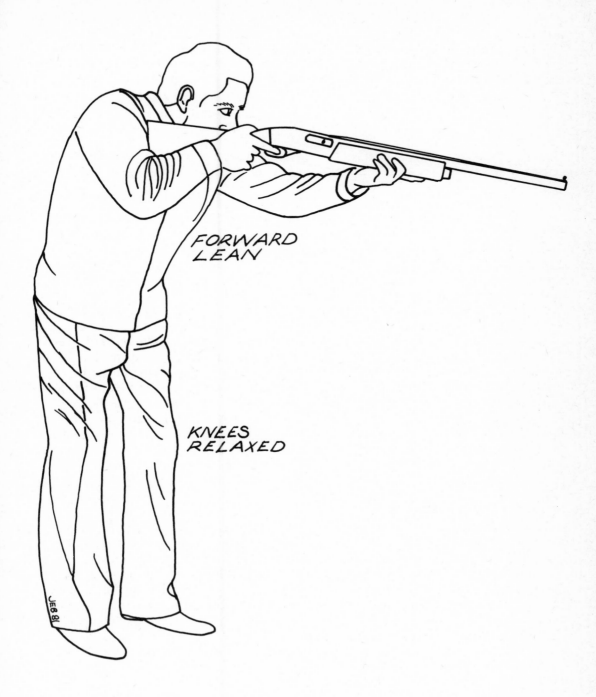

FORWARD
LEAN

KNEES
RELAXED

Figure 116 Gun mounted, Ground Game

ahead of the target the distance that experience proves to be correct, this causing the muzzle to accelerate ahead of the target. The trigger is pulled while the gun is kept moving. This method skeet shooters refer to as "pointing out". Most of them see and remember the apparent lead as a visible space between muzzle and target. At Station 8, the muzzle has to be accelerated so fast from so far behind the target that if the trigger is pulled with the muzzle on the target (or its front edge anyway!) the latter will be hit. The resemblance to the "Churchill" style (a resemblance already noted) is obvious.

But that isn't how all skeet shooters hit their targets (except, I think, for Low 7 and the two Station 8 targets). In fact, nowadays the majority of shooters bring up the gun ahead of every singles target, and the first target of doubles, by about the distance they have found to be the correct lead for that target when the muzzle is travelling at the same apparent speed as the target, adjust this lead while keeping the gun moving, and pull the trigger (still of course, keeping the gun moving). This is, of course, the "sustained lead" method of Chapter 1. It is particularly favoured by International rules skeet shooters, since the *actual* speed the gun has to be moved in shooting these very fast targets is then slower (and hence more controllable) than that in any other method of leading. Note that the target is still used as a moving reference-point, and that the gun moves for a short but appreciable distance, and time, with the target, the muzzle at a fixed visual distance from the latter, as we saw in the first chapter. On the second target of doubles the gun usually comes to the target from behind the latter, but with the controlled, smooth swing aimed at by competition skeet shooters, all these targets need some visible lead, though from Stations 1 and 7 this may be very slight.

Still other skeet shooters, by keeping the gun perfectly still until the target has travelled visually well beyond the muzzle (forcing them then to accelerate the muzzle fast up to, and beyond, the target) are able to shoot directly (i.e. without any lead apparent to themselves) at High 1, 2 and 3, and Low 5 and 6, as well as both targets from Station 8. Some shoot thus also at 4 High and Low. A tiny minority shoot thus at every target on the field. This method of leading is usually termed "swing through" by skeet shooters.

Sporting Clay Targets

Competitions over "sporting clay" layouts are extremely popular in Britain and becoming yearly more so in Europe and some other parts of the world (e.g. Algeria and South Africa). Such layouts, wherein the clay target provides the ultimate in practice for the game and waterfowl shooter are common in Britain, less so in Europe, and quite rare elsewhere in the world. However, unlike the development that has taken place in skeet, the provision of such practice (rather than the staging of competitions) remains the primary purpose of such layouts, though it appears that their use in competitions may soon outweigh that as practice sites for field shooting (in terms of numbers of targets shot, if not in importance).

There is no standardization of such layouts. The better ones show a wide variety of targets, both singles and doubles, at an equally wide range of speeds, crossing and quartering, incoming and outgoing, high and low, in level flight as well as climbing and descending, at ranges from 15 to 50 yards. Clays of normal configuration and size (as used in trap and skeet shooting) are the type most frequently used in practice for game shooting, or when the shooter is being coached or fitted for a gun on such a layout with field shooting as the ultimate purpose. However, in competitions, as well as the "normal" clay target (in the "tough" version used in International trap and skeet, as well as the "softer" variety used in "national" clay target games in Britain and

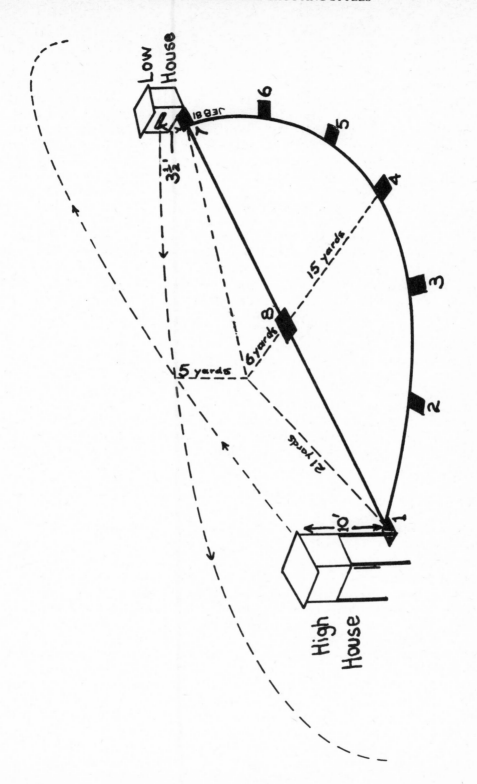

Low House

High House

6

5

4

3

2

8

7

18 yd.

3½'

15 yards

6 yards

15 yards

21 yards

10'

1

Figure 117 Skeet Field

America) half-size ("mini") and three-quarter size ("midi") clay targets (of normal proportions as regards diameter vs. "doming") are used, as well as thin flat clays of normal diameter ("battue") and thicker flat clays of normal diameter ("rocket"). All these have their own flight characteristics, not only in differing initial velocities from a certain trap, but in how well they sustain these. The behaviour of the flat "battue" and "rocket" clays in the latter part of their flight is unpredictable, both types tending to veer and sheer off the line of the early part of their flight. The roster of targets is rounded out by clay "rabbits" of various sizes, these being thick-rimmed discs bowled along the ground by traps fixed on their sides for this purpose. The "rabbits" are also used for training the field shooter of course.

For competitions the traps are adjusted (and often moved bodily) between competitions so as to show a different selection of shots from one competition to the next on any layout.

Naturally, on such a variety of targets, a variety of methods of leading are used. However, the approved general method, the one used by those who coach the highly successful British team, is our good, old "majority method" of putting the muzzle visibly on the flying target (keeping pace with it) then, as the gun is mounted, looking (and pulling out the muzzle) ahead of the target the requisite distance, and pressing the trigger while gun and shooter continue to swing as a unit.

Trapshooting

Every kind of trapshooting was always a game in its own right, and not "practice" for anything else. Figure 118 is a sketch of the field used for British and Commonwealth "Down the Line" as well as for American-rules trapshooting. The traphouse extends above ground level. Targets begin their flight a foot and a half above ground level and are thrown 50 yards, their elevation being therefore constant. Singles targets are thrown at random lateral angles within (in North America and Britain) a 44 degree field. In Australia and New Zealand the lateral spread of targets tends to be wider, and there (as in Britain) two shots (scored differently) are permitted at each singles target. North American rules permit only one shot at any target. Doubles are everywhere thrown at constant angles, the left target some 22 degrees left of the centre-line of the field, the right one a similar angle to the right of that line. Singles targets are shot from 16 yards behind the trap, from five stations, and handicap matches from the shooters' handicap distances (up to 27 yards behind the trap in North America). Doubles are shot from 16 yards. A round of singles (16 yards or handicap) consists of 25 targets, five from each station. A doubles event is usually 50 targets, three pairs from each station, followed by two pairs from each station the second time around, so to speak.

All forms of "International" trapshooting (15-trap, 5-trap and single trap) have in common targets starting their flight some 20 inches below the horizontal plane of the shooter's feet, thrown anywhere within a 90 degree angle measured at the line of traps (or the single "ball" trap) at widely variable elevations, and fast enough to travel 75 to 80 metres at the optimum elevation for distance. All competition is at singles targets from a distance of 16½ yards behind the traps (or trap). Two shots may be fired at each target and a hit with either scores the same. As in all other forms of trapshooting it is permitted to put the gun to the shoulder before the target is called for, and the target appears immediately on call. The acoustic release system is now the norm. After shooting at each target, the shooter proceeds toward the next station ready to occupy it as soon as its tenant has shot and moved on.

The 15-trap layout (called "Olympic Trap" or "Olympic Trench") is the one used in world competitions. The traps are in five groups of three traps (Figure 119), each group having a shooting station behind it. The left trap in each group throws its target to the right of a line joining the centre trap and the shooting station, while the right trap throws to the left of this line. The centre trap throws its target within 15 degrees right or left of this line. Thus, target trajectories cross a short distance ahead of the trench. Traps are reset for elevation and direction before every competition, and the selection mechanism for targets is such that all shooters get the same total mix of targets.

Olympic Trench is without doubt the most difficult form of clay target shooting that takes place on a set, constant, layout (i.e. excluding Sporting Clays). However, the scores made on the 5-trap "Universal Trench" layout shown in Figure 120 average only slightly higher. Here again the outer traps (now four in number) throw their targets inward across the trajectory of the centre one, and, again, traps are reset before competitions and according to approved combinations of lateral and vertical angles. There is keen international competition in this game in Europe.

Scores made over the single, oscillating, "Ball Trap" are considerably higher than those made over Olympic or Universal Trenches. The field is laid out concentric on the trap, as for American-rules trap or for DTL (Figure 118) and thus the shooter knows what the general directional flow of the targets will be. Too, all targets have approximately the same velocity (all coming off the same trap). This is not true in the 15-trap and 5-trap game, since the traps in these are first set for elevation and direction, and then the spring-tension of the trap adjusted to give the desired target range.

ZZ Pigeon trapshooting was developed in Europe in the 1960's, the first installation having been in Monte Carlo where it was hoped it would lure back the live pigeon trap-shooters (their game having been banned there). It is now shot at a number of centres in western Europe. Attempts to transplant the game to Britain have met with limited success so far. There are presently two installations in the United States, being looked at by officials of trapshooting clubs, and others, as a possible further, and future, avenue for trapshooting to take in North America.

The game has many physical resemblances to live pigeon trapshooting. The shooter faces a line of five traps, five metres apart, from a distance of between 22 and 30 metres, depending on the nature of the competition being shot and on his allotted handicap. The traps are at ground level, but each is hidden from the shooter's view by a small screen which looks like the back of a live pigeon trap. Each trap consists of a target holder, a clutch mechanism, and an electric motor running continuously at between 4000 and 8000 rpm. Each trap oscillates continuously through a lateral angle of 120 degrees. The target itself is a plastic, two-bladed "propellor" about a foot long, with a detachable plastic disc, about the size of an ordinary clay target, in its centre.

Calling for a target results in electronic random selection of one of the traps and instantaneous connection of motor and target holder on that trap, via the clutch mechanism. Now spinning rapidly, the propellor lifts itself off the target holder. The initial flight path is slightly above the horizontal, and in whatever direction the oscillating trap happened to be pointing when the target was called for. As the propellor flies its axis of rotation tilts farther from the horizontal. This effect combines with that of the slightest air movement present to cause a sudden and unpredictable change in flight direction at a certain stage in the flight. A gusty, variable wind produces the violent zigzags which give the target its name.

As in live pigeon trapshooting, there is a boundary fence a short distance beyond the traps. Two shots are allowed at each target, either scoring the same. To score, the

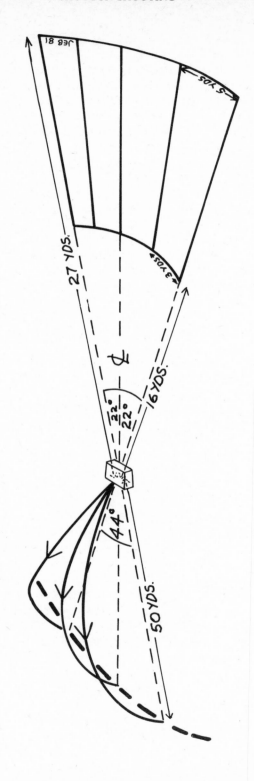

Figure 118 Field for American Trap and British DTL

central disc must be smashed, or be separated from the propellor, and fall on the shooter's side of the fence.

Also in common with live pigeon shooting, only one shooter is on the line at any time. However, the shooting is quite difficult (in Europe, 10 targets are sufficient to separate shooters in local matches, and 20 in National competitions). Thus, large numbers of competitors can be "processed" on even a single field! Live pigeon trapshooters agree that in moderately breezy conditions, ZZ is more difficult than the best of live pigeons shot on the same kind of field.

The primary problem of all trapshooting arises from the simple fact that one can only point a gun in one direction at once! In skeet, and in most Sporting clay target shooting, this presents no problem to the shooter — or should not. He knows the approximate track that each target will follow (often quite exactly) and for single targets can so dispose himself and the gun that the latter can be triggered on the target after a short, controlled swing. In skeet doubles, too, after the first target is shot, the gun is pointing somewhere in the vicinity of the second one, and this too can be covered by another relatively short movement of the gun. This situation pertains, too, in shooting many Sporting clay doubles. When it does not, when the second target is relatively far from the broken shards of the first one, the state of affairs is like that in shooting the second target in doubles trap (American or DTL) and it is one whose consideration I should like to defer until we have looked at other kinds of trapshooting.

In all of these the preliminary point of the mounted gun, before the shooter calls for his target, can be right only for one of (or a small range among) the variety of targets that can result, and he does not know which one it will be. This means, too, that after the trap is sprung he has first to look for and find the target, and *then* shoot it. I propose to look at the various kinds of trapshooting in turn to see what difficulties, if any, these factors present, and what further problems the shooter has to solve to be consistently successful. In doing this it is simpler to tackle them in the reverse order from that in which they are dealt with above.

In ZZ (and live pigeon trapshooting) only 20 per cent of the time (over a long series) will the shooter be presented with a target (or bird) from the particular trap at which he is pointing when he called "Pull". Often right-shouldering shooters point at the trap second from the right, and left-shoulderers at the trap second from the left, in the line of traps. There is no problem in these games of knowing at once which trap was pulled, since the change in appearance of the trap and the general easy visibility of the relatively large target (certainly by comparison with the clay target) make this obvious. The first problem in both these games is that on 80 per cent of occasions the gun has first to be moved so that it points in the area of the sprung trap, usually virtually stopped there, and operations to shoot the target or bird then recommenced instantaneously. Occasionally target or bird will have commenced its flight along a path which is virtually a prolongation of that of the initial movement of the gun, but simply to continue the latter movement on these rare occasions risks spoiling the shooter's general system and timing. Control (plus speed!) is essential to the first part of the operation and, paradoxically (the second problem!) great speed and a willingness to allow the subconscious mind to control are essential to the latter part, since the boundary fence and the limit of the effective range of the gun and ammunition are both too close to admit of any delay. On his better days the crack live pigeon shot will be found to be hitting birds with his first shots when they are but a few yards from the trap, even when the birds are small, swift, and extremely "wild" (as they should be).

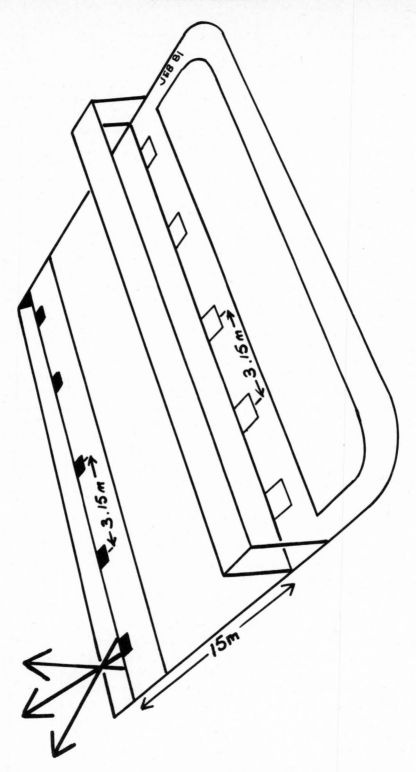

Figure 119 15-Trap Olympic Trench

However, it is not possible to perform in like fashion on the ZZ target which will normally be past its original lifting flight and moving (more or less) erratically when shot at, such movement constituting a problem in itself!

In all forms of "International" trap the relatively high speed of the targets is a problem, partly in requiring them to be shot with despatch before they are out of range and partly because their speed makes them invisible (as an entity rather than a mere blur) until they have travelled ten yards or so from the trap. This cuts down further the actual time available to shoot them. Commonly the first shot is got away half a second after the trap is released when the clay is some ±35 yards from the shooter. However, this is considerably less than 0.5 seconds after the shooter sees the target clearly enough to move the muzzle after it. Since some targets are low (but a yard and a half, or less, higher than the level of the roof of the trench or trap-pit at the 10 yard point in their flight) the initial point of the gun has to be relatively low too, since apart from the risk of not seeing the low straightaway targets at all if the gun is pointed higher, one cannot bring the gun *down* to any of the lower targets (which are still effectively rising) with much hope of consistent success. For every target from the 15-trap trench the shooter has the array of traps from which that target will appear symmetrically in front of him. The same is not true of the four stations off the centre-line in the 5-trap and single-trap layouts. In shooting from these the shooter's preliminary point passes to one side of the centre of the trench or traphouse: it has a lateral component and is centred out in front of the trap or traps in such a way as to take advantage of the biased flow of the target array as seen from these off-centre positions (to the left or right according to whether the shooter is left or right of centre). The advantage of being able to adopt such a preliminary point (because of the curtailment and hence the greater control-lability and shorter time taken in the swing onto the target) from four out of five stations is reflected in the *somewhat* higher scores registered, on average, in 5-trap as compared to 15-trap Trench where every shot is from the "centre station". Scores over the single ("Ball") trap layout are still higher since the flow of targets as viewed from those stations off the centre-line of the field is still better defined, particularly if the trap oscillates no farther than 30 degrees each side of the centre-line (which is the minimum required, and hence a setting often seen . . . . . alas). Too, all single-trap targets have the same speed. Many people are able to shoot all these fast, International-trap, targets by swinging the gun in a continuous, accelerating movement from the preliminary point and triggering it just as the muzzle visually passes the clay (which method they term "shooting by instinct"). However, shooters with short reaction-times often have to see "daylight" between target and muzzle to succeed, and this with either barrel. The targets are so fast that, despite the relatively great movement required of the gun on wide and/or high targets, few people have problems of shooting behind the target with a stopped gun (whose muzzle *had* got far beyond the clay).

Such a thing is all too common, especially among beginners, in shooting singles (from 16 yards or from handicap distances) at American-rules trap or British and Commonwealth DTL. Here the shooter possesses the same advantage as in Ball Trap in having a known flow of targets as viewed from positions out of the centre-line of the field, indeed his advantage is greater since the trap usually oscillates no more than 22 degrees each side of the centre-line. Further, since target elevation is constant, those who shoot with both eyes open (and hence can see under the gun) can adopt a relatively high preliminary point, so that upward movement of the muzzle to the target is minimal. However, since the targets are so slow, a single movement of the gun from the preliminary point, past the clay, triggering as the muzzle goes by it, is a consistently

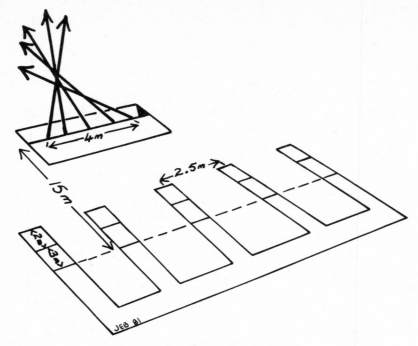

Figure 120   5-Trap Universal Trench

successful way of shooting these targets for only a proportion of people (those who see the target very quickly and move the muzzle to it with equal despatch). Most people who try to shoot these targets thus do not see the target so close to the house, and hence have a long run-up to it with an accelerating gun. The usual result is to get the muzzle far beyond the target before the trigger can be pulled, and the shooter, seeing this, stops the gun. The clay does not stop, of course, but goes on its merry way, and triggering the stationary gun results in the charge passing behind the target. Most people, therefore, have to shoot these targets by a kind of two-stage process of first reaching the visual vicinity of the clay with the muzzle, and then (while keeping the gun moving, of course) mentally starting afresh, as it were, from there. They may accelerate the gun forward from the target (triggering it with a suitable lead) or from a little behind the bird (triggering as the muzzle passes the target) and in either instance the analogy with the "majority method" of leading is obvious. Some swear that they use a "sustained-lead" method on targets shot from 16 yards. For most shooters who have begun their careers outside trapshooting, because the gun is at the shoulder throughout (where, except for those with experience in American or English skeet, it has been previously only during the final act of gunmounting and moving the gun to point somewhere ahead of the target) it is difficult to perform the initial action of bringing the muzzle into the visual vicinity of the target *without* simply continuing this to a point beyond the bird. Usually this is a point too far beyond the bird, and the shooter, knowing this, stops the gun, with the results we have seen. It does help such a shooter mentally to separate the shooting of these slow clays into two parts. The main problem for most people in American-rules trap, and the similar British and Commonwealth DTL, then, is in producing a smooth, controlled, slow movement of the gun, despite the fact that this movement cannot be reduced below a certain length (even on stations farthest from the centre-line of the field) by holding the preliminary point far out in the general flow of the targets lest the shooter put himself in the position of having to come back a long distance as a preliminary to shooting certain targets. Smoothness without speed will get one nowhere at International trap, but smoothness is virtually *all* in successful shooting of these slower targets. Shooters of this kind of trap often talk of the fast swing or quick shooting of certain of their colleagues, but, everything is relative, and if (as is common) they do no other kind of shooting, they sometimes scarcely know the true meaning of the words "fast" or "quick"! The singles target thrown in these games is shot by the average shooter one full second after it leaves the trap, though the targets are slow enough to be discernible almost as soon as they cease to have the roof of the traphouse between them and the shooter's eyes. The very quick shooter referred to above (who isn't always the highest scorer, notice) often breaks birds in *half* that time.

The need for controlled smoothness of gun movement applies with especial force in shooting the second target of doubles. Having been discharged at the first target, the gun necessarily begins its travel to shoot the second one pointing far away from that target, which was slow to begin with and is now perhaps as much as 25 yards from the trap. Some restraint is necessary in moving the gun and getting it onto the line of travel of this second clay, and even given this, most people can trigger the gun just as they reach or pass it, with no lead visible to themselves. Again, since the gun is already at the shoulder, such restraint is difficult for those who come to this kind of shooting from almost every other, especially since the target is obviously far away, and getting farther. To shoot the first target (whichever one of the pair is chosen) the gun is placed so that this target can be covered with a short, quick, controlled movement of the gun, and the resemblance to skeet and Sporting clays is obvious.

As might be expected from the above, guns of differing weights and inertias are desirable for different kinds of trapshooting, and indeed are essential if the highest scores are to be obtained. This will be examined in Chapter 6. Really there is no such thing as an "all round" trapgun, any more than there is an "all round shotgun".

THE STOCKS

Skeet

The American-style "field and skeet" stock of average dimensions (drops at comb and heel of about 1½ and 2½ inches respectively, no cast, and a length of about 14 inches) mounted in what is termed in this book the "American classic" fashion, would seem to be ideally adapted to skeet. Such a stock with modifications (generally minor) for the individual shooter tends neither to high nor low shooting (and skeet has apparently diving as well as climbing targets) and its natural pointing elevation, mounted thus, accords well (as we have seen) with the average elevation at which skeet targets are shot.

In fact, such stocks, or slight modifications of them, are to be found on the majority of guns used in International-rules skeet. Often a recoil pad is incorporated, not so much to decrease apparent recoil as to prevent the butt slipping down the shoulder when the gun is fired (thus leaving it in the right place for the second shot of doubles). Since most of the pads used have a hard heel, and this is mounted in the shoulder pocket, they provide no cushioning of recoil. The rear face of the pad should be stippled or corrugated, or otherwise formed into a non-slip surface (a smooth finish,

Figure 121 Ready position, International Skeet, American style with High-Comb Stock

with or without, say, vertical ribs, does not fulfil this function effectively). The *sides* of the pad and its *top* surface ahead of the heel (but no part of the *rear-facing* surface) should be varnished or taped over so that the pad does not impede rapid gunmounting. One now sees some stocks with a heel of solid wood, the rubber pad occupying only the lower three-quarters of the butt. Such stocks mount easily but slip down the shoulder almost as easily as if fitted with a smooth buttplate. It must not be lost sight of that the stock is lifted up and *back* into the shoulder: it is not a long stock "skidded" up the surface of shirt or jacket into place at the shoulder. There is little agreement among International-rules skeet shooters on the right pitch for the butt. In addition to those who fit the butt to the shoulder as described for the "classic" American style, others seek to prevent the butt moving at the shoulder when the first shot of doubles is fired by means of increased downpitch. Still others favour stocks with extremely prominent toes (the pitch on the rest of the butt being independent of the toe, and usually "normal") with the idea of preventing the stock being mounted, in haste, too high.

In the last few years in Western Europe and America, respectively, such stocks have been joined on International skeet fields by two other types. One of these incorporates some cast and a Monte Carlo comb, the heel being as low, or lower, than that of the American type stock discussed above. These cast stocks are intended to be mounted higher on the face than is the castless stock, and the stepped-down heel of the Monte Carlo type of stock comes nicely into the pocket between the chest and a relaxed shoulder when head and body are fairly erect. The resemblance to the East European field stock discussed earlier is obvious, and no matter where a skeet gun wearing such a stock originates, such stocks show the influence of the redoubtable Russian International skeet shooters, many of whom used such stocks before they were adopted by shooters from other countries. Such stocks usually have about $\frac{3}{16}$ inch cast where contacted by the shooter's face. This is too much for very few people when a gun is mounted and shot quickly with the head erect. It can be increased easily by removal of wood on the side of the stock where this is contacted by the face, producing a flat, or flatter, surface in that area. Such stocks are increasingly prominent in Europe.

Some American International skeet shooters have recently adopted stocks with high, often level, combs, shot in a canted-head style. Such stocks require a much more forwardly-inclined preliminary position (Figure 121) than do lower-combed, lower-heeled, stocks (Figure 122).

In recent years increasing numbers of North American-rules skeet shooters have taken to the use of similar stocks with high, level (or almost level) combs. The shooter either cants his head sideways over these, or turns his face sharply towards them, or combines these attitudes to whatever degree is necessary to bring the eye over the breech. Stocks with drops of 1½ inches at both comb and heel are now not unusual. A stock of these dimensions requires that the shooter hold well under those skeet targets which are, from his viewpoint, descending, but this seems to be no handicap to their users. The small heel-drop is useful when shooting the 12-gauge events in giving minimum upward rotation of the gun in later stages of recoil. This helps in shooting doubles (since the gun is little disturbed by the first shot) but it is especially beneficial when the shooter is involved in long, drawn-out shoot-offs of several hundred targets (and this is where the use of stocks like this in skeet had its origin). If the stock were cast to suit the shooter, this would remove any necessity for canting or excessive turning of the head. The shooter sticks to the same stock dimensions for the smaller gauge skeet guns of course. It must be said that much American skeet (and virtually all English skeet) is still shot with guns carrying the traditional American-style "field and

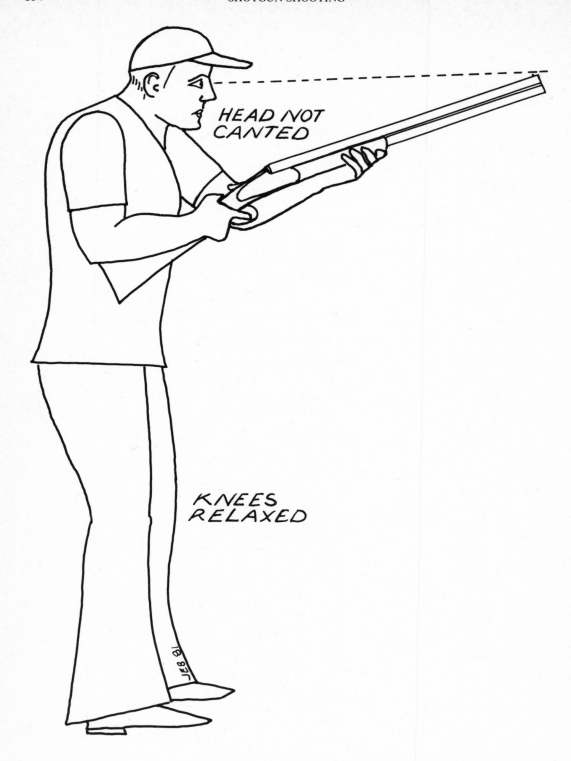

Figure 122 Ready position, International Skeet, Conventional style

skeet'' stock, premounted before calling for the target in what is termed in this book the ''classic'' American style.

Sporting Clay Targets

In International (FITASC) Sporting clay target competitions ''gun down'' rules obtain, though the butt does not have to be dropped as far from the shoulder as in International skeet. English Sporting rules allow a pre-mounted gun. The guns most commonly used in Britain and Europe for this kind of competition are over-and-unders with the American style of field and skeet stock, with little or no cast, and generally without a recoil pad. Gas-operated autoloading guns are becoming ever more prominent. These are stocked similarly. Generally the gun is mounted in what I have called the ''classic'' American style, though the style termed in this book ''Modern British'' is also evident. A small minority of shooters use a level-combed, castless stock with a dropped heel (Figure 123). These stocks resemble the Greener ''Rational'' stock in outline, there being a slope rather than a step between the rear end of the level comb and the heel of the stock. As the reader will be able to anticipate, the users of such stocks cant the head sideways over the comb to a degree varying with the width of their jaws, thus putting the eye in line with the rib. Few such stocks are available on guns from the factories, and they are usually produced by cutting the comb off an ordinary field-type stock, inletting a suitable piece of walnut, and shaping it into a level, rounded comb. Such stocks may reflect the influence of American literature!

A fair number of Sporting clay competitors also shoot skeet. Few are also trap-shooters. Competitions are rarely over more than 100 targets except in international competition when 150 may be shot. Local matches are often over as few as 50 or even 30 targets. Though a score of 100 has been obtained (once!) in first class competition over 100 targets, scores of 90 per cent will usually win in such circumstances. Shoot-offs of over 10 targets are rare.

Trapshooting

In considering the stocks used for trapshooting it is important to bear in mind that all trapshooting (at *clay* pigeons at least) takes place at targets which are, to a varying degree, rising, and also receding at what is, for consistent success with the shotgun, long, or very long, range. Not all live pigeons act thus.

As is done in this book in regard to shotgun stocks as a whole, it is possible to trace the development of the stocks in use today for trapshooting in an historical framework. However, as virtually every type of trap stock that has been developed is still in use (and indeed, still being manufactured) the record is still more obviously one of successive additions to the types in use, rather than of total supersession of older types by newer ones. Too, trapshooters, more so than any other class of shotgunner, are much given to personal experiment with, and alteration of, stocks, and in the course of this the individual trapshooter may repeat in microcosm part, or parts, of the larger history of stocks designed for trapshooting. He may indeed repeat some of it backwards in his search for the best possible stock for him!

The British live-pigeon trapshooting stock of the late 19th century (page 52) with drops at comb and heel of about 1½ and 2 inches and little or no cast, a stock copied by trapshooters of the period everywhere, may be regarded as the progenitor of all later stocks designed for trapshooting at inanimate targets. Except for the work that has been done on trap stocks by Italian shooters with the gunmakers of that country (largely since World War II) most of the developments that have taken (and are taking)

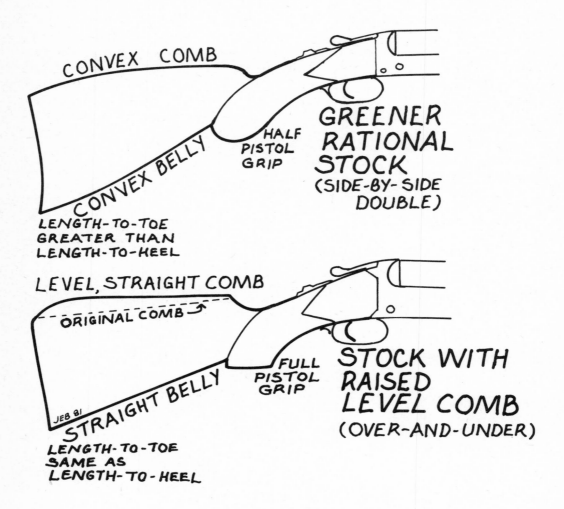

CONVEX COMB

CONVEX BELLY

HALF
PISTOL
GRIP

GREENER
RATIONAL
STOCK
(SIDE-BY-SIDE
DOUBLE)

LENGTH-TO-TOE
GREATER THAN
LENGTH-TO-KEEL

LEVEL, STRAIGHT COMB

ORIGINAL COMB

STRAIGHT BELLY

JEB 81

FULL
PISTOL
GRIP

STOCK WITH
RAISED
LEVEL COMB
(OVER-AND-UNDER)

LENGTH-TO-TOE
SAME AS
LENGTH-TO-HEEL

Figure 123   Greener "Rational" Stock, and Stock with raised, level Comb

place in the 20th century in stocks for clay target trapshooting have been either in America, or as a direct effect of American influence, or in response to the demands of the American market. This despite the fact that, except for Britain and some parts of the British Commonwealth, there has been no parallel copying of American-rules trapshooting outside North America. The rest of the world has stayed with the 15-trap trench, supplemented by the cheaper 5-trap (and now single Ball-trap) layouts.

The old British live-pigeon trap stock usually had a straight grip. Almost all today's trap stocks have a pistol grip. Though the latter affords a more comfortable attitude for the hand and a more secure anchor for consistent trigger-pulling for the same degree of grip in the hand, the transition period from one type to the other was long: the first 40 years of the century in fact. The change was first apparent on the pumpguns used in America for both singles and doubles trapshooting. Shooters found (or imagined they found) the pistol grip useful in holding the gun to the shoulder when closing it on the second shell. The development of single-triggers for double-barrelled guns that were both reliable in use and gave good, sharp, ''pulls'' paved the way for the near-universal adoption of the pistol grip by users of the double-barrelled trap gun in games where two shots are fired. While two-trigger double guns had predominated many shooters had believed (as do many users of two-trigger game guns, and the few two-trigger trap guns in use today) that a straight-grip stock was necessary to them, to enable them to slide the hand back and forth on the stock for easy access to the separate triggers. In fact, a properly shaped pistol grip allows easy and equal access to either trigger of a two-triggered gun (as any good gunmaker or stockmaker can demonstrate) as well as providing a better anchor for the hand than does any straight grip. Where such a pistol grip is fitted I think it would be difficult to demonstrate that the two-trigger gun is at any disadvantage compared to the single-trigger, except that the latter makes it possible to use a glove on the rear hand in cold weather (an important consideration in some climates). Observing the excellent scores in trap-shooting in North America, and the wins by the outstanding American trap teams in International rules competitions in the early years of the century, the rest of the world copied features of their equipment where they felt they could. They saw no advantage in the current repeaters over the double-barrelled gun, but the pistol grip and the single-trigger (and a beavertail fore-end to protect the hand from the heat of the barrels) became everywhere the norm on trap guns.

Until after the second World War, the normal trapshooting stock everywhere did not differ greatly from the live-pigeon stock of 1880 or 1900. The changes, mainly made after World War I, were in the increasing prevalence of pistol grips, described above, a very slightly higher comb (drops of 1⅜ inches and 1⅞ inches at comb and heel became, and remain, the norm for this type of trap stock) and the near-universal use of some kind of recoil pad. Usually such stocks were (and are) used in what is termed in this book the ''classic'' style (the comb running under the angle of the jaw) and with a marked forward lean of the body when the gun is horizontal (Figure 124). This forward inclination is made necessary by the higher heel of the trap stock as compared with the American field stock. The natural pointing elevation of this kind of trap stock mounted in this way is about 22 degrees for many people, and the line of sight is higher above the breech than it is for the lower-heeled field stock (Figure 125). Though this sight-line gives the high *shooting* desired by trapshooters on their rising targets, the naturally-high *pointing elevation* is scarcely useful in any form of trapshooting. In American-rules trap and British-style DTL the highest targets allowable (presuming no strong headwind is raising them!) are shot some seven degrees above eye-level, and

Figure 124   Trap Stock, "classic" style mounting

the highest targets in International trap but a couple of degrees higher (despite appearances). Too, preliminary points over the traps are rarely as high as four degrees above eye-level in American trap, and often six degrees below eye-level in other forms of trapshooting. Further, as can be seen in Figure 125, the eye is looking out of the very top of its orbit, right beneath the eyebrow, and in fact, because of this, stocks with the order of drop cited above (1⅜ × 1⅞ inches) represent a practical limit in comb height (particularly as regards the heel) for stocks to be shot in the American "classic" fashion. To be used thus, they are fitted to the shooter in a fashion analogous to that described earlier for the American field stock, remembering that an eye somewhat higher above the breech is desired. It will be noted that the higher natural elevation of pointing results in a stock with less pitch in fitting a certain shooter.

The type of stock just described was not the only one in use in the period between the two World Wars. A certain number of trapshooters used, and vehemently advocated, a type of Monte Carlo stock with a relatively deeply dropped heel (3½ inches was common), a level comb (a drop of about 1½ inches was normal) and a length of about 14 inches (a little shorter than the general run of "classic" trap stocks (Figure 126). In using such stocks the shooter adopted a pretty upright stance, mounting the gun, low-elbowed, with its butt in the shoulder pocket. Though the neck was upright as viewed from the side (Figure 127) most such stocks lacked cast and the shooter canted his head sideways over a comb purposely left thick and rounded (Figures 128, 129). Because of the upright stance and the relatively short stock, the recoil pad had to be set on at an angle giving a lot of down pitch in order to fit the shoulder pocket.

I do not know who invented the Monte Carlo comb, though presumably it was a live-pigeon trapshooter who was wont to shoot at Monte Carlo and who designed it to sit atop a field stock to give his gun the high-shooting quality he needed for live pigeon

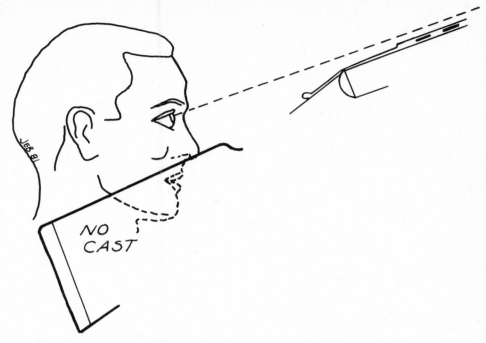

Figure 125   Fit, Trap Stock, ''classic'' style

trapshooting (it being the desire of all live-pigeon trapshooters to kill the bird as soon as possible after its initial upward spring from the trap, and before it has made much progress in its flight proper). It seems possible that its inventor was an American or a European, field stocks in these places being usually lower-combed than in Britain and hence more in need of a ''lift''! The British pigeon shooter, too, would be fitted by his gunmaker with a ''pigeon'' stock with a relatively high, unstepped comb.

There remains one more factor to be borne in mind in the pre-1940 trapshooting scene, which is that about 1925 or 1930, a pair of Italian immigrants to America returned to their native land taking with them their keenness for clay target trapshooting that they had acquired in America. They managed to infect huge numbers of their countrymen with their enthusiasm (though the disease took the 15-trap International-rules form for the most part). Today the membership of trap clubs in Italy exceeds a million, some ten times that of American trapshooting clubs.

After the second World War, trapshooting resumed with renewed vigour everywhere that the game had been pursued prior to hostilities, but nowhere so much as in America and Italy. It also had new beginnings (together with International skeet) in some places where it had been virtually unknown in 1939.

In North America, with increased participation and expertise, shoots involved more and more targets to decide the winners, the sole move to increase the intrinsic difficulties of the American-rules game (which was and is still the only one with more than a toe-hold on the North American continent) being to increase distances in handicap matches, which are but a part (though an important one) of the total game. Thus recoil-effects on the shooter became more and more important. The ordinary trap stock (14½ inches long with drops of 1⅜ and 1⅞ inches at comb and heel) mounted in the ''classic'' fashion also proved to have limitations in this new era of long races and

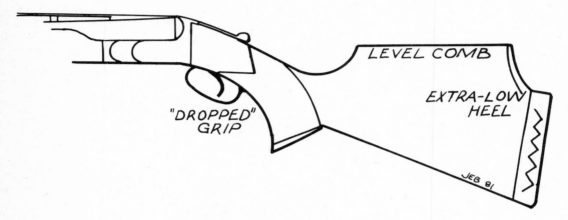

Figure 126   Old-style Monte Carlo Trap Stock

sometimes even longer shoot-offs. Though the head is well placed with the neck behind it not to be snapped down onto the comb by recoil, still, the comb crosses the jawbone where this is but thinly covered by muscle. This presents no problem with a field-type stock for a reasonable amount of shooting, but does so when very many shells are fired with a high-comb stock, perhaps day after day. Seeking relief, more and more shooters ceased leaning forward, and, mounting the butt somewhat higher (in the shoulder pocket, on the shoulder joint, or even on the upper arm, as felt best to the individual shooter) canted the head sideways over the comb of the stock, the comb then coming into contact with the cushioning pad of muscle over the angle of the jaw. In seeking a better stock fit for such an attitude shooters learned to adopt level-comb stocks, with or without a Monte Carlo step at the heel end, according to the height of their shoulder and the extent to which they raised the rear elbow in shooting. Monte Carlo stocks with deeply dropped heels largely disappeared in the general realisation of the connection between heel drop and uncomfortable upward rotation of the gun into the face in the later stages of recoil. Raising of the rear elbow allowed the general use of a soft-middled, concave-faced, "trap-style" recoil pad mounted either on the shoulder joint or, less often, the upper arm, with one "horn" above the shoulder and one in the armpit. If the *base* of such a pad is set on the stock with zero pitch it suits most people. Such a pad is useful in all trapshooting when the butt is thus mounted since it ensures consistent gunmounting and keeps the butt in place when the first shot is fired, which is a great help in games where two shots are fired. Combs became thicker on these level-comb stocks, the better to spread the forces produced by upward rotation of the comb against the jaw muscle of the canted head. The castless stock suited the canted-head style. Indeed, cant plus *any* cast puts the eye of most shooters *beyond* the breech-end of the rib, so to speak.

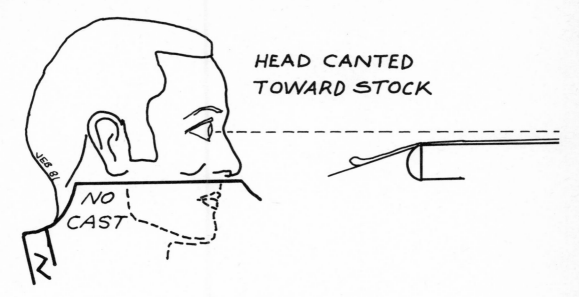

Figure 127 Fit, old-style Monte Carlo Trap Stock

Figure 128 Preliminary hold, old-style Monte Carlo Trap Stock

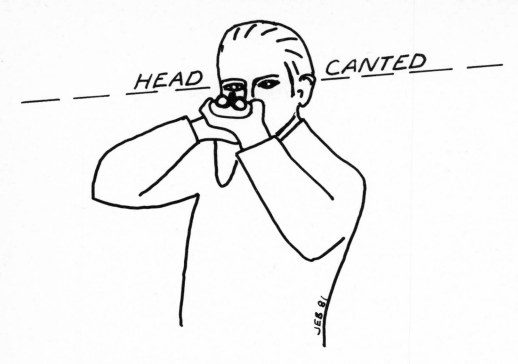

Figure 129　　Canted Head, old-style Monte Carlo Trap Stock

If the stock has a drop of 1½ inches where the face touches it (a very usual figure) a cant of 10 degrees of head, or gun, or the combination of the two (again, a very usual amount) gives an effective cast of $\frac{5}{16}$ inch at the face (assuming the eye is the usual distance above the breech) (Figure 130).

Many people who are quite prepared to accept a certain amount of canting of the head sideways over the comb as a harmless expedient become quite worried if the gun itself is canted towards the head of the shooter to produce the same effect. This effect aside, canting the gun has two others. One is that the gun shoots a trifle lower, the other that it centres its patterns to the side towards which it is being canted, to the extent of several inches at the 35 to 45 yards range at which trap clays are hit. Or, it would do these things *if* the shooter in pointing the gun looked down the centre of the canted rib from breech to muzzle. In practice the line of sight passes from the front-sight over the *high side* of the breech end of the rib (Figure 131) the result being "automatic" compensation both for the low shooting tendency and for the lateral offshooting. It must be added that it would be better if ribs on trap guns which might be used canted were very slightly convex from side to side on their upper surfaces (rather than being flat or concave). This would ensure that all shooters, including the gun-canters, would look over a *nearly*-flat surface from breech to muzzle, rather than one which for the canters is very obviously tilted over at an angle. Particular care would be necessary to make the rib quite matt and non-reflecting (Figure 132).

Note that if the (usually convergent) setting of the barrels of an over-and-under gun brings the shots from both barrels to a common centre when the gun is not canted, then the patterns will still be effectively at one centre when the gun is canted to any usual, useful, degree. Barrel convergence corrects differing rotation of the gun about its

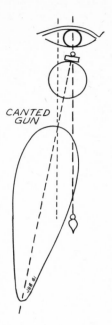

Figure 130   Fit, Canted Gun

centre of gravity in the initial stages of recoil when one barrel is fired as opposed to the other, as we saw in Chapter 1. This convergence is required whether the barrels are disposed one above the other, or one beside the other, and hence for every canted angle between. However, the barrels of many over-and-under guns intended for trap-shooting are purposely converged to shoot to different heights. Traditionally they have been set so that the lower barrel shoots a good deal higher than the upper one (adjustably so on an increasing number of models) but this is reversed in some newer models. A difference of six to 12 inches at 40 yards is usual. For most shooters this makes such guns more useful for doubles shooting as well as for International Trap. In each of these the first shot is at a more-or-less sharply rising target. Not only is the subsequent shot at a target which is now flatter in its flight, being farther out on its trajectory, but the shooter's head may be less tight against the comb than for the first shot. On both counts a flatter-shooting second barrel is desirable on the over-and-under trap gun. Canting an over-and-under gun whose barrels are set to shoot to different points causes some *lateral* separation of the centres of the patterns from the two barrels. The effect is slight, but there is little room for error on trap targets, particularly distant ones, and such a gun should be used uncanted by a suitable combination of stocking and posture.

It may be noted that the side-by-side double gun cannot be used canted with success (as a trap gun nowadays, such a gun would be unusual other than on a live-pigeon field). Due to the breadth of the barrels at the muzzle the cant is very obvious, and dissatisfying, to the eye. The eye insists that the muzzles be brought level before the trigger is pulled. If the gun has been canted to get the eye centrally above the breech, this action can result in the most consistent missing imaginable.

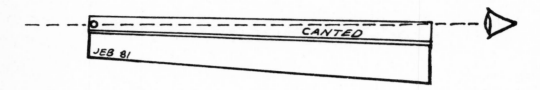

Figure 131   Alignment, Canted Gun

Since World War II, American-rules trapshooting has seen the development of techniques to take advantage of the constant height reached by all targets, aimed at requiring shorter vertical movement of the gun to the rising target. The less "chasing" of the target by the muzzle (i.e. the shorter and more controlled the movement of the gun) the more accurate is shooting likely to be, both from being less hurried, and by virtue of the decreased chance of over-running the required lead (which on the relatively slow American-rules trap target is never large). Whereas it was normal for the pre-World War II American trapshooter to have a preliminary hold on the top, or even the back of the traphouse (as some British DTL shooters seem still to have) nowadays in North America such a hold is largely confined to shooters who close one eye and who hence cannot see under the gun with the other one. Among American-rules trapshooters who keep both eyes open we now have many who point the gun three feet (or even more) above the house, often with a gun which, for them, places its pattern centres three feet above the frontsight at the ranges where targets are hit. Such an inherently high-shooting combination of gun and gunner means that little vertical movement of the gun is needed on any target, and all targets (including the straight-away) can be kept in sight, higher than the muzzle, until broken. A stock comb high relative to the breech is part of the equation producing a high-shooting gun, though it may be found necessary, too, to increase the pitch of the rib (by raising its breech end) if the view of its total length laid out before him is unsatisfactory to the shooter. Ribs of adjustable pitch are a feature of certain modern single-shot trap guns for American-rules shooting. Upward bending of barrels has suffered a corresponding decline. This never was wholly reliable, certain barrels persistently resuming their original straightness (or slighter bend!) when heated by shooting. Level-comb stocks

Figure 132   View down Canted, Convex, Rib

with drops of as little as 1⅜ or even 1¼ inches, with or without a little extra drop, Monte Carlo style, at the heel are now common in American-rules trapshooting. Usually these are shot off the shoulder joint or even the upper arm, with a canted or canted and turned head.

A rib which as a *whole* is extremely high relative to the barrel or barrels is a help to the shooter who has a preliminary point high over the traphouse, since it allows him to see deeper under the gun, over the forward hand (Figure 133). It makes necessary the use of a stock with a comb and heel which are extremely high relative to the barrel or barrels. This provides a bonus in reducing upward rotation of the gun in recoil, and hence its potential to punish the shooter over a long series of shots.

Guns which are built and/or fitted to shoot *very* high are not useful outside American-rules single-target shooting. In other forms of trapshooting, singles and doubles, the *constant* angle of rise of the American singles target when the single shot allowed at it is discharged, is absent. Thus, vertical leads required are variable, setting a limit to how much built-in elevation of the charge (or "high shooting") is useful.

Italian guns are very prominent in International-rules trapshooting. Italian trap-shooters, living in a great gunmaking country, did not have to look elsewhere for guns suited to the game they have taken up with such gusto. The Italian trap gun resembles those from other countries in its high, level, or nearly level comb (with or without a step down at the heel) but the Italian gunmaker, being fully conversant with the use of cast on field stocks to allow the shooter to use these without sideways cant of head or gun, does not hesitate to turn out stocks with cast to allow the trapshooter to do the same. Thus it is that the trapshooter who goes to an Italian factory to be fitted, will be provided with a more or less cast stock which will do just that. The fit of such a stock

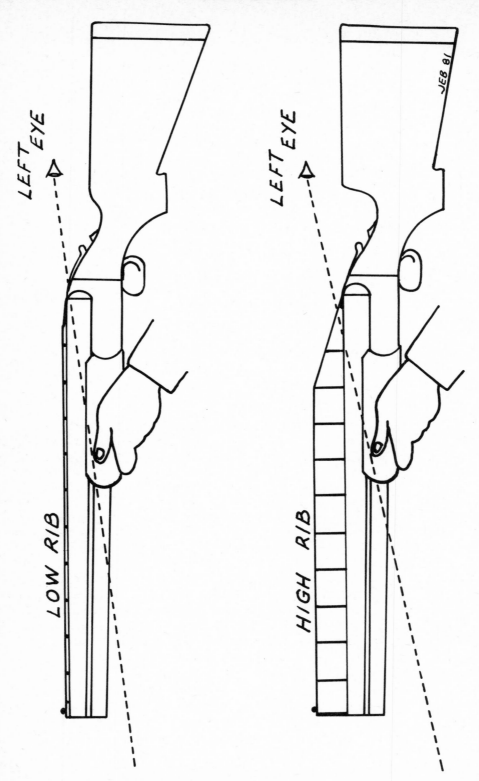

Figure 133   Low-Rib and High-Rib Trap Guns

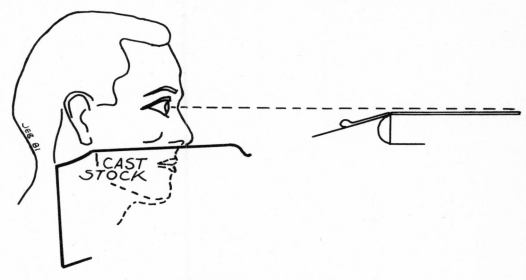

Figure 134   Fit, Cast Trap Stock

is shown in Figure 134. This one happens to have a slight Monte Carlo step required to fit this particular shooter. The "standard" trapshooting stocks turned out by the Italian factories generally have a slight cast (varying in amount) combined with a thick comb. Stocks suitable for the left shoulder, as well as for the right-shouldering majority will be found. Unlike those stocks fitted to the individual shooter, most Italian trapshooters use these "standard" stocks in a style like the "classic" one of Figure 124 (comb under cheek bone and jaw-angle) but with lower elbows. The slight cast and the thick comb add together to give the same effect as the somewhat thinner comb and zero cast of American stocks. The butt is mounted inside the shoulder on muscle rendered thicker by the low elbow.

We saw earlier (page 97) that as much as half an inch of cast may be necessary where the face of the shooter contacts the stock, when the stock is mounted against the closed jaw of the erect head of a shooter in hot action against live game (Figure 21). Perhaps half this amount suffices for all but a small proportion of trapshooters who cant neither head nor gun, yet mount the stock covering the angle of the jaw, and it is interesting to see why. Good trapshooting technique (like that of every other game, be it a shooting game or not) requires that the participant be as physically relaxed as possible, with tension only in those muscles that maintain his posture when in readiness for action, and when in action only those necessary to posture and movement. In any game where the gun is mounted to the shoulder before the target is called for there is no need for the jaw to be closed, nor indeed for tension anywhere except in those muscles holding the shooter's head, body, and gun in position (they should not be pulling the latter forcibly back into the shoulder) and a trifle in the shooter's rear hand, so that it affords a secure anchor for trigger-pressing.

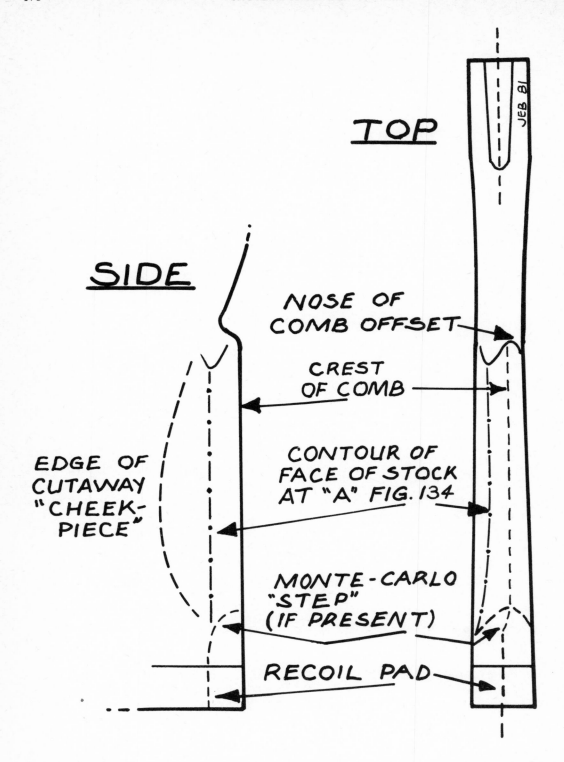

TOP

JEB 81

SIDE

NOSE OF
COMB OFFSET

CREST
OF COMB

EDGE OF
CUTAWAY
"CHEEK-
PIECE"

CONTOUR OF
FACE OF STOCK
AT "A" FIG. 134

MONTE-CARLO
"STEP"
(IF PRESENT)

RECOIL PAD

Figure 135   Trap Stock with cut-away Cast

Thus, the trapshooter's jaw is open (Figure 22) and properly so. Even his mouth may be open too, remaining thus after he calls for the target, and while he shoots. Many trapshooters say things like: "'Ull" or "Ool", from the throat, not even putting the tension in their facial muscles required to say "Pull". The jaw being open, the big muscle over its rear corner is untensed and flat. Further, the jaw may be pushed slightly sideways relative to the rest of the head by pressure against the side of the stock without this being either noticed by the shooter or causing him any discomfort. The total effect is that the trap stock for mounting against the relaxed facial musculature of a shooter requires less cast than does a field or game stock for the same shooter to be mounted against the side of a closed jaw with more or less tension in the musculature over its rear corner (the head in both instances being uncanted). Usually a third to half as much is correct, whether this is integral cast (hopefully dog-leg!) of the stock as a whole, or obtained by cutting away the face of a thick-combed stock (Figure 135) thus letting the face "into" it, nearer the centre-line of the gun, such a cast being best measured by the thickness of wood removed from that face (A on Figure 136) and not at the crest of the comb (B on the same Figure). In this way a cheekpiece, flat from top to bottom and slightly concave fore-and-aft, is cut *into* the thickness of the stock.

Many Italian trap guns have been reaching the American market over the past 15 years, gradually becoming more suitable in weights, barrel-lengths and stock-comb height for the American-rules trapshooting for which they have mainly been intended by their purchasers. The stocks of most show some cast. Perhaps it has been the presence of such guns that has emboldened trapshooters in America and elsewhere who are averse to canting head or gun, but who would like to mount the stock higher on the face, to produce effective cast on their castless stocks by cutting away the stock where it contacts the face. Most of today's thick-combed trap stocks have plenty of "substance" in them for this to be done to an extent to accommodate the widest, relaxed, jaw. If the cutaway is carried forward properly to the nose of the comb, there is produced a stock which in recoil decreases the pressure on the face. This is particularly marked if the comb also slopes slightly downward from heel to comb-nose (as is true of more and more trap stocks as received from the factory). It is, in any event, a modification easily carried out by the trapshooter himself or by a neighbourhood gunsmith. Cast produced by cutting away the face of the stock both moves the comb over slightly (about ⅛ inch, for example, for the removal of $\frac{3}{16}$ inch thickness of wood from the face of the stock in Figure 136) and lowers the comb a little. If it is also desired to modify the stock by sloping a level comb slightly forward, obviously one has to begin with a thick-combed stock having a comb higher than the one desired at the end of the work.

There is, of course, no real difficulty in altering the cast of a stock by bending it laterally at the thinnest part of the grip after this area has been softened by the application of hot linseed oil, though the resulting cast will not be of the ideal, "dog-leg", kind. Any professional gunsmith can do this, and it is not beyond the skilled amateur. With stocks that are deeply bifurcated at the head (as are those of most over-and-under guns) care has to be taken not to splay the cheeks of the stock in this process. When a stock is attached by a bolt (as are the majority nowadays) this may have to be replaced by a headless stud, suitably threaded, and screwed into the butt bolt socket after being bent suitably to fit the hole in the cast stock. It should be secured there with a lock-nut to prevent it from rotating. The stock is kept in place by another nut (with a washer under it) screwed onto the end of the stud. The hot-oil process can be used to alter the drop of any stock, too, of course, or drop and cast simultaneously.

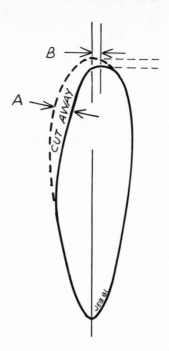

Figure 136   Section, cut-away Cast

It would be idle to pretend that this is the full story on trap stocks in use at the present day. Trapshooters are highly individualistic by nature, and having found a formula for any aspect of equipment or method that affords them a high degree of success, are apt to stick to it. Many shooters, for example, substitute a marked turn of the head (Figures 76, 77) for the head-canting that others adopt (Figure 75). As noted earlier, the turned-head style is one in which the shooter is particularly vulnerable to recoil, and heavy guns are virtually a sine qua non for its exponents.

In International-rules shooting, many Russians use what is essentially a very short, cast, East European style, field stock, so short in fact that the face is at the very front end of the comb (and hence held higher than it would be were the stock longer).

Some Americans who use gas-operated, self-loading trap guns (often weighted to around 10 lbs) have revived the Monte Carlo stock with a deeply dropped heel (three inches or more). These custom-made stocks have a ''Roll-over'' comb of suitable height, the crest of which is cast well away from the centre-line of the gun (more or less, to suit the individual shooter). It is unusual for the heel or toe of these stocks to be much cast. The weight of the gun, and the nature of its mechanism, serve to bring effective recoil well within manageable limits despite the low heel of the stock. Users affect a low-elbow style with a suitable, suitably pitched, recoil pad. These stocks differ from earlier deep-drop Monte Carlo trap stocks in having offset combs which allow shooting with an uncanted head.

The extent to which the American trapshooter (alone among his countrymen) is becoming familiar with cast and its function is apparent in the stocks of some of the present (1982) production of American trap guns, which show as much as ⅜ inch cast at heel on their high (often level) combed stocks. These guns include individual examples of the most popular autoloader. The tube running through the stock of this model was commonly supposed hitherto to preclude the incorporation of any cast in its stock. Examination shows the tube bent laterally the requisite small extent at its junction with the back of the receiver. Such stocks are mounted with the butt in the shoulder pocket or on the shoulder-joint.

Outside Britain (where for reasons we have seen he finds even more work coming to him from game shooters in the "Standard British" and "Churchill" styles) the maker of custom shotgun stocks has the trapshooter as his major client. Two factors combine to make this so. One is that the trapshooter must hit, and go on hitting, with the very centres of his patterns if he is to be successful in first-class competition. The other is that the trapshooter, of all shotgunners, puts his face into the least-varying contact with the stock. Thus, if that stock does not fit him perfectly (for whatever attitude and disposition of head, neck, shoulders, torso, and gun butt he habitually adopts) then quite consistent failure is assured.

To sum up the stocks in use for trapshooting today in a list which is probably not in order of importance, and has scant chance of being exhaustive:

1. Stocks with little or no cast, and a thick, approximately level, comb. The heel of the stock may be slightly dropped below the level of the comb, in continuation with it, or even raised slightly above it, as best fits the shoulder of the individual user. The butt carries a concave-faced, "trap" style recoil pad. The pad is mounted on the shoulder-joint, or even on the uppermost part of the upper arm. The heel of the pad is above either of these, and the toe in the armpit. The rear elbow is more-or-less raised. The head is canted over, or canted over and turned towards, or simply turned towards, the stock. The gun may be canted towards the face in addition.

2. Stocks as in 1 (except for the raised-heel variety), but with cast, generally integral but possibly cut into the face of the stock, used without cant of head or gun, or marked turning of the head. The comb covers the rear angle of the jaw, and the stock (usually carrying an "ordinary" style of recoil pad) is usually mounted inside the shoulder-joint in the shoulder pocket. Some shooters do mount such stocks farther out, on the shoulder joint. The elbows are usually lower than in the style described in 1.

3. The "old style" of trap stock, generally with some downward slope from comb-nose to heel (no Monte Carlo notch) used in the style termed "classic American" in this book, with an "ordinary" recoil pad mounted in the shoulder pocket. Some large-jawed shooters use an American-style *field* stock, short enough to leave the face well forward on the comb.

4. Stocks as in 3, but with cutaway cast, mounted higher on the face, recoil pad in the shoulder pocket.

5. Short, East European style "field" stock, mounted with the butt in the shoulder pocket, the face well forward on the comb.

6. Deep-drop Monte Carlo stocks, comb alone well cast, little or no cast on heel or toe of stock. Mounted with low elbows, the butt may be in the shoulder pocket (with an ordinary style of recoil pad) or on the shoulder joint (with a trap-style pad). These stocks are most often seen on gas-operated, autoloading, shotguns.

Head Raising

Any shooting style in which the head is tilted to meet the comb of the stock carries with it the possibility that on some shots the shooter will straighten up his head to see target or bird better, thus taking the face out of contact with the comb and shooting over the top of the target. This does not apply only to the bad style of Figure 65 in which the head and neck are bent down relative to the torso, but also to all styles in which the head is canted sideways over the comb. To put it shortly: it is as easy to straighten up the head as it is to tilt or cant it!

The canted head style solves some problems for trapshooters as we have seen, but carries with it this potential for head-raising by the shooter on some shots. A parallel danger exists when the shooter's head is turned markedly towards the stock to get the eye in line with the rib, for, to get a better view of what he is shooting at, the shooter is apt to turn his head more squarely towards it, thus moving his eye from the correct position.

There is much less inherent tendency to head raising in those styles where the head remains relatively erect relative to the torso (the "classic" American style, the British styles, and the styles in which the crooked stock and the Eastern European stock are used) though even these are not free of the possibility.

It is noticeable that most trapshooters who have retained the "old style" stock (drops at comb and heel of 1⅜ and 1⅞ inches approximately, respectively) and shoot it in the "classic" style, and those who use a cast stock with an uncanted head, rarely miss due to raising the head from the comb. Reader take note!

Tailpiece
Before we leave the subject of stocks for competition shooting the reader should note that only in the case of Sporting Clay targets has any style of shooting been mentioned which involves any tension about the neck and shoulders.

It is an axiom of all kinds of athletic competition that physical tension is a handicap (to say the least) and that tension (involuntary or deliberate) anywhere in the body beyond that necessary to maintain stance and posture will beget unwanted tension elsewhere and reduce performance. The "Standard British" and "Churchill" styles are therefore unsuited to any kind of competition shooting. Whether the Modern British style is advisable either, the reader may judge for himself.

CAST vs DROP

Before we leave the subject of stocks and gunfitting something is due to the reader on the subject of **cast vs stock-drop**, in the matter of their degree of interchangeability for the shooter. Greener's dictum on this subject in his 1888 book "Modern Shot Guns" is typical: "The object of cast-off is to bring the mean centre of the barrels in a line with the shooter's eye, without having to press the cheek hard against the stock. Too much cast-off is a great mistake. The same object can be gained by having a more crooked stock."

Some "factory" stocks will be found that have the usual American-style "field and skeet" stock dimensions as regards length, and drops at comb and heel, but which also incorporate some cast, often about ¼ inch. These are suitable for use in the American "classic" style, mounted with the comb under the rear angle of the jaw. The slight cast allows the comb to be mounted slightly higher on the slope of the jawbone when the eye is centrally above the breech. Slightly less drop on the comb, compared to a cast-less stock, will then be found correct for a certain shooter. It is in these circumstances that this notion arose and has validity. Its principal effect on the shooter is that he must face his target a little more squarely with a given length of stock.

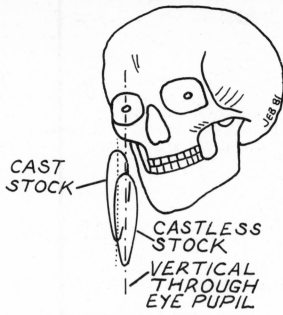

Figure 137 Cast vs. Drop

The upright section of the jawbone behind and *above* the rear angle (Figures 13, 14, 15) remains pretty vertical when the erect head is turned normally toward the stock, and the gun fitter has a choice of providing enough cast to allow the comb to run by the side of this part of the jaw, *or* enough drop (with or without a little cast) to allow the comb to run under it, as it does in the "classic" American style, or when using a true, crooked stock.

However, canting the head sideways towards the comb tilts this rear part of the jawbone off the vertical, producing an inclined plane along which cast and drop are again interchangeable in producing a fit allowing the comb to come in its right place above the breech and in a continuation of the line from muzzle to breech (Figure 137).

The shooter with a wide jaw needs a *lot* of drop on a stock without cast if he is to use it with a canted head and against the side of the rear part of his jawbone, a good deal more than is thought of as normal these days, particularly on the comb of a Monte Carlo or Greener Rational type of stock (Figure 123). A stock of either of these types, suitably proportioned, will generally be found to be the best type for field shooting by any shooter who cants his head noticeably, unless he also raises his shoulder (British fashion) behind the butt (which is quite unusual among head-canters).

But the usefulness of such stocks is not restricted to head-canters! In this regard, it is interesting to note that in fitting a Rational stock to a particular shooter, it was quite usual for Greener to alter only the length and cast noticeably from "standard" measurements. The comb usually had a drop of 1½ inches for most of its length, rounded down to a 2½ inch drop at heel. Hence Greener's dictum, quoted above, was not applied in fitting this kind of stock! "Universal" fit for the butt-end was achieved by shooting off the shoulder-joint, making a prominent toe to the stock a logical thing for all shooters. The cast required for a particular shooter was a function both of the width of his jaw and his customary head-cant (if any).

It will be noted in Figure 137 that the cast stock contacts the face over a larger area than does the uncast one, and, unlike the latter, could be shaped to fit over a still larger area, thus spreading the force of recoil. This is generally true of cast as opposed to uncast stocks, whether or not the head is canted, and is ever a point in favour of a fit incorporating some cast (unless the shooter has a narrow jaw and truly needs no cast).

The author hopes he will be pardoned for stating the obvious in noting that drop cannot be substituted for cast and the gun still fitted for "Standard British" or "Churchill" styles. These are high-shoulder styles with the gun well up on the face, and, strictly, in either there should be no cant of the head (which would make such substitution feasible).

Shooters with short and/or thick necks and wide jaws (these things often going together) and whose (laudable) predilection is to mount the butt in the shoulder pocket may find no comfort *except* with a cast stock when they need a high comb (for trap-shooting, for example). Usually such shooters have no desire to cant the head because of the discomfort this brings. Depending on the thickness of the comb, such a shooter may also find extra comfort in a few millimetres of cast when using lower-combed "field and skeet" stocks, mounted in "American classic" style below the rear angle of the jaw. Italian "factory" stocks of this (and "trap") type often have a thick comb and 5 mm to 7 mm of cast at heel.

Though accustomed to fit stocks in other styles, the gun fitter should never forget that for those shooters who (for example) will not lean forward in shooting low birds (as is required in the American "classic" style) nor raise and bring forward the shoulder behind the butt (as is necessary in "British" styles) nor cant the head (supposing that he, as a professional fitter could bring himself to contemplate fitting for such a posture) or when the shooter, due to disability *cannot* do any of these things, there always remain, for field shooting, the East European style of stock and the crooked stock, either of which can be proportioned to fit.

Which, so to speak, is where we came in.

Much of this chapter is summarised in Table III.

Stock Comb *under* Rear Angle of Jaw (Figure 17)

1. **Crooked Stock.** Pages 47–53; Figs 44, 45.

2. **American Field & Skeet Stock** (no cast) **"Classic" Style Mounting.** Pages 54–86, 147, 161, 165, 181; Figs 48, 49, 61–64, 66–69, 71, 115, 116, 122.

3. **American Field & Skeet Stock** (no cast) **"Modern British" Style Mounting.** Pages 91, 93; Fig 78.

4. **Trap Stock** (generally "old-style": rearward-sloping comb, no to slight cast) **"Classic" Style Mounting.** Pages 167–168, 181; Figs 124–125.

Stock Comb *on* (over) Rear Angle of Jaw (Figure 16)

1. **Field Stock** (no cast) **Head Canted Sideways over Comb, Butt in Shoulder Pocket or on Shoulder Joint or Upper Arm** (best with thick, rounded, level, Monte Carlo comb). Pages 84–89, 163; Figs 72–74.

2. **Field Stock** (no cast) **Head turned towards Stock, Butt Mounted on Shoulder Joint or Upper Arm** (best with rounded, level, Monte Carlo comb). Pages 89, 90; Fig 76.

3. **Trap Stock** (no or slight cast, level comb with or without Monte Carlo step) **Head Canted Sideways over Comb, Butt Mounted in Shoulder Pocket or on Shoulder Joint or Upper Arm (Gun may also be Canted towards Head).** Pages 168–173; Figs 75, 121, 126–130.

4. **Trap Stock as 3 (above), Head turned towards Stock, Butt Mounted on Shoulder Joint or Upper Arm (Gun may also be Canted towards Head).** Pages 180, 181; Fig 77.

5. **East European Field Stock** (cast) **Butt Mounted in Shoulder Pocket.** Pages 53, 54, 163, 180, 181; Fig 46.

6. **Made-to-order British Game Gun Stocks** (cast) **"Standard British" and "Churchill" Style Gunmounting.** Pages 93–147; Figs 79–81, 88, 91–114.

7. **Made-to-order Trap Stocks** (cast) **Butt Mounted in Shoulder Pocket** (high, level, comb, with or without Monte Carlo step). Pages 175–179, 202; Fig 134.

Table III – Stocks and Gunmounting

Chapter 3

Patterns, Strings
and Penetration

THE PELLETS

Having left the muzzle of the shotgun, a load of shot begins to spread both laterally and longitudinally. It forms a little flying cloud of pellets, a cloud which has length as well as diameter, and which is denser at the forward end. The farther the distance from the muzzle, the greater becomes the lateral spread, and the greater the distance, too, between the leading pellets and those trailing along at the tail-end of the cloud.

It is easy for the shooter to check the lateral spread and distribution of pellets resulting from the firing of a particular cartridge in a certain barrel, at any desired distance. This is done by shooting at a suitably large (preferably plain) sheet of paper, or at a steel plate (6 feet square is a useful size) covered with some kind of non-drying, white "paint". The non-drying quality means that the plate can be brushed over after each shot, thus obliterating the pellet marks and making it ready for the next one. One part of white, oil-base primer paint mixed with three parts of some kind of vegetable (cooking) oil makes a good "paint" of this kind. It is even better if a half-pound of powdered zinc oxide is thoroughly mixed into each gallon. Every pellet except the wide "fliers" (of which there are always a few) and those exactly on the track of another, records its position as it reaches paper or plate. The result is termed the "pattern", and the process itself "patterning".

To be sure of getting a truly representative sample of the patterns produced by a certain barrel with a certain load at a certain distance requires the firing of 15 to 20 shots. However, even four or five shots serve to demonstrate the kind of results the combination is giving. The chamber and the barrel bore should be wiped quite dry before shooting starts, and recording of patterns should not begin until the barrel has been fouled (and further cleared of traces of oil) by having at least a couple of shots fired through it.

It is usual to pattern game and trap guns at 40 yards, counting the pellets that fall within a circle 30 inches in diameter, centred in what is judged to be the exact middle of the pattern. If the pattern is symmetrical, and lacking in large obvious gaps, and the circle is divided into quadrants for the purpose of counting the pellets (as are many patterns reproduced in periodicals and other literature) then if the number of pellets in the upper half of the pattern differs widely from that in the lower half, and/or the number of pellets in the left half of the pattern differs widely from that in the right half, this is because the effective pattern-centre was not well chosen (as regards the pellets in the 30 inch circle at least) and reinspection of the pattern will demonstrate the truth of this.

The number of pellets within the 30 inch circle is calculated as a percentage of those in the whole load, and the average of these percentages calculated for as many shots as the shooter fires. The actual number of pellets in, say, five cartridges, dissected for the purpose, should be counted and averaged for use in these calculations. Assumptions about the average number of pellets in a factory load, based on the shot-size marked on the exterior, are often far from valid. Home loaders should ascertain the actual number of pellets per ounce in any batch of shot to be used in pattern testing. In America patterning distances are measured from gun-muzzle to pattern-sheet, elsewhere from the breech of the gun to the sheet. This can make a difference of a couple of percent in high-percentage patterns, less in low-percentage patterns.

In America it has become usual to pattern .410 guns, other than skeet guns, at 25 or 30 yards. This not only makes comparison with other game guns difficult (since these are tested at 40 yards) but has given rise in America to the belief that there is something different about the way the .410 acts with its shot loads when compared to larger guns. In fact, with loads up to ½ oz at least, no fundamental difference is apparent, and elsewhere in the world .410's are patterned at the same range as other guns. It is true that 40 yards is far beyond the practical game-killing range for the .410, but so it is for some other guns too.

Skeet guns of all gauges are patterned everywhere at 21 yards, this being intended to reproduce the distance from Stations 1 to 7 to the crossing-point of the targets in mid-field. Guns for International skeet are more appropriately patterned at 25 yards, a lot of outgoing targets being hit well beyond the crossing-point. Considering the number of shoot-offs in American-rules skeet which are settled by doubles at all stations (except 8) or sometimes just from Stations 3, 4 and 5, 25 yard patterning may be more appropriate for guns for American skeet too.

The degree of longitudinal spreading of the shot-cloud in flight (the so-called "stringing") is less easy for the ordinary gun owner to ascertain than is the lateral spreading demonstrated by patterning. However, if he shoots at a steel patterning plate from, say, 50 yards, he can compare loads, factory or home-prepared, by *ear*. Of course, this is only qualitative, but it is easy to hear the difference between loads with shorter and longer strings. If all birds and targets flew directly away from, or towards, the gun, on a line of sight, patterning would record the only kind of spread of the shot pellets which could be of any interest to the shooter. But with reference to shooting at crossing targets, live or clay, particularly those at longer ranges, much ink has been expended in attempts to show that it is important that the shot string be as short as possible. An almost equal volume has been used to reassure shooters that the length of the shot string simply doesn't matter, and we now have some skeet shooters who believe that a long shot string will help them to hit targets, and who believe that they have found a way to increase the length of the shot string to an appreciable extent via barrel-boring methods.

The truth is that, to all intents and purposes, the length of the shot string produced by a certain combination of barrel and ammunition has little or no effect on success in any kind of shooting.

In demonstration of the truth of this let us consider shooting at a bird crossing the shooter's front at right angles at a range of, say, 40 yards, with two different loads, one producing a shot string only 5 feet in length at that range, the other a string 20 feet long (respectively half and twice as long as the 10 foot string usual from many modern factory-loads at that range). Let us further assume that the shot pellets have an average velocity at this range of 800 fps and the bird one of 80 fps, these being typical values. In Figure 138 it has been assumed that the shot cloud, apart from "fliers", is 3 feet across, approximately cylindrical, and that a spot, D, in the middle of the cloud, some 45 per cent of the length of the cloud behind the leading pellets, is the centre of the most effective part of the cloud (where the cloud is most densely populated by pellets). Thus, a perfectly-led bird or target will, at some stage, find itself in this part of the shot cloud, its successive positions lying along the arrowed line. Note the shallow angle of this line to that of the direction of shot flight, and the fact that if the bird were slower (as many are) or not crossing at a full right-angle (as many do not) the angle X would be still smaller. Note the actual difference in lead required for a perfect hit with the two strings: a matter of 7½ inches. In practice the difference would not exceed a couple of inches, since the usual difference in length between a "long" shot string and a "short" one is 3 or 4 feet rather than 15!

The bird or target is really being shot by a slightly elliptical pattern (the projection of the shot cloud being circular in its own direction of flight but elliptical when projected in the direction of the arrowed lines in Figure 138). The ellipse has its long axis in the direction of the bird's flight, and is obviously more elongated the longer the shot string. The effective spreading of the pattern as regards the bird or target by this effect results in some decrease in density. As regards birds or targets crossing at right angles to the direction of fire, such reductions in density usually amount to 3 to 6 per cent at 40 yards and 6 to 12 per cent at 50 yards (these being percentages of the pellets in the stationary 30 inch circle at these ranges, not percentages of the total load). These are not such decreases in pattern density as to have marked, let alone devastating, effect on success. The decreases are smaller on birds and targets crossing at less than 90 degrees, and of course on the quartering clay targets of the trapshooter.

Following some remarks by a well known and highly successful Russian International skeet shooter on the value of a long shot string in making targets easier to hit, at a time when the rest of the world was seeking any explanation (old-style ammunition, strange bell-shaped "chokes", diet, meditation, etc., etc.) other than the sheer excellence of the Russian team for the success of the latter, many skeet shooters under the same rules persuaded themselves that what he said must be so. Whether or not any of the variety of chokes and ammunition they have since adopted actually produces a longer shot string is yet to be shown, but despite anything that has been said or written on this subject, since the shot travels at about 10 times the speed of the target, again it is the diameter and not the length of the cloud of shot that counts in making the target easier to hit. The left side of Figure 138 could well represent a 21 yard crossing skeet target about to be hit by shot travelling at 1000 fps.

From their writings it would appear that some skeet shooters have an ideal picture in mind which is the reverse of this, one in which the *shot string* (one of immense length, though it is never explained how this is to be obtained over a flight of a mere 21 yards) *is hit from the side by the fast clay target* (Figure 139)! The argument is that the longer the shot string under these circumstances the more likely is it to be intercepted by the clay target on some such path as the one shown. But the (imaginary) state of affairs shown in the drawing requires the clay target to be travelling *as fast as the shot*! Nothing else needs to be said, except perhaps that there is also involved a belief that,

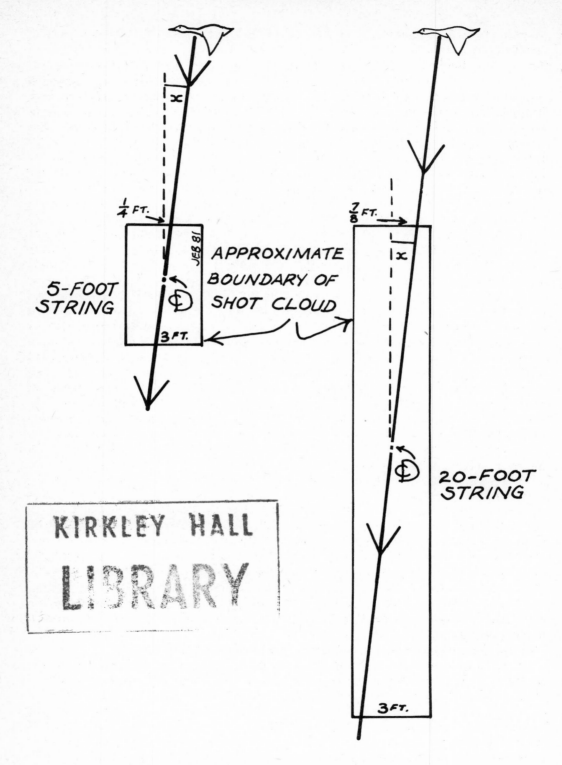

Figure 138   Short and Long Shot-Strings

no matter how long the string into which the shot is drawn, there are always enough pellets of No. 9 shot in the 12-gauge skeet load to give density everywhere in the string to hit the target with certainty. Which simply is not true. Some of the believers are prepared to argue that though in the widespread patterns they have sometimes managed to produce there are gaps of a size to let a clay target slip through unscathed, such "tunnels" through the pattern do not exist when it is, in effect, drawn into a still more sparsely populated ellipse by the movement of the target. Well has it been said that someone can always be found who will believe anything, just so long as it is contrary to common sense, experience, logic and the laws of Physics. The same people are usually those wanting very-high-velocity International skeet loads to cut down on required leads. This added velocity of course decreases angle X in Figure 138, thus making the length of the shot string still more meaningless.

It is well for the shotgun shooter to forget all about shot string length as any kind of curb on performance, and treat the pattern as essentially the story on pellet distribution and density as viewed by the target.

Air pressure ("wind" if you wish) between the pellets begins to pry apart the load of shot as soon as it has left the muzzle. This "launch effect" is greater on loads shot from cylinder as opposed to choke barrels. From the former the shot load emerges still in the flat-fronted, cylindrical shape that it had in its passage up the barrel. Within inches of the muzzle the cylinder is appreciably wider in diameter as air-pressure begins to separate it into individual pellets. From a choke barrel the shot load emerges in a conical mass, flying point foremost, and much longer than the space the load occupied in the cartridge or in its travel through that part of the barrel behind the choke. The greater the amount of choke (up to a certain limit) the more apparent is this effect. The cone maintains its identity, though spreading somewhat laterally and longitudinally, for quite some distance from the muzzle. The leading pellets thus tend to protect those of the main mass of the cone behind them from being as easily pried apart by air-pressure as are those in loads shot from cylinder barrels. Hence, individual pellets do not start on deviant paths immediately outside the muzzle, as happens with cylinder barrels. Shot from the latter, the pellets become individual, tiny, missiles at once, whereas, projected from a barrel with a good deal of choke, a shot load maintains some spatial cohesion for many yards from the muzzle, shedding peripheral pellets as it goes, until, at last, air-pressure begins to pry apart the main mass of pellets, and, again, each pellet becomes an individual projectile and a law unto itself.

It may be noted here that while any part of the load stays reasonably well together as a single mass, this mass is ballistically superior to the individual pellets which compose it (and those which have left it). For this reason, everything else being equal, a load shot from a choke bore reveals greater average pellet velocity over any range than the same load shot from a cylinder barrel, though the difference becomes less marked the greater the range.

In the flight of individual pellets which have separated from the main mass of the load, two factors are of importance. One is that not all pellets in a load are exactly the same size, and the larger a pellet is (other things being equal) the better able it is to overcome air-resistance. The other is that when a gun is fired the pellets lose their initial spherical shape (to a varying degree) due to being flattened by pressure from the wad, or from other pellets, or by being pressed against the walls of the case. Pellets noticeably deformed in this way are most common at the rear end of the load. Further: if not protected by an effective sleeve-type wad, or a shot-wrapper, pellets on the outside of the load are abraded and flattened during their passage up the barrel. Due to their irregular shape, all deformed pellets tend to deviate from the path on which they were launched (due to forces other than simple gravity which acts on perfectly spherical pellets too!). They also lose their velocity quicker than do pellets which retain their spherical shape. The sum of both factors, termed ''in flight'' effects by the ammunition factories, is to increase the lateral spread and longitudinal stringing of the shot load over what it would be were all pellets perfectly spherical and exactly the same diameter and weight.

Thus, two approaches are open to us in controlling the lateral spreading and longitudinal stringing of the shot cloud:

a) To delay (or advance, if that is possible and desired) the onset and completion of the disintegration of the load as a single ballistic entity, into individual pellets each having a ballistic life of its own.

b) To try to decrease the deformation of the pellets of shot on their way to the muzzle (or, rarely, to increase this either on their way to the muzzle or before loading, if added spread of the shot is desired).

Control of the behaviour of the load by the first of these approaches is achieved by choking the barrel: in its original (and strict) sense a gradual, slight, decrease in the internal diameter of the barrel just behind the muzzle (decreasing as the muzzle is approached) thus forming a conical section there. The choked portion of the barrel varies in length from a fraction of an inch to several inches, and there is often a cylindrical portion between the end of the choke-cone and the muzzle (Figure 6). It will be observed that choke in the true sense is what it says it is: a squeezing down, or strangulation indeed, of the barrel at the muzzle end. Nowadays, however, the term includes any modification of the barrel bore at or near the muzzle with the idea of modifying the lateral and longitudinal spread of the shot in any way, and it is in this sense that the term is used here.

It seems that virtually every gunmaker, and every gunsmith who does choke work, has his own idea on exactly how a choke should be dimensioned. Variations are therefore endless. Apart from a simple conical constriction, or this plus a cylindrical section immediately behind the muzzle, one sees chokes with an enlarged portion of barrel bore behind, or ahead of, the narrowest point of the constriction, variations in taper (both gradual and relatively abrupt) and outwardly-opening cones (often termed ''reverse-chokes'') just behind the muzzle. Some of the variations from the cone, or cone-plus-cylinder, styles are the result of the owner of the gun (or one of its previous owners!) wishing to have a different choke (often a greater one) than that originally present.

However, unless you are interested in choke as such (in the engineering sense) neither the form nor the actual constriction of chokes need concern you very much. This is because chokes are classified and judged by the results they produce on the pattern plate or sheet with the load it is desired to use. Which brings up the point that there is no set of standard loads for testing chokes in different guns, which makes it hard indeed to compare results from different sources. Such standard loads would have to be quite exactly specified, not only as to shot-load and velocity, but also shot-size, shot hardness, wad type and pellet protection. All these things affect patterns. In fact, the only proper way to define the kind of performance we are discussing is to say that a barrel produces such-and-such a pattern at a certain range with ammunition loaded thus and so. Which is exactly the kind of information that used to appear, together with the maker's label, inside the lid of the case supplied with high grade British guns.

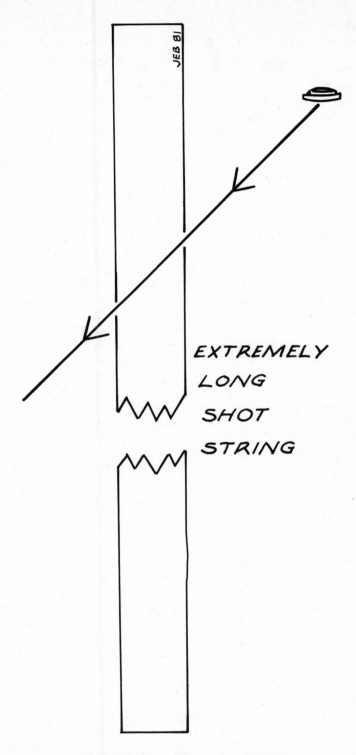

Figure 139   Erroneous mental picture:
Very long Shot-String and very fast Skeet Target

Chokes are loosely classified, then, on performance, from "Full" (hopefully giving the densest, smallest patterns the barrel borer can obtain with whatever load he uses) down through "Improved Modified" (or "Three-quarter choke") "Modified" (or "Half choke") "Quarter choke", "Improved Cylinder" (which varies from what some other makers would term "Quarter choke" down to tiny constrictions of a few thousandths of an inch) to "Cylinder" (which is, or should be, zero choke) and (uninformative term!) "Skeet". The reader who suspects from terms like "Half choke" that nomenclature is also affected by the actual constriction in the barrel, is correct. Skeet guns in 12-gauge show the greatest variations of any in the forms of boring they exhibit. They include not only true cylinder barrels and ordinary slight conical and cylindro-conical chokes, but others with enlarged sections of the bore, abrupt tapers (or "steps"), cylindrical sections in mid-choke, "reverse" chokes at the muzzle, and so on. What is being sought in these "others" varies from maker to maker. Sometimes it is simply an extra-large pattern! Other types have the avowed intention of mangling pellets to produce a longer shot string (the futility of which was discussed above). It is doubtful if any of them accomplish what a true cylinder barrel, soft shot, and high velocity cannot, *if* so scattered a pattern at the farther skeet ranges were desirable even with the 12-gauge load (which is a matter discussed in the next chapter). "Skeet" chokes in 28-gauge and .410 guns may be anything up to an actual Modified choke, since the relatively light loads used in these guns have to be kept well together if they are to break the farther skeet targets with certainty.

Some so-called "Cylinder" barrels actually have a little choke, their makers wishing to be able to say that *their* "Cylinder" barrels shoot "better" (i.e. with a little added density in the pattern at all sporting ranges) as compared to those of rival makers. There is a tradition in this, for the "Improved Cylinder" boring began as a slight, long, conical choke with no cylindrical portion just behind the muzzle. It was thus not apparent to the eye (indeed, a tight choke bored in this way may not be) and it was only the use of a barrel-gauge that disclosed the reason for the smaller patterns produced by these "improved cylinder-barrels" (from discussion of which their originators were careful to exclude any mention of the term "choke"!). As may be imagined, their "secret" was soon out. These early Improved Cylinders were developed at the time when British sportsmen were swinging towards the use of cylinder barrels again after an early over-enthusiastic adoption of heavy chokes for all kinds of shooting, including much for which they were not suited.

Choke nomenclature is obviously quite inexact, for one can only determine the behaviour of a certain barrel with a certain ammunition by actual test, and hence *define* its choke performance (for that ammunition). Just to give some idea, in 12-gauge barrels (nominally .729 inch diameter, though as we saw in Chapter 1 this varies widely from maker to maker) choke constrictions are often within the following limits:

Full Choke: .030 to .040 inch.
Improved Modified (Three-quarter Choke): .025 to .035 inch.
Modified (Half Choke): .016 to .025 inch.
Quarter Choke: .008 to .015 inch.
Improved Cylinder: .005 to .015 inch.
Skeet: .000 to .005 inch (conventional choke) plus the variety of "Skeet" borings noted above.

Choke constrictions in the smaller gauges (except for skeet chokes) are proportionately smaller. Skeet chokes in gauges smaller than 12 are almost always the conventional conical or cylindro-conical type. They should have more actual constriction than does the 12-gauge skeet gun, and the successful ones do.

Too much choke constriction in a barrel, the so-called "over-choked" condition, produces a spread of shot wider than that of somewhat smaller constrictions. A choke cone which is too steep produces similar effects. "Full Choke" .410's from a number of makers are over-choked. The true "Full Choke" is whatever is the optimum amount, and conformation, in that barrel to produce the smallest-diameter patterns with a certain load. A barrel that shows over-choke symptoms with a certain shot load at a certain velocity using a fast-burning propellant, sometimes produces tight "full choke" patterns with the same shot load (and wad column) at the same velocity, when driven by a slower-burning propellant. Presumably the pressure on the base of the shot load given by the latter, as the shot goes through the choke, is greater than when a fast-burning propellant is used. But this is far from saying *why* this should produce the effect noted. American trapshooting ammunition (for American-rules trap) has tended to be loaded with faster-burning propellants than are used elsewhere in the world for comparable loads, and American complaints about "over-choked" European trap guns have been common. The ever-greater numbers of imported guns being used in American trapshooting (including many carrying American brand-names) may account for the advent of American trapshooting ammunition using slower powders.

According to the ammunition used, and the amount and form of the actual constriction, the chokes named above can produce a wide range of patterning behaviour. The percentages of the load within the 30 inch circle at 40 yards are, however, usually within the following limits:

> Full Choke: 55 to 100 per cent.
> Improved Modified (¾ choke): 50 to 90 per cent.
> Modified (½ choke): 45 to 80 per cent.
> Quarter Choke: 40 to 70 per cent.
> Improved Cylinder: 35 to 70 per cent.
> Cylinder: 30 to 40 per cent.

Skeet guns are usually patterned at 21 yards. American 12 and 20-gauge skeet guns generally give 80 to 90 per cent patterns in the 30 inch circle at this range. For the 28-gauge skeet gun, the custom barrel-borer likes to see the whole load just within the 30 inch circle at this range, and that of the .410 skeet gun well within the circle. Note that in testing one load from one barrel, the percentage of pellets in the circle will not usually vary more than 10 per cent above and below the average. With good competition ammunition the variation may be less than half this. Table IV gives (in round figures) the 30 inch pattern percentages at greater and lesser ranges of patterns of from 40 to 90 per cent at 40 yards.

One useful way of looking at the effect of choke is as deferring farther down-range the start of the trumpet-shaped spread of the shot (Figure 140). Note in particular the less-than-proportionate spread at short ranges of loads shot from the choked barrel. Note, too, that at ranges far beyond those that are useful, choke and cylinder barrels may have a similar overall spread. In parallel fashion, a load from two different, slightly choked, barrels may give precisely similar patterns at 40 yards with, say, 35 per cent of the pellets in the 30 inch circle, yet at half that range one may put all the load well within the 30 inch circle and the other put 10 per cent of the load outside the circle. Again, two barrels may each put 40 per cent of the pellets of a good duck load in the 30

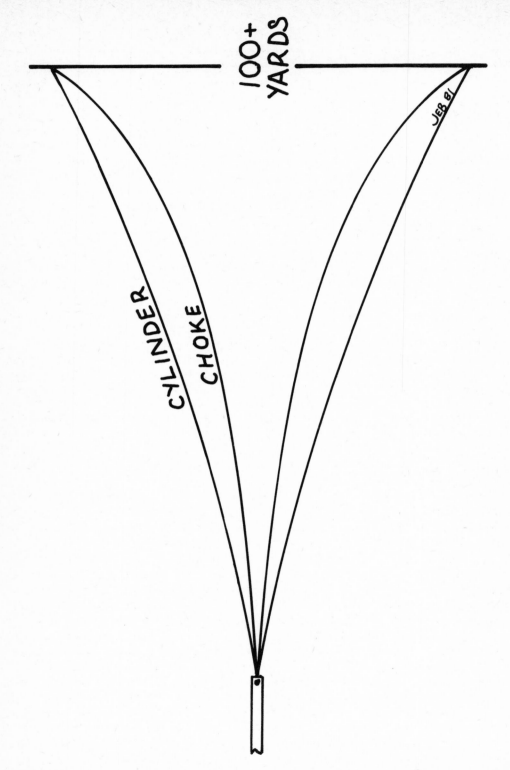

Figure 140   Relative spreading with Range, Choke and Cylinder (diagrammatic)

	Distance — Yards									
	15	20	25	30	35	40	45	50	55	60
↑ INCREASING CHOKE					100	90	80	70	60	50
				100	90	80	70	60	50	40
			100	95	85	70	60	50	40	30
		100	95	85	70	60	50	40	30	25
	100	95	85	70	60	50	40	30	25	20
TRUE CYLINDER	100	85	70	60	50	40	35	25	20	15

Table IV — Variation of Patterns with Distance

inch circle at 60 yards, but give 40 yard patterns differing by more than 10 per cent of the load in the 30 inch circle. In the end, to know how a certain barrel and load perform at a certain range the combination has to be tested at that range.

A point not to be lost sight of is that air-pressure tending to pry apart the shot load in the early part of its travel increases with increasing velocity of the load. The higher the latter, the shorter the distance in which air-pressure is able to produce a certain degree of disintegration of the load, and the wider the eventual spread of the shot at ranges of interest. The effect is reinforced by the increased deviations of the individual pellets due to their added velocity. The faster a deformed pellet is forced to fly, in general the farther will it depart from the direction in which it was launched. Well has it been said that cylinder barrels, soft shot, and high velocity do not go well together, unless you wish to spread shot all over the map!

This brings us back to consideration of the steps that can be taken to decrease shot-spread (and stringing) due to deformation of shot. These are:

1. The use of shot with a high proportion of alloying material (antimony) thus making the shot harder and less easily deformed. Loads for trapshooting (especially that of live pigeons) have the hardest shot of all, followed by some American skeet loads. In these games, unlike game shooting, someone is always keeping score, and it is important to the ammunition manufacturer that his products compare well with those of others in these circumstances. Since most of his customers have interest neither in competition shooting nor its results, it is hard to see that excellence or otherwise of his trap and skeet ammunition could have any effect on sales of his other kinds of shotgun ammunition. In these days of heightened consumer-consciousness it is doubtful any-way if anyone would believe that the quality of one kind of ammunition produced by a manufacturer would necessarily be reflected in the quality of another kind, used for a purpose where results might be quite hard to judge. Antimony currently costs about ten times as much as lead, and so the attempts of ammunition manufacturers to cut costs and keep prices down has resulted in the shot in much factory-loaded game and waterfowl ammunition (including American) becoming steadily softer in recent years. The snag is that, as we shall see later, the harder the shot the better is the *quality* of the patterns it produces. Thus the effects of softness cannot be overcome by added choke (within the maximum) nor by the best of pellet-protection in shotshell and barrel (and the average percentage of antimony in field loads has gone down sharply since plastic sleeves around shot became common) nor by a combination of these things. Reloaders in particular are now as awake to the desirability of the hardest-possible lead shot as the trapshooter has always been, and certain shot-making companies are now marketing premium grades of shot of guaranteed hardness (which is to say guaranteed minimum antimony percentage). These cost more but give noticeably superior results. I have no current analyses of shot as loaded by individual factories, but the best European loads for International Trap and live-pigeon competition have shot with about 6 per cent antimony, the best loads for less demanding forms of trapshooting and for skeet about 4 per cent antimony. Good game loads these days may have shot containing up to 2 per cent of antimony, but others can be found in which the shot is virtually pure lead.

2. Plating shot so that the pellets slide over each other more easily in the early part of their travel when the gun is fired than do those of unplated shot. This has the effect of equalizing the pressures on all sides of any pellet, so that deformation takes the form of numerous tiny "flats" on its surface, rather than a few large ones. The general sphericity of the pellets is thus better maintained, and hence they fly faster, over any range for a certain initial velocity. Crushing tests of pellets to show (what we could have guessed) that plating pellets makes them virtually no more resistant to such crushing than are unplated ones of the same alloy, thus do not tell the full story on their actual performance. Plating the shot prevents cold-welding of the pellets by pressure when the gun is fired. The principal effect of such cold-welding is to decrease the number of discrete projectiles and to spoil pellet-distribution. In this, plating is much more effective than the graphiting of unplated pellets, which is often done. Ironically, the harder unplated pellets are (due to their antimony content) the greater is their liability to cold-welding. Thus, in general, plated pellets give better distributed patterns, a shorter shot-string, and hit harder, than do unplated pellets of the same alloy, but unless velocity is reduced patterns tend to spread wider with the sizes of shot used in clay target shooting. Plating is yet another thing that cannot substitute for overall pellet hardness, and considering the cost of plating (plated shot costs about double the price of good, unplated shot) it is a waste of money to plate any but the hardest shot. Some clay target rules (including those for American trap and skeet) do not allow the shooter to use plated shot.

3. By mixing "fillers", such as ground plastic or flour, with the shot load. While this may or may not allow the pellets to slide over each other when the gun is fired (thus helping them to remain more nearly spherical) it seems to the writer that their more important role is probably played beyond the muzzle, where their effect may be to make the emerged shot load more "solid" aerodynamically, thus helping delay the prying apart of the shot load by air pressure. If you load ammunition for yourself or others do NOT mix such fillers with shot except in approved, tested "recipes" (for which see American literature). Added to loads designed for use without it, it drives up pressures very noticeably. Such fillers are not allowed in any kind of clay target competition.

4. The use of wads which are designed to cushion the base of the shot load, and sleeves to prevent abrasion of the outer pellets on the walls of the barrel. These may be combined into a one-piece plastic moulding, or may be a combination of card, fibre, cork, or other materials, with a cup or wrapper around the shot. Developments in wadding and shot protection are fairly continuous, and I cannot know where they will be when you read this. Note that some patterns of plastic wad with integral shot sleeves are good at protecting peripheral pellets from abrasion, but have poor cushioning qualities, basal pellets in the load becoming highly deformed. Others are good in both these respects.

5. Using the slowest-burning propellant that will give a certain load of shot the required velocity. This results in the most gradual acceleration of the shot from rest when the gun is fired, thus deforming the pellets less than when a quicker-burning propellant is used. However, greater weights of such slower-burning propellants are needed, which raises costs. It seems to me, too, that the slower burning the propellant used, the hotter the barrels become if shooting is virtually continuous over a period. American ammunition factories are now following the rest of the world in using slower powders than of yore in ammunition for trap and skeet shooting.

It may be noted here that modern commercial trapshooting ammunition with hard, unplated shot will average patterns of over 80 per cent of the load in the 30 inch circle at 40 yards from suitably choked barrels. Percentages higher than this are regularly obtained with larger, plated, hard, shot and the best wadding. Careful assembly of hard, plated shot, suitable wadding and shot-sleeves, and flour or ground plastic in the shot load, has made the 100 per cent, 40 yard pattern a repeatable reality.

Control of pattern percentage should be through choke (or this combined with muzzle velocity) and not via shot deformation from the use of soft shot and/or lack of shot protection. The less deformed the shot the better is its distribution within patterns of a certain percentage. This means there is less concentration of the shot in the middle of the pattern. Proponents of skeet chokes purposely designed to mangle shot to give a wider pattern overall, should bear this in mind and ask themselves if they are getting anything useful. The less deformed the shot, the slighter the actual choke constriction needed to produce patterns of a certain percentage. Soft shot, hard wads, and a lot of choke result in patterns with a small, dense, centre and a wide periphery of pellets too thinly distributed to be useful. Patterns with the same percentage of the load in the 30 inch circle but made with hard shot and better wadding from barrels of less choke, have a larger area in their middles which can be relied on to kill birds or break targets, *and* the load has the potential of being able to be put usefully through a tighter choke where this is necessary to produce a denser centre in a higher-percentage pattern for shooting at longer range.

It is time to say something in general about the distribution of shot within patterns. All normal patterns from smoothbore barrels are denser in the middle than they are at the edges. To put this another way: If one takes a certain small area (say 25 square inches) in the middle of a pattern it will be found to have more pellets in it than does a similar area nearer the edge of the pattern. The higher the percentage of the load in the (standard) 30 inch circle, the more marked is this central thickening of the pattern. The increase in density of pellet strikes from pattern-edge to pattern-centre is gradual. Plotted on a graph, the density on any diameter drawn across the pattern is rather like the bell-shaped "normal" curve beloved of mathematicians, the higher the percentage of pellets within the 30 inch circle, the higher the peak of the curve.

Figure 141 summarizes all this for patterns from 40 to 90 per cent of the load within the 30 inch circle. For purposes of analysis and demonstration, the 30 inch circle has two concentric circles drawn within it, one 10 inches in diameter, the other 20 inches. Fairly hard shot, and reasonably good protection for it when the gun is fired and during its passage up the barrel, are requisite in producing patterns distributed as

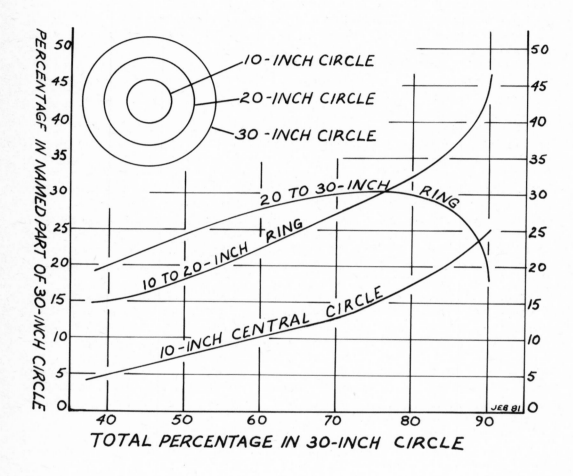

Figure 141 Shot distribution within Patterns of various Percentages

shown in the graphs. It is interesting to note that distribution of pellets across a pattern is about the same for patterns of a certain percentage from a certain lot of cartridges, whether these are long-range patterns from a choked barrel or short-range patterns from a barrel with little or no choke.

Note that it is possible to produce a pattern of, say, 50 per cent of the load in a 30 inch circle at 40 yards in a number of ways:

1. Hard shot, protective wadding and sleeving, very slight choke.
2. Hard shot, non-protective wadding, no sleeving, more choke than 1.
3. Soft shot, protective wadding and sleeving, more choke than 1.
4. Soft shot, non-protective wadding, no sleeving, still more choke than 2 or 3.

There are other options, but these will serve for the purpose of demonstration.

The first option will produce patterns with the minimum extra density in their centres for their percentage, while the fourth option, at the other end of the scale, will give patterns with a relatively small dense central area surrounded by a wide ring of thinly-distributed pellets inside and outside the 30 inch circle. Options 2 and 3 will give patterns falling somewhere between the other two in their characteristics. A 12, 16 or 20-gauge gun giving 50 per cent patterns at 40 yards with certain cartridges containing, say, an ounce of shot, ought to be suitable for shooting game at 20 to 30 yards. The combination of option 1 certainly would be. With option 4, however, one has a small, dense, pattern-centre, liable to put far too many shot into a close bird, surrounded by a wide, sparse fringe, as liable to wound as to kill any bird within it. We shall discuss such ill-distributed patterns again later in this chapter. The point to be grasped here is that pattern *quality* is largely a function of *ammunition* quality, rather than anything to do with the gun.

Note in Figure 141 that as the percentage of the load in the 30 inch circle increases from 40 to 90 per cent, the density in the middle of the pattern becomes *very much* higher, disproportionately so in fact. Note, too, that the outer 5 inch ring of the 30 inch pattern has its highest density in patterns of 70 to 80 per cent. Only when pattern percentage exceeds this do we start to get less pellets in the outer ring.

Long experience by shooters, and experiments by amateurs as well as the ammunition factories, have resulted in reams of material on effective patterns, scattered through the literature on shooting and too voluminous to reproduce here. It can be summarized as follows:

Taking the 12-gauge 1⅛ oz load as an example (probably the most-used load in the world) it is not possible to obtain patterns acceptably effective:

a) For game shooting: outside a central circle about 25 inches across.
b) For the farther skeet targets: outside a central circle about 20 inches across.
c) For trap targets (even American-rules singles, and DTL, targets shot from 16 yards behind the trap) outside a central circle about 15 inches across.

All measurements are give or take an inch of course. ''Acceptably effective'' means for a) that most birds, say 90 per cent, hit by the central 25 inch circle of the pattern will be put in the bag (including gathered cripples). For b) and c) it means that all the farther skeet targets hit by the central 20 inch circle of the pattern, and all the trap targets hit by the central 15 inch circle, will be broken.

What this really amounts to is that at the range where a bird or target is struck there is no point in the pattern from the 1⅛ oz load we are using as an example being under 75 to 80 per cent in the 30 inch circle for game shooting and 80 to 85 per cent for skeet. For it is at these orders of percentage that the area of pellet-density in the centre of the pattern that can be relied on to do the job to the standards specified above is at its largest diameter. Reducing the percentage of the pattern in the 30 inch circle *reduces* the size of the effective central area. It also means that even at the 34 to 38 yards at which most American-rules and DTL targets are hit when shot at from the 16 yard mark (let alone the ranges at which handicap targets from the back yardages, and targets shot with the second barrel at International Trap, are struck) no trap gun and load presently available will produce patterns of percentages high enough to reduce the diameter of this fully-effective circle: as we go through 80 and 90 to 100 per cent patterns at the target, down to patterns but 2 feet across, the size of that fully-effective circle (within which *all* targets will be broken) goes on increasing. Were the whole pattern (excluding obvious stray "flier" pellets) still smaller than this, the size of the fully-effective circle might at last be smaller too. Thus, the use by most trapshooters, including those of long experience, of the combination of choke and load that will give them the smallest, tightest patterns they can obtain, on all singles targets in every variety of trapshooting, is undoubtedly correct. No barrel and load available combine to produce patterns which have a fully-effective central area on every shot at the ranges at which trap targets are hit from the longer handicap marks, or with the second shot at International Trap.

For a while we had advocates of Modified chokes for trapshooting. Ironically, most of them were not trapshooters. Recently their numbers have declined to near vanishing-point. The first target in American and DTL doubles is shot by most people appreciably closer than the range at which they hit any other kind of trap target. For this reason, for that first target, the fast doubles shooter does not need the tightest patterning combination of choke and ammunition he can find (though such a thing is certainly advisable for the second one!). A barrel and load patterning 75 per cent at 40 yards is a good one for the first shot on doubles targets.

Turning again to skeet: small-gauge skeet guns, the 28-gauge and .410 in particular, need to throw patterns of higher percentage than those of their sister 12-gauge skeet gun if the score potential is not to be lower. Some custom barrel-borers understand this very well and have taken the lead in this field.

A good deal of what has been written above may come as something of a shock to the novice shotgunner. For example, there is a pretty general belief around that if pattern percentage at the range of the bird is reduced from, say, 80 to 60, then not only will it be easier to put the pattern on the bird (which is true) but that the pattern will still be dense enough to be relied on to kill the bird over a big, big area extending well outside the 30 inch circle! The truth is that, with normal game loads, no pattern one can put on a bird is reliable at its *optimum* range (let alone nearer or farther) outside a circle about 2 feet across (which is well *inside* the 30 inch circle, notice) and reducing the pattern at the bird below some 80 per cent merely reduces the size of the fully-effective circle inside the pattern. Even at the optimum range, what is outside a two foot circle is a wide zone of thinly-distributed pellets that could not be relied on to kill even were the two foot circle itself completely *emptied* of pellets and these pellets spread in that fringe, adding to those already there! It is just too big an area. The matter of how many pellets it takes to kill birds, and break clay targets, consistently, is covered later in this chapter and in the next one.

In short, a shotgun has to be pointed remarkably straight to do much good, certainly if consistent hitting is to result. Ill-informed folk-mythology (of people who don't use shotguns) says the opposite. Forget it.

At ranges beyond that at which the fully-effective circle within the pattern reaches its greatest diameter, the pattern does not suddenly become wholly ineffective and

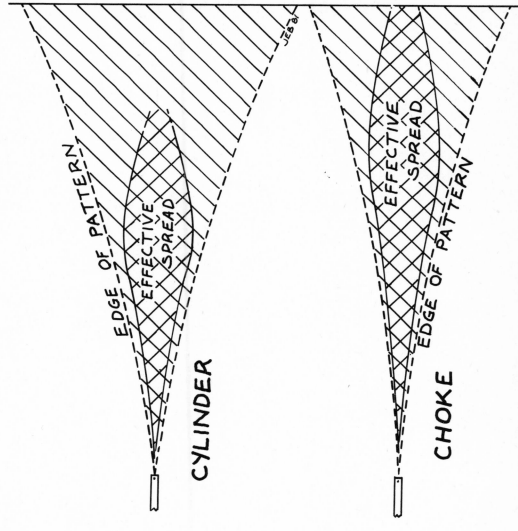

Figure 142 Total Spreads and effective Spreads, Cylinder and Choke

unreliable over its total diameter. What happens is that the part of the pattern effective for a given purpose becomes smaller and smaller in diameter until pattern density and pellet energy fail. German texts have been better than anything in English at depicting this, and Figure 142 is typical. It is diagrammatic and not to scale.

Anyone who has ever shot a shotgun at sheets of paper or at a patterning plate could scarcely fail to notice that patterns are denser in the middle than they are at the edges. References to this are found in the literature of the 19th century indeed. But it was not until the 1930's that mathematical analyses of this phenomenon began to appear in magazines on both sides of the Atlantic, and the realization began to dawn generally that this was a characteristic of patterns from ordinary shotgun barrels. Not until the 1960's was the recognition of the phenomenon dignified by analyses in books with hard covers! This was due largely to the work of Oberfell and Thompson at the University of Oklahoma, and to the excellent presentation on the subject by Winchester-Western at the Third Sportswriters' Conference in January 1962 at Alton, Illinois.

Until then most existing "authorities" on the shotgun had just gone on talking about the necessity for "even" patterns. Usually they meant by this that there should be no obvious clustering together of shot in some areas of a pattern, and corresponding gaps in others. However, the inherent, overall clustering together of shot in the central area of all normal patterns went unremarked by almost all of them.

Even when it was drawn to their attention, they could fail to grasp its importance. Burrard, the well-known British writer on shotguns, makes no mention of this pattern characteristic (let alone of its being an inevitable one, governed by the laws of Physics and capable of being represented mathematically) in his monumental work "The Modern Shotgun", which went through several editions and reprintings between the 1930's and the 1950's. Yet Burrard was the editor of a magazine in which, in the 1930's, he had published an article by the perspicaceous Edmund Bernard, cleverly analyzing patterns for pellet-distribution within them.

Bernard drew two concentric circles within the 30 inch one, one 17.2 inches across, the other 24.5 inches across, thus dividing the 30 inch circle into three equal areas. He found that "even" pellet-distribution across the 30 inch pattern was a myth. He demonstrated that the 60 per cent pattern shot by a cylinder barrel at 30 yards was indistinguishable from the 60 per cent pattern shot by a half-choke barrel at 40 yards. He noted that when the true cylinder barrel and the half-choke barrel were both shot at 30 yards, they put a similar number of pellets into the area between the 17.2 inch circle and the 30 inch circle: all the extra pellets the half-choke barrel put into the 30 inch circle at this range went into the central 17.2 inch circle, these amounting to about a quarter of the total load. And he satisfied himself that no pattern from normal game guns and loads was a reliable killer outside a two foot circle at any range.

Burrard, having had put before him a splendid, brief, demonstration of an important aspect of shotgun ballistics not dealt with rigorously in published print anywhere before, totally ignored it in his authoritarian book. In fact, and worse, he says therein, time and time again, that it is important that pellets be evenly spread over the 30 inch circle, and makes it quite clear that by this he means just that!

But Burrard is not alone. A few years ago an article appeared in an American shooting journal of the highest prestige from the pen of a well-known writer on guns and shooting. In this article the writer advised his readers to analyse the patterns given by their shotguns, to make sure that these had the same density of pellet-strikes *all over* the 30 inch patterns. He gave details of how to perform such analyses, said he owned barrels which gave this kind of pellet-distribution, and implied that any barrels that did not do so were falling below the standard possible.

The magazine published a disclaimer with the article, but it is difficult to say why they published it at all.

Consider that the usual distribution of, say, a 70 per cent pattern which results from the firing of good ammunition with 100 pellets in the load is approximately:

    10 inch central circle: 13 pellets
    10 to 20 inch ring: 27 pellets
    20 to 30 inch ring: 30 pellets.

Since the 10 inch circle has 11 per cent of the area of the 30 inch circle, the 10 to 20 inch ring 33 per cent, and the 20 to 30 inch ring 56 per cent, a perfectly even distribution of the 70 pellets in the 30 inch pattern (as required by the article) would be:

    10 inch central circle: 8 pellets
    10 to 20 inch ring: 23 pellets
    20 to 30 inch ring: 39 pellets.

However, even in a 40 per cent pattern (which of course shows less extra density in the centre than does a 70 per cent pattern) 70 pellets would be distributed as follows:

    10 inch central circle: 9 pellets
    10 to 20 inch ring: 26 pellets
    20 to 30 inch ring: 35 pellets.

Which is to say that not even *it* would pass muster with the writer referred to, whose "ideal" pattern is of course quite abnormal and something one gets in one pattern out of thousands examined (if then).

Other, current, writers have suggested that these kinds of patterns, showing the same density of pellet-distribution all over their spread, are indeed what we want could we but attain them. However, we should be quite clear that unless we could also control the overall spread of patterns much better than we can at present, such patterns would be of little use except for short-range shooting. As we have seen, the patterns we produce at the moment at the ranges of interest are only dense enough to do the job required of them with certainty over quite *small circles* (15 to 25 inches in diameter) in their centres. If we were able to make the pattern of the same density everywhere, then, to be effective overall it would also have to be only slightly larger in *total diameter* than are *these circles*. For the excess pellets from the small area in the very centre of the pattern of normal distribution where the density is *greater* than is absolutely required, added to the pellets from the unreliable (and hence useless) fringe of the pattern, would result in a ring of pellets (of the same density as the rest of the truly evenly-distributed pattern) adding but a few inches to the diameter of these 15 to 25 inch diameter circles. Incidentally, no clay target shooter would wish to have such patterns anyway, because a clay hit by *any* part of the pattern would show the same kind of "break", giving no indication whether it was struck by the denser centre of the pattern or the less-dense periphery. Nor would it give any indication of the direction of the centre of the pattern relative to the clay. Both kinds of information are used by the clay target shooter as valuable "feedback".

It should be noted that we are able to produce patterns of even pellet-distribution over their total spread by the use of barrels, or chokes, with shallow rifling of slow twist (having one turn in, say, 60 or 70 inches). However, these barrels spread shot very widely. At 10 yards the pattern is usually about 30 inches across. Such barrels are used by some European shooters on 7 to 15 yard rabbits and woodcock in dense cover. However, excellent patterns for short-range shooting can be produced by the simple expedient of using ammunition of higher than normal velocity, from cylinder barrels. Normal shot loads are quite suitable for this (slightly reduced if recoil is felt unpleasantly) and, as ever, the harder the shot used, and the better it is protected, the better the *quality* of the patterns in terms of the minimum of central thickening. Patterns suitable for 10 to 20 yard shooting are easily obtained. When ranges are really short the writer prefers another formula (page 219).

It seems appropriate to note here that certain choked barrels, to the despair of the barrel borer and the custom gunmaker, refuse, no matter how their choke is re-cut and otherwise modified, to shoot other than a well-distributed pattern that would be wide even from a true cylinder barrel using the same ammunition. The reason is interesting. Most shotgun barrels, carefully measured, prove to be slightly oval in cross-section, rather than truly circular. Not only that, the ovalness of the bore does not always maintain the same attitude, but varies along the length of the barrel. In a few barrels the ovality varies in such a way that the barrel for more or less of its length is really a smooth-bore rifle (reminiscent of Lancaster's famous "oval-bore" rifles) and the axial twist applied to the shot-charge by such a barrel, and the resulting centrifugal force, will partially or totally nullify the effect of any choke. Thus is produced the phenomenon of a choked barrel shooting a cylinder pattern (or one even wider) with any ammunition. The choke itself may lack ovality, but only a few inches of barrel behind the choke showing ovality with the axis of the oval consistently turning in one direction in this length, is required to provide this effect. Having found such oval-bore rifle barrels on a number of guns (purporting to be trap guns, no less, though it seems hardly likely that they were patterned at the factory) one American maker of screw-in interchangeable choke tubes now finishes his tubes with low, narrow, straight, internal ridges parallel to the bore axis, running the full length of each tube. By this means he ensures that the shot-charge is delivered from the muzzle virtually free from axial rotation. Suffice it to say that there seem to be no barrels that shoot a higher pattern percentage than those fitted with these "straight-rifled" choke tubes from this maker.

It is common to find an author recommending guns giving quite low percentages in the 30 inch circle at 40 yards, for general game-shooting, not just for game at short to moderate ranges (say, 15 to 30 yards). This is an aspect we must examine further. It is possible to derive the following table from Figure 141, remembering that the shot distributions shown in that figure are typical of ammunition with reasonably hard shot and reasonably protective wadding:

30 inch pattern percentage:	40	50	60	70	80	90
Percentage of load in 10 inch circle:	5	7½	10	13	17½	25

Patterns from ammunition with soft shot, relatively poorly-cushioning wads lacking shot sleeves, of perhaps somewhat higher velocity, and reaching their percentage with more choke, can give results as follows:

30 inch pattern percentage:	30	40	50	60	70
Percentage of load in 10 inch circle:	8	10	12	15	20

Worse examples, with yet more marked central thickening of the patterns, could have been cited. Percentages over 70 at 40 yards are rarely reached with such ammunition. Patterns of 30 per cent, even from barrels with slight chokes, at the same range, are plentiful.

The thing to notice is that patterns of this kind of distribution are what are behind at least some of the stories of guns that give quite low percentages in the 30 inch circle at 40 yards, yet, used by accurate shooters, will kill fairly regularly at full ranges. Such stories are a constant feature of British shooting literature. Note that:

a) Only recently have any pellet-protection devices been incorporated in *any* British ammunition for game and wildfowl shooting.

b) British guns are normally regulated with loads lacking such protection. If a barrel puts 45 to 50 per cent of the pellets in the 30 inch circle at 40 yards it is called "Improved Cylinder" regardless of the actual amount of choke, and of course of the actual distribution of shot within the pattern (both things being quite fair and within the spirit of choke nomenclature).

c) The shot in most British game cartridges is soft, containing, it is said, but 1 per cent of antimony. It must be said that the shot in American game loads is often softer still these days.

A recent British book proudly reproduces a pattern with 47 per cent of the pellets in a 30 inch circle at 40 yards. In the central 10 inch circle are 11 per cent of the total pellets in the load: something typical of 60 per cent patterns from better ammunition, and which here leaves but 36 per cent of the load to cover the rest of the 30 inch circle. The caption says that the pattern shows "good pellet distribution"!

With ammunition incorporating hard shot cushioned by suitable wads and protected by some kid of sleeve (e.g. a good trap load) it is quite likely that the barrel which produced this 47 per cent pattern would produce patterns of at least 60 per cent. With the same shot size there would likely be about the same number of pellets, the same 11 per cent of the load, in the central 10 inch circle. However, while fully-effective spread of the badly-distributed 47 per cent pattern at 40 yards scarcely exceeds that 10 inch circle, that of the better-distributed 60 per cent pattern would be 18 or 20 inches.

At the shorter ranges more usual in British driven game shooting, this barrel with the ammunition giving the poorly-distributed 40 yard patterns, will show patterns having a small dense centre (which will put too many pellets in any bird hit by it — after all the idea of shooting game birds is that they shall subsequently be eaten) surrounded by a fairly broad ring with pellets at perhaps about the right density. With the better ammunition, the patterns resulting from this barrel at these closer ranges will be denser than is desirable over a quite large area in their centres, and the ring of pellets at suitable density will be quite narrow. At first sight this may seem to be an argument for the use of "old-fashioned" ammunition and for the sort of patterns it produces in barrels of appreciable choke. However, the fact is that a good shot, properly fitted, finds it only too easy to hit close birds with that destructive little pattern-centre, bird after bird. For normal driven game shooting, then, with birds at 15 to 30 yards, it is far better that the shooter use ammunition with hard shot, preferably well-protected, from barrels of very little choke. In fact, the best trap ammunition obtainable with shot running around 340 to the ounce, will be hard to beat! By this means he gets patterns which at the usual ranges will kill over a large area of their spread (for those days when he is not on top of his form) yet which have central areas which will not put too many pellets in birds on those days when his accuracy is at its best and he is hitting all his birds with the very centres of his patterns.

It is generally supposed that driven pheasants are shot at ranges greater than any other driven birds, but in fact they are rarely more than 20 yards above the shooter. When they really *are* 40 yards up, the best ammunition obtainable, larger shot sizes, and heavily-choked barrels are appropriate.

ENERGY AND PENETRATION

It remains to say something about pellet energy and the penetration of pellets. As the pellets fly through the air, they not only spread laterally and string out, they also slow down of course. In doing so they lose energy. The farther they fly the less the energy they retain, and the poorer become their powers to penetrate game or shatter clay targets.

In choosing a pellet-size a balance has to be struck between pattern-density and pellet-energy. The necessity for such a balance has constantly to be borne in mind. It is of no use to have a pattern which will strike the bird with a large number of pellets if these lack the power to penetrate, and so kill, the bird. Conversely, the energy of pellets whose penetration is more than adequate is wasted, unless enough of them strike and pass through vital organs, and thus kill. To ensure this requires patterns at the range where the bird is struck which are of a certain minimum density.

"Adequate penetration" for shooting game and waterfowl is such that the pellets will traverse most, or all of, the thickness of the bird at which they are shot, at the range at which it is hit, whatever view of itself the bird presents to the shooter, even tail-end on (the view presented by a bird flying straight away on a line of sight). This last is the hardest of all birds to kill outright, of course, since its vital organs, from the viewpoint of the shooter lie on the far side of a mass of other tissue. Pellets that strike the thick central area of the breastbone, from any angle, cannot be expected to travel farther, but this is about the only exception to the general rule stated above. Pellets having adequate penetrative powers as there defined will obviously be able to traverse any vital organ in their path. They will, too, usually break even the larger wing-bones if these are struck, stressed as these bones are in flight.

Game is killed by damage to one or more vital organs: brain, spine, heart, the major blood-vessels, and so on. It is not killed by "shock". Birds struck by a single bullet which sheds more energy in its passage through them than do a dozen pellets of the usual sizes, will often fly 100 yards or more if that bullet misses all the vital organs. They then die of loss of blood, or of asphyxia, but not of "shock".

Autopsies and X-ray photographs of large numbers of shot birds, both game and trap-pigeons, have led to the same conclusion: A bird hit by six or more pellets of adequate penetration will usually be killed outright, five pellets will generally render a bird immobile (at least) but four pellets may not do so. Few birds hit by three pellets or less would (or do) find their way into the bag. Birds killed by a single pellet which happened to hit them in a vital spot are very much the exception!

Detailed recommendations of shot sizes for game, waterfowl, and clay target shooting will be found in Chapter 4.

With regard to clay target shooting, it may be noted here that to ensure that all targets are hit by at least two or three pellets (essential minima for breaking the target, depending on the shot size and the range) the *average* number of pellets hitting a target must be several (about five) times this. An average of less than this means that, due to the variability of patterns and the shot-distribution in detail within them, some targets will then be hit by one pellet or none at all. Some targets will be hit by double that average number! Not for nothing does the experienced clay-target shooter like to see a proportion of his targets "smoked". Choke requirements to give the kind of results required in clay target shooting are also discussed in Chapter 4.

In some areas of the United States only steel shot is legal for use on waterfowl since large numbers of ducks are said to have died in these areas by ingesting spent lead-alloy shot. Compared with any kind of lead-alloy shot (including plated types) steel shot patterns more evenly in the sense of having fewer clusters and blank spaces in the pattern, and of showing less central thickening for patterns of a given percentage. It gives higher-percentage patterns, too (all things being equal). However, due to its relative lightness it has lower striking energy at all ranges than does lead alloy shot of similar diameter, or even of the same weight, when the initial velocity is the same. Due to its hardness (which as *steels* go is very soft) its use in thin and/or relatively soft barrels will bring their useful life quickly to an end. Its good points compensate to some extent for its relatively rapid loss of energy, but no load of steel shot can be raised to the level of effectiveness of the better loads of hard lead alloy shot. No handloading data for steel shot has been published by the powder makers at the time of writing, and no manufacturer has placed the shot itself on the market for the home loader.

If in patterning the shooting is carried out with the same style and speed used on birds or clay targets, and there is a prominent mark (say 6 inches across) on the middle of the sheet or plate (as there should always be) the test will also serve to show:

a) Where the gun, with that ammunition, throws its patterns relative to the mark for that shooter, and

b) For double-barrelled guns, whether or not the patterns from the two barrels are centred at the same point, that is, whether or not the two barrels shoot to the same place.

The centres of a succession of patterns from any shotgun barrel scatter over a circle a few inches across at 40 yards (the usual distance for patterning tests) and in arriving at a pattern-centre for a certain barrel and load it is necessary to fire about 10 shots. If paper sheets are being used to ascertain patterning behaviour, individual patterns can be collected on sheets changed for each shot (and retained for analysis of variation in patterning behaviour over a series). These sheets should be fixed one at a time in front of a sheet left in place for the whole series and on which the composite pattern centre becomes very obvious.

Taking a) and b) in turn: a) is almost the same as saying "Whether or not the gun fits the shooter", and certainly this test should reveal no appreciable lateral variation between the composite pattern centre from the barrel (or *barrels*: see below) and the mark. With regard to vertical placing of the pattern-centre: it may be said at once that there is virtually no kind of shooting for which a gun throwing its pattern-centre below the mark is suitable. Guns exist (and are still being made today) which are *inherently* low-shooters, that is to say when the gun is shot with the frontsight covering the mark and the line of sight passing a reasonable distance above the breech (say ¼ to ⅓ inch) the centre of the resulting pattern will be found below the mark (a foot below at 40 yards is not uncommon). Such guns include repeaters whose barrel receives poor support from the magazine tube due to flimsy fixing of the latter to the receiver. Movement of the gun in the first phase of recoil causes hinging at the junction of the receiver with the barrel, the barrel then pointing, and shooting, below the mark. The other common kind of inherently low-shooting gun is the side-by-side double with thin-walled, usually long, and hence relatively flexible, barrels. Downflexing of these (Figure 37) in the first stage of recoil results in shooting below the mark.

The shooter is well advised simply to avoid such inherently low-shooting guns, for two reasons. One is that though shooting on, or above, the mark can be produced by raising the comb of the stock (and with it the shooter's eye) this results in the whole top surface of the gun forward of the breech being displayed to the shooter when the gun is in position, as a long upward slope. This means that the shooter will have to stick to such a gun, or guns, for it is not possible to shoot such a gun alternately with others which shoot to the desired elevation when the line of sight passes a normal short distance above the breech, the rib (and the rest of the top of the barrel or barrel-assembly) being then more or less fully foreshortened to the eye. Or not with any satisfaction or pleasing results at least! The only person such a gun might suit (as a game gun, that is) would be the trapshooter who desires extremely-high shooting from his trap gun (or guns) and who gets it solely by means of very high stock-combs. He, too, sees the whole of the upper surface of his trap gun as an upward slope before his eye. A side-by-side double with 30 or 32 inch barrels, very light in their forward parts, might suit such a shooter very well as a game gun! Conversely, the trapshooter who shoots other kinds of clays, and perhaps game too, with guns that are *not* chronic low-shooters, would be well advised to ensure that the ribs on his trap guns are so pitched that his line of sight passes the same distance above the breech-end of the rib on *all* his guns when each shoots to an elevation suitable to the purpose for which it will be used. The alternative can be confusion supreme to the shooter, and much missing above and below targets and birds. Some trap guns have ribs so pitched that the gun shoots well above the mark when the line of sight passes close above the breech end of the rib, and the pitch of the rib on others is readily adjusted by the shooter.

The other reason for avoiding the inherently low-shooting gun is the variation in its performance (in regard to where it shoots) with variations in the ammunition used in it. This is worst in the case of the repeaters mentioned, and worsens steadily as use loosens the anchorage of magazine-tube and barrel. I should add that I have never seen an American-made repeater that suffered from this congenital defect. The thin-barrelled side-by-side doubles are equally sensitive to ammunition variations, but at least get no worse in use. With ammunition resulting in the barrels shooting together (see below) and which is loaded to high standards of uniformity (little variation on shot and powder loads, velocity, etc.) such a gun is at least usable.

How far above the mark it is desirable that a gun should centre its patterns with the ammunition it is wished to use depends both on the kind of shooting it is intended for and on the personal preferences of the shooter. However, if in testing the gun is shot with its frontsight covering the mark, in general it may be said that:

 a) A skeet gun should centre its patterns about 6 inches above the centre of the mark when tested at 20 or 25 yards.
 b) A game gun, or a gun for sporting clays, should centre its patterns 6 to 8 inches above the mark when tested at 40 yards.
 c) A gun for trapshooting should centre the patterns from the first barrel fired (or the only barrel in the case of American-rules singles targets) not less than 8 to 12 inches above the centre of the 40 yard mark. The second barrel fired (in doubles, British DTL, and International Trap) is better for most people if it shoots a little "flatter" (say 6 inches high at 40 yards) but it certainly should never shoot higher than the first one. Over-and-under trap guns with barrel-convergence readily adjustable by the shooter are now on the market and are increasingly popular for obvious reasons.

The trap gun to fire two shots provides the sole exception to the rule for double-barrelled guns that they should, as nearly as possible, superimpose the patterns from the two barrels with the load it is desired to use. This matter is discussed further below.

Trap shooters vary very much in their ideals in regard to the height (or heights) the gun should throw its patterns relative to a fixed mark, depending on which game they shoot, where they point the gun before calling for the target, and the way in which they prefer to move the gun after seeing the target. The figures given above would suit a lot of International-rules shooters, British "Down the Line" shooters, doubles shooters, and even most American-rules singles shooters. However, some of the latter would regard a gun shooting its pattern centre a foot above the mark as providing the minimum elevation for 16 yard singles targets, and would prefer up to twice that amount for handicap targets shot from 25 to 27 yards.

As we have seen earlier in this chapter, pellets are *not* distributed evenly across patterns. In general (with the exceptions also noted above) patterns are denser in the middle than they are at the edges. For this reason a gun which does not fit the user quite exactly for the style in which he uses it is a chronic, discernible handicap, and (except for those specialist over-and-under trap guns discussed above) a double-barrelled gun which does not shoot the pattern-centres from both barrels to the same point is an anathema.

It has been suggested in literature that a side-by-side double gun which throws its patterns no more than 5 or 6 inches laterally wide of the mark at 40 yards is no cause for concern, and can be tolerated. This implies, too, that the performance of such a gun is acceptable if it centres the patterns from the two barrels 6 inches apart at 40 yards, if one of these centres is laterally in line with the mark (and both are a little way above it) and acceptable if the pattern centres are a *foot* apart if a point halfway between them is exactly in line with the mark in a lateral sense, and a suitable distance above it.

It is noticeable that the perpetrators of this kind of statement are much more exacting in their requirements when it comes to where the gun throws its patterns in vertical relationship to the mark. I would suggest that the shooter be much more rigid in his standards, both in regard to gun fit as a whole, and for relative pattern placement by the barrels of double guns, than not to be worried by discrepancies of 6 inches at 40 yards. Habitually hitting things with an area of the pattern 6 inches from its centre when the shooter has done everything right not only makes a greater percentage of misses a certainty, but because of the nature of pellet-distribution within patterns it makes nonsense of matching patterns to the requirements of successful shooting of a certain target or bird at a certain average range. As we saw earlier in this chapter, the effective diameter of the optimum patterns from the usual guns and cartridges used in game shooting is about a couple of feet. Patterns 6 inches off-centre leave but a further 6 inches of tolerance to play with to the nearer edge of the effective pattern. To take another example: in trapshooting the very philosophical basis of the game is that a tight choke and accurate placement of the resultant small patterns shall be necessary to high scores, and, as we saw above, the certainly-effective diameter of patterns in trapshooting (even at the American-rules game, or DTL, from 16 yards) is only about 15 inches. When the target is farther away when hit, the diameter of the consistently-effective and reliable part of the pattern decreases to a small area indeed in its very centre. Gunfitting, gun-pointing, and relative pattern-placement of double-barrels to tolerances like 6 inches at 40 yards would constitute an insuperable barrier to anything but laughable trapshooting scores.

I suggest that no one should be satisfied with the fit of a gun which shoots more than a couple of inches laterally-wide of the mark (with the centre of the composite pattern of both barrels if the gun is a double) at 25 yards for a skeet gun, and at 40 yards for game and trap guns. Final refinements in gunfitting for elevation can only be arrived at in shooting at targets with the "picture" of muzzle and target that "comes naturally" to the shooter, which is to say with the vertical relationship of these that *his* eye prefers. This is easy for the shooter himself to carry out. On a skeet field, Low 7 targets are perfectly suitable, as are straightaway targets on the trap field (the shooter standing right behind house or trench). The key is that when a clay target is hit, but not centred in the pattern, the larger pieces tend to fly away from the centre of the pattern. With observation, then, it is possible to arrive at a fitting for elevation thus, quite as exact as that for lateral shooting provided by the stationary mark. There is no harm in availing oneself of an observer who is competent at seeing the shot-cloud in the air (page 256). The final check of course is to shoot at clays at all the speeds, distances and angles of the targets or birds the gun is intended for, and to observe the manner of their breaking.

Turning again to the matter of the barrels of a double gun, side-by-side or over-and-under, shooting to the same point b) page 210): it was noted in Chapter 1 that to produce this effect requires that the barrels be in a particular relationship with each other, specifically that they converge by a certain, precise, degree towards their muzzles. However (as noted there) there are two matters concerning barrel-convergence which must be borne always in mind. One is that a convergence (it may be virtually zero) that causes the gun to superimpose the patterns from the two barrels at the testing range with a certain load will not necessarily give this result with any other loads except those closely resembling the first in shot load, muzzle-velocity, propellant burning-rate, and even wad-type. This can mean a lot of testing of factory and hand loads in a certain gun. The other matter is that the convergence given to the barrels of a factory-made gun sometimes suits only a load, or loads, that are not the one, or ones, that the gun would appear to be designed for in all other respects. Strange this may be, but it is sometimes true for all that. Further, though individual guns of a certain factory-made double seem as alike as peas in a pod, they usually do vary in regard to their superimposition (or otherwise) of pattern centres with a certain load. This is due to variations in barrel convergence. Therefore a test of one such gun neither qualifies nor invalidates all others of that model for use with a certain load. As we shall see, some pairs of barrels will not shoot together with any load!

It is well to be clear what kinds of standards are possible in this regard. The shooter who orders a custom-built double-barrelled gun from a reputable maker is able to specify the load which will be used in it, and to require that, using this load, the gun superimpose the patterns from both barrels at a certain range (usually 40 yards). Any gunmaker worth his salt will be prepared to guarantee that the gun will do this. When the gun is tested, it will then often be difficult to discern *any* consistent difference in the placing of the pattern centres from the two barrels (the pattern centre from each barrel being arrived at as the average of several shots). There may be an inch or two separation at most. Contrast this with the common state of affairs when a double gun is shot with ammunition fitting its chambers and safe to use in it, but picked at random from the variety of loads available today in most gauges (but particularly the 12) when the pattern centres from the two barrels may fall anything up to a foot apart at 40 yards.

It may be noted here that gross "shooting apart" (say 6 to 18 inches) of the barrels of double barrelled guns with loads appropriate to the gun, is very often due to barrels unintentionally bent, either before assembly or in the process of assembly. The *effective* convergence of a pair of barrels, one or both of which are bent, is that existing over the last few inches behind the muzzles, of course. Thus, in a certain model of "factory made" over-and-under gun, say, on all guns the barrel axes will be found to measure the same distance apart at the breech, and the same distance apart at the muzzles (different distances, naturally) yet, tested with identical ammunition, examples may be found that superimpose pattern centres from the two barrels at 40 yards, while others may place their pattern centres a foot or more apart at the same range. Examination usually reveals that bent barrels, the bends differing from gun to gun, are the cause.

If the upper barrel is bent concave upward, and the lower barrel concave downward (bringing the barrels nearer together at the mid-point of their length than they would be if straight) and if the convergence is sufficiently reduced by such bending, the barrels may be effectively parallel (or even divergent) near the muzzles, and they will not "shoot together" with *any* load, the upper barrel always shooting higher than the lower one.

The occasional over-and-under gun will be found with barrels bent in the opposite sense (top barrel convex upward, lower barrel convex downward). In such examples, the barrels may have been bent thus deliberately prior to assembly if the gun is a trap model, since this is liable to result in a high-shooting lower barrel and a flat shooting top one, which with the usual firing order is desirable for trapshooting.

Lest the reader should go away with a false idea on the subject, it must be said that few shotgun barrels (indeed) are perfectly straight. If a barrel (or barrel-assembly) is so far bent as to cause the gun to shoot noticeably out of line with a sighting taken over the centre-line of the breech and the frontsight, then the correct stock measurements for a particular shooter with that barrel (or barrels) will be different from those for a gun with a straight barrel or barrels. This is yet another reason for the shooter to check the fit of each gun he uses, and with each barrel, or pair of barrels that he uses. Trouble can arise when a gun has interchangeable barrels, for it is far from uncommon for these to be bent to a different extent and in different directions!

A pair of barrels may also "shoot apart" due to the choke in one or other barrel being cut or formed with its axis at an angle to that of the rest of the barrel bore. This, again, affects the *effective* convergence of the barrels, and is something to be checked if a pair of barrels behave thus without apparent bends to account for it. Deliberate cutting of a choke in this way can be used to adjust where a barrel (a single or one of a pair) shoots, and this is regularly resorted to by gunsmiths specialising in choke work, particularly those catering to trapshooters. For some guns using screw-in, interchangeable, chokes, these are now obtainable with various degrees of angularity to the bore-axis behind them, specifically to alter the direction in which the barrel shoots.

Thus, the first thing to be done with a double-barrelled skeet or game gun of unknown performance is to find a load with which the two barrels shoot to the same point (or not more than 2 to 3 inches apart) at the testing range appropriate to the gun. If such a load can be found, and if it is suitable for the shooting contemplated (and in the case of competition, allowed by the rules) gunfitting can proceed. If such a load cannot be found, a different gun has to be sought. For over-and-under trap guns, the relationship of the pattern centres from the barrels has to be checked for every trap load that circumstances may force the shooter to use. As we saw in Chapter 2, we now have trap guns with barrel-convergence that is adjustable by the shooter to suit any ammunition he wishes to use, and his own style and preferences.

Some shooters, having been badly "stung" at some time in their experience by a double gun whose barrels shot far apart, lose all faith in doubles, and use a repeater for all their shooting. Here again, when different guns and interchangeable barrels are used, the shooter has to make sure that all shoot to the same "zero".

Even when barrels (and chokes) are perfectly straight, and converged correctly for a certain load, double-barrelled guns may prove unsuitable for their avowed purpose. In North America, for example, imported over-and-under guns can sometimes present a problem. American trap, skeet and game loads are as a whole lower in velocity than are such loads elsewhere in the world. The imported over-and-under gun often shoots such ammunition to different "zeros" with its two barrels (the upper barrel often shooting higher than the lower one).

It may be noted that the relative elevations to which the upper and lower barrels of an over-and-under gun shoot can be affected by the way, and particularly the tightness, with which a gun is held. A relatively short stock, little downpitch, and a loose hold in general, permit the gun to rotate more freely about the centre of gravity in the first phase of recoil when the upper barrel is fired, than would a longer stock (tighter against the shoulder by reason of its length) less downpitch, and a tighter hold (primarily with the rear hand, but possibly including some grasp by the forward hand at the moment of discharge). By contrast, the "zero" of the lower barrel may be little affected by variations in these things, since the force produced when this barrel is fired is almost in line with the centre of gravity and produces little rotation of the gun in the first phase of recoil. In these circumstances the upper barrel tends to shoot higher than the lower one. American practice tends to shorter stocks, less downpitch, and a looser hold than is typical in Europe, a combination which tends to lead to "shooting apart" of over-and-under guns which "shoot together" in Europe!

The lighter an over-and-under gun is in relation to the charge that it shoots, and the less the resistance to rotation about the centre of gravity in the first stage of recoil by reason of the lightness and/or shortness of its barrels, the more the convergence its barrels need to shoot to the same elevation. This is something of a problem in light game guns, but an acute one in making relatively light trap guns intended for live pigeon trapshooting with the 1¼ oz load. It is almost as much of a problem in making light trap guns intended for Olympic Trench shooting if the normal firing sequence of: 1, Under. 2, Over, is adhered to.

Extra separation of the breech ends of the barrels (thus allowing extra convergence), or suitable bending of the barrels before assembly, are two possible solutions. However, a well known Italian maker of such guns now turns them out to be fired in the *reverse* sequence: 1. Over, 2. Under. These guns have a shallow action combined with a very high rib and a correspondingly high comb (Figure 133). Since these guns have barrel-convergence no greater than that of guns of greater weight, and greater barrel-inertia, regulated to shoot the same ammunition but in the 1. Under, 2. Over, firing sequence, they shoot higher with the first-fired top barrel than they do with the lower one, fired second. The shallow action, high rib, and high stock combine to raise the C. of G., so that the gun is not greatly disturbed when the upper barrel is fired.

A chapter on patterns and patterning would be incomplete without comment on the recurrent stories of famous shotgunners who never pattern a gun on paper or plate. In fact, there have always been a few such people, and the reasons are interesting. One is that patterning most shotguns (i.e. fixed-breech guns in gauges larger than 28) is a miserable business physically. The recoil is particularly noticeable when shooting at a stationary (or should I say "stationery"?) target. Nor is there much fun in counting patterns!

In avoiding all this, the kind of shooter we are discussing takes the new gun and several boxes of ammunition he can trust, and, standing a suitable distance behind a clay target trap (the distance depending on the load, and the choke in the gun) shoots at a large number of straightaway targets (inevitably some of them will fly at slightly quartering angles). Gradually, but quickly, he learns from the way the clays break (the larger pieces flying away from the centre of the pattern) where the gun throws the centres of its patterns, for him and with that load. He finds out, too, how dense on average is the pattern-centre produced by the barrel, or barrels, and whether or not there is much variation in this from shot to shot (some clays being "smoked" perhaps, and others broken into many small, or even a few large, pieces). Unlike the process of patterning, this one is fun, to some extent at least, and integrates all the information such a shooter feels he needs to know about a gun.

It has been said that shooters who test guns thus do so because they don't want to have their confidence in a gun shaken by seeing on the pattern sheet the poorer patterns in a series shot by the gun. This is nonsense. Such a shooter is as interested in these as is any other shooter, and sees the results of such patterns on the clay targets they are put on. Be cautioned however that to test a gun in this manner requires extremely precise gunpointing, *quite* constant in relation to the target in fact, and keen discernment of quite slight differences in the way a target breaks. It's up to you, but the pattern plate is the more reliable method for most people. It is interesting to test a gun and cartridge combination as outlined above and then by patterning at the plate.

Chapter 4

Choosing a Choke
and a Load

GEESE, AND FLIGHTING
(American: Pass-Shooting) DUCKS

For these we need the densest long-range patterns we can obtain. The way to get them, using tight chokes, heavy loads of hard (possibly plated) shot with "filler" in the load, and the best-possible wadding and shot-protection will be obvious to the reader of the preceding chapter. Not all factories load ammunition incorporating all these features, but the home loader can. Barrel and load combinations should be tested at 60 yards, where differences in performance scarcely noticeable at 40 yards often become startlingly apparent.

In practice (rather than theory) shot in the range of 50 to 70 to the ounce (British and American BB) is the best size for geese, and one about 140 to the ounce (British No. 3, American No. 4) for ducks. Table V shows British and American shot sizes in terms of diameter and approximate numbers per ounce (the latter varying with the alloy used, of course).

Where the law requires the use of steel shot there is no way to come near to the performance given by the lead-alloy shot loads referred to above.

ROUGH SHOOTING AND
DUCKS OVER DECOYS

The term "rough shooting" is intended also to cover what are called "upland game hunting" and "rabbit hunting" in North America. Though it must be said that bob-white quail shooting on some Deep South estates can be pretty smooth! It is meant to embrace all those situations where game is shot over dogs, or by "walking up", rather than those when the game is driven.

The loads used for these purposes are usually from 1 to 1¼ ounces, but in North America as much as 1½ ounces is commonly shot from the 2¾ inch chambered 12-gauge gun, especially at ducks and such game as late-season pheasants.

DIAMETER (inches)	SIZE (Am) = American (Br) = British	NUMBER PER POUND
.36	LG (Br), 000 Buck (Am)	99
.33	SG (Br), 00 Buck (Am)	130
.32	0 Buck (Am)	145
.30	Spec. SG (Br), 1 Buck (Am)	175
.27	SSG (Br)	240
.25	3 Buck (Am)	300
.24	4 Buck (Am)	340
		NUMBER PER OUNCE
.20	AAA (Br)	35
.18	BB (Am)	50
.16	BB (Br)	70
.15	2 (Am)	90
.143	1 (Br)	100
.13	3 (Br), 4 (Am)	140
.12	4 (Br), 5 (Am)	170
.11	5 (Br), 6 (Am)	220
.102	6 (Br)	270
.10	7 (Am)	290
.095	7 (Br), 7½ (Am)	340
.090	8 (Am)	410
.087	8 (Br)	450
.085	8½ (Am)	500
.080	9 (Br), 9 (Am)	580

Table V — British and American Shot Sizes

The combination of gun and ammunition should be such as to give patterns of 75 to 80 per cent in the 30 inch circle at the farthest *usual* range at which birds are shot. This may be as little as 25 yards for woodcock (and ruffed grouse in North America) and as much as 45 yards for various species of partridges and grouse. The appropriate barrel for the purpose thus may be one with virtually no choke, or one giving the densest patterns that can be obtained, but the shooter who is looking for a certain performance has to test chokes and loads for himself, especially nowadays. As we saw in the preceding chapter, a pattern of about 75 per cent at the range of the bird is the one giving the greatest *overall* density in the pattern at that range.

Among those whose shooting is always in open countryside (and virtually never in woodland or bush) there is a school of thought which holds that in these circumstances the shooter should always use the tightest-patterning combination of choke and load he can obtain, allowing those birds that flush at short range to increase their distance to a suitable point before he shoots. By adopting this approach, which has had some notable adherents, the shooter can deal effectively with birds that rise near and far, while more open borings restrict him to shooting at birds that rise at short and medium ranges.

Usual shot-sizes are 8 and 9 (British and American) for snipe (and for American woodcock), American No. 8 for American quail, British No. 7 and American No. 7½ for partridges (and the North American ruffed grouse), British No. 6 for red grouse, British No. 5 (American No. 6) for early-season pheasants and for teal and rabbits, and British Nos. 4 or 3 (American 5 or 4) for larger species of grouse, all other ducks, for late-season pheasants and for hares. Some British shooters use but three British sizes: 8's for snipe, 4's for ducks (and when specifically looking for a hare for the pot) and 6's for everything in between. Some of these would use the 4's on geese too, rather than buying a couple of boxes of something bigger.

For game birds, pheasants, partridges or grouse, that rise at long ranges in late season, British No. 3 (American No. 4) shot in the kind of loadings mentioned above in connection with duck flighting, and delivered from tightly-patterning chokes, is the best bet.

For really close work in dense cover with the .410 (page 238) British No. 5 (American No. 6) is the best size in loads of ½ to $\frac{11}{16}$ oz. Because of the denser patterns it produces, shot smaller than this will smash birds at really close range. Shot larger than this is too thinly distributed beyond 10 yards or so, unless there is quite a lot of choke in the little gun, which there should not be. What a barrel borer would call "Improved Cylinder" or "Quarter choke" is the right thing. In these increasingly enlightened days, .410 "Skeet" barrels are often (and rightly) about Quarter choke, or even a little bit tighter than this. If your close cover shooting with the .410 is predominantly at birds and rabbits at 10 to 15 yards, rather than 5 to 10 yards, then, obviously, a smaller shot-size is indicated, and you might also consider the 28-gauge with its $\frac{9}{16}$ and ¾ oz loads.

DRIVEN GAME

Driven game is usually shot somewhere between 18 and 28 yards from the gun, and the usual shot-loads are between 1 oz and 1⅛ oz. Thus in getting the largest useful pattern (about 75 per cent) at the farthest useful range, barrels giving patterns of 50 to 55 per cent in the 30 inch circle at 40 yards with the chosen load would seem to be indicated. In fact such barrels are the norm on guns intended primarily for this kind of shooting. The usual gun is the double, and both barrels (or all four barrels of a pair) should be bored the same. To have any variation in borings between the barrels is to ensure finding oneself firing the more tightly choked barrels at closer birds, and vice versa.

In a very few places driven pheasants are shown which really *are* "high", passing perhaps 40 yards and more above the shooter. In these circumstances the densest patterns obtainable by the use of tight chokes and suitable ammunition are called for.

Some driven game shooters use British No. 6 (or a near equivalent) for all their shooting. Others use British No. 7 (American No. 7½) for partridges, British No. 6 for grouse, and British No. 5 (American No. 6) for pheasants (or European equivalents of these sizes in each case). The usual ranges are such that any of these sizes provides adequate penetration on any of these species. However, really high pheasants, black grouse, and late-season red grouse should not be tackled with a size smaller than British No. 5 (American No. 6). For driven hares, alone, British No. 3 (American No. 4) is probably the best size.

SKEET

Skeet loads in each gauge and game are laid down by the rules. American rules require that the shot-size shall not be smaller than No. 9. International (and English) rules call for 2 mm shot (which is slightly smaller than No. 9) but also specifically allow American No. 8 and No. 9 shot. American No. 10 shot was given a protracted trial on International skeet targets, but seemed to lack breaking-power on outgoing targets beyond midfield.

In fact, almost everyone uses No. 9 shot for every variety, and in every gauge, for skeet.

At 21 yards, the usual patterning range for testing skeet guns, the percentages in the 30 inch circle for competition guns should average:

12-gauge (1⅛ oz load):   80 to 85 per cent (90 to 95 per cent where American-rules "all doubles" matches and shoot-offs are a possibility).

20-gauge (⅞ oz load):   85 to 90 per cent (95 to 100 per cent for the barrel to be used in "all doubles").

28-gauge (¾ oz load):   95 to 100 per cent.

.410 bore (½ oz load):   100 per cent (with a virtually pellet-free margin 2 or 3 inches wide within the 30 inch circle).

Average percentages less than these can result in lost targets over a long series, those patterns at the low end of the inevitable variation in pattern over such a series being simply too sparse to do the job. Every generation seems to have to discover for itself that barrels producing the widest-possible patterns are not the right medicine for skeet competition, not even in 12-gauge, and that it simply doesn't pay to risk not breaking some of the outgoing targets through a too widely spread, sparse, pattern, because such a barrel confers no counterbalancing advantage in ease of hitting the closer incomers (which are relatively easy to hit anyway) and even if it did, all the outgoers have to be broken to score 100 per cent! The increasing use of appreciable choke in .410 and even 28-gauge skeet barrels (they would now be unsaleable without, and .010 inch and .005 inch are now usual) has been the single most important factor in the rapid rise in small-gauge skeet scores in recent years, followed by improvements in ammunition.

SPORTING CLAY TARGETS

All rules, British and International, for Sporting clay targets specify 12-gauge as the largest gun that can be used, but provide no compensatory features for shooters using smaller gauges. A wide variety of targets are used, as we saw in Chapter 2.

Under British rules the shooter may use as many guns as he wishes in a single competition, but International rules allow the shooter to use only one gun in a competition, and he may not change any part of it (e.g. barrels or even choke tubes). British rules allow the use of up to 1⅛ oz of shot, International rules up to 36 g (1¼ oz approximately). Shot must be between 2 mm and 2.6 mm in size in British competitions, between 2 mm and 2.5 mm in International-rules events. Table VI shows shot of this range of diameters in terms of British, American, French, Italian and Spanish shot sizes.

DIAMETER	BRITISH	AMERICAN	FRENCH	ITALIAN	SPANISH
2.00 mm	—	9	9	—	10
2.03 mm	9	—	—	9	—
2.16 mm	—	8½	—	—	—
2.21 mm	8	—	—	8	—
2.25 mm	—	8	8	—	9
2.41 mm	7	7½	—	7	8
2.50 mm	—	7	7	—	7
2.51 mm	6½	—	—	6	—
2.59 mm	6	—	—	—	—

Table VI — Shot Sizes for Competition Shooting

If the International-rules shooter chooses a gun with a conventionally-bored choke of 10 to 12 thousandths of an inch (which may be called Improved Cylinder or Quarter choke by the manufacturer) or, if he uses an over-and-under gun (these being in the majority in all Sporting clay target competitions) and feels that something is to be gained by having the barrels choked differently, chokes of about 8 thousandths and 14 thousandths, he will find that by choosing suitable ammunition as regards velocity, shot-size, shot-hardness and wadding-type, he can obtain pattern-spreads and densities suitable for targets at all ranges from 15 to 35 yards in the case of edge-on targets of normal size, and to 45 yards if the clays are presented with their greatest area to the shooter (e.g. overhead clays from a high tower). If edgewise, distant (35 to 50 yard) clays (or smaller or thinner edgewise clays closer than this) are part of a competition course, inevitably some will fail to be hit due to pattern sparseness.

Skeet loads with shot around 2 mm in diameter are suitable for ranges to 30 yards, trap loads with shot of about 2¼ mm for targets to 35 yards or a little more, and the best obtainable trap loads (and 1¼ oz pigeon loads for International-rules shoots) with shot of about 2½ mm for targets in the 35 to 50 yard range. Patterning of the gun with all available trap and skeet loads is indicated and advisable. It may be noted that shot of 2.6 mm (British No. 6) is the favourite size of British game shooters. British rules allow this size specifically to accommodate the British game shooter who wishes to use his usual ammunition in casual competition (or perhaps in a wisely casual attitude to competition).

Many of the most successful British-rules Sporting Clay competitors also stick to one gun, with one set of barrels, or one barrel, choked as suggested above, for all targets, using a variety of trap and skeet loads. Others use as many as three guns, identical in everything except chokes, or sometimes three interchangeable barrels or pairs of barrels, or a selection of choke tubes in an over-and-under or gas-operated autoloader, choosing both choke and load to suit the "stand" they are on as they go through a competition.

TRAPSHOOTING

All trapshooting is with the 12-gauge gun. Loads for all trapshooting except ZZ and live pigeons are restricted to a maximum of 1⅛ oz. For live pigeons and ZZ shooting the maximum is 1¼ oz.

Concerning clay target trapshooting: there is a great deal of evidence that the tightest patterns we can regularly obtain with present-day guns and trapshooting ammunition are required to *guarantee* scores of 100 per cent (even on American-rules and British DTL singles shot from 16 yards behind the trap) presuming the shooter is skilful enough to do his part perfectly. As pointed out nearly 20 years ago in the Winchester-Western analysis referred to in Chapter 3, positively to guarantee breaking every trap target (presented to the shooter almost edge-on, remember) the average pattern at the target with 1⅛ oz of shot running 340 or 350 per ounce (American No. 7½, British No. 7) must have virtually *all* the load within the 30 inch circle, and the gun must be pointed very accurately too (an aiming error *averaging* not more than a couple of inches at the target). These requirements must be satisfied to ensure that every target will be hit by at least two pellets, despite inevitable variations in percentage and pellet-distribution from shot to shot. Patterns of a slightly lower percentage ensure similar results when American No. 8 shot (or its close equivalent) is used, and this appears to be the best shot-size for American-rules trap, and British DTL, singles shot from the 16 yard mark, both shots at doubles, and the first barrel at International trap games. Some American trapshooters use American No. 8½ for 16 yard singles. However, three of these are required to do the work of two American 7½'s (or 8's) and there are not half as many again No. 8½'s in the load, nor will they pattern to as high a percentage as 7½'s or 8's. Note that if the average pattern at, say, 35 yards is to be one that can be just enclosed by the 30 inch circle (apart from a few "flier" pellets) the combination of barrel and load must average 90 per cent in the circle at 40 yards.

A fast doubles shooter may hit the first target consistently at only 30 yards from his feet. A 100 per cent pattern at this range should result from a "Modified" barrel patterning some 75 per cent at 40 yards. This seems to be one of the two cases in trapshooting calling for patterns somewhat less than the tightest obtainable. The other case is that of the novice trapshooter, who, at the outset of his career, needs a barrel of less than maximum choke until he learns where he must point to put the pattern on 16 yard singles, or for the first shot on International targets. Patterns from such a "Modified" choke barrel will break the vast majority, but not all, of targets centred in them, up to 40 yards or so. For the American-rules trap, and British DTL, shooter, this barrel can be the lower, Modified choke, barrel of an over-and-under gun which will serve as his doubles gun in the next stage of his career. Screw-in chokes on a trap gun mean that it can advance in pattern-tightness parallel with the owner's increasing expertise.

The lower averages in shooting at American-rules trap clays from long-handicap distances (as compared to the averages from 16 yards) and in second-barrel shots (as compared to first-barrel shots) at International trap, are due largely to the thinner patterns at the ranges where the pellets catch up to these clays, rather than to shooter-error, no matter what the shooter himself chooses bravely to believe to sustain his efforts. At the ranges where these targets are hit, patterns have spread to a degree where if any part of the pattern can be totally relied on to break clays (every time, remember) it is a small area a few inches across in the very centre of the pattern. Every extra yard of range reduces the effective diameter of the pattern (Figure 142) as well as the striking-energy of the pellets. Thus, in American trap, shooting from 27 yards is a completely different game from 16 yard singles, and the second shot at International trap, if the shooter is a little slow in making use of it, a quite different proposition from the first one.

The longest ranges at which the pellet sizes usually used on clay targets possess adequate energy to break these (depending on the load, the hardness of the pellets, the hardness of the targets, and so on) are about as follows for American shot sizes (see Table VI for equivalents):

No. 7½ — 50 yards (two pellets required for a certain break)

No. 8 — 45 yards (two pellets required for a certain break to 40 to 42 yards, three beyond that)

No. 8½ — 40 yards (three pellets required for a certain break)

No. 9 — 35 yards (three pellets required for a certain break).

A whole chapter could be written on chokes and loads for live pigeon trapshooting in Europe and America, but it would be of other than esoteric interest to very few readers. The reader who might have been directly interested will be already aware of the constant back and forth in arguments on this matter in European and American periodicals, and among live pigeon trapshooters. These arguments have been going on for over a hundred years. Trapshooting is a game for individuals, and no division of it more so than live pigeon shooting.

GENERAL

A few final notes concerning ammunition:

1. **Price is an indication of quality (and hence of performance) though not a complete one. British and American ammunition is thoroughly reliable. So are trap (including pigeon) and skeet loads from virtually all sources, as a rule containing hard shot and good wadding (it is not possible to deceive competition shooters concerning ammunition quality). Thus, these are splendid ammunition for game shooting if the load and shot size are right.**

2. **Plastic-cased ammunition is a godsend to the waterfowler, and to the game shooter who goes out in the rain (some don't, though they aren't driven game shooters, whose show, like that of the competition shooter, must go on, having cost so much to stage). It is a godsend, too, to the home loader because of the durability of the better plastic cases. Clean the chamber/s of the gun thoroughly after using this kind of ammunition, or (unless they are chromed) they will rust.**

3. **Paper-cased ammunition is the best kind for autoloaders (presuming it can be kept dry) especially in competition shooting, as less gas leaks back past the sides of the case to be deposited on the mechanism within the receiver. Thus, paper-cased ammunition helps such guns to go on functioning reliably between thorough cleanings.**

4. **For the handloader:**

Loading machines are undergoing continuous development. Before buying one, find out what the current best ones are. Magazines dedicated to clay target shooting carry loading-tool reviews, but may not take seriously good tools of low output per hour, since clay target shooters use a lot of ammunition. Which brings us to the point that, unless you personally get a special enjoyment from making your own ammunition, handloading is really for the clay target shooter, the assembler of special long-range waterfowling loads, and the ballistics experimenter who knows what he is about. With the exception of some North American crow hunters and British woodpigeon specialists, most British and North American rough shooters who do not also shoot trap, or skeet, or sporting clays, would be many years amortizing the cost of the more expensive tools, let alone showing a profit. No matter what tool you use, follow the manuals (and current advice in reliable journals) religiously. Do not be satisfied until you have adjusted the tool (presuming it is so adjustable) to produce folded crimps any factory would be proud of. A plastic wad that "hangs up" in being loaded into a plastic case often has had its skirt slit by one of the folds in the mouth of the latter. Thus, any hesitation of a wad of this kind in sliding into a plastic case should cause the loader to stop, fish out the wad, and check it. If its skirt is cut he should throw the wad away and load another. It is false economy to turn out a suspect load, possibly wasting the other components, just for the price of a wad.

Chapter 5

Guns

SIDE-BY-SIDE, DOUBLE-BARRELLED GUNS

The side-by-side double-barrelled gun is the oldest type of multi-shot shotgun. It remains highly popular as a gun for game and waterfowl, and to a lesser extent as a live-pigeon trap gun. However, it is nowadays used by very few clay target competitors. I believe that this state of affairs, as regards most forms of clay target shooting, has its origins largely in historical accident rather than an inherent unsuitability of the side-by-side double for the purpose. Here a digression is necessary.

The mechanical clay-target trap was an American invention (the target itself, in its present form, seems to have been the brainchild of a Scot) and clay target shooting was indulged in by only a handful of people in any country outside North America until after World War I, and not at all in many countries until the 1930's. There is, by the way, a folk-belief among older American clay-target shooters that they still outnumber clay target shooters in the rest of the world put together, and that, eventually, the International Shooting Union will replace International Trap by American Trap in international competition. This despite the fact that, for example, Italian trapshooters alone outnumber American trapshooters by 10 to one, and that only four other countries in the world (out of the 97 in the ISU) all of them (not surprisingly) English-speaking, shoot a form of trap resembling the American-rules game. None of the four wants, or expects to see, International Trap (which each shoots in its own country) replaced in international competition by the American game. Though the latter can no more be "mastered" than can any other form of trapshooting, it lacks the athletic quality required to qualify it for inclusion in, for example, the Olympic Games, where there is certainly not the time available, either, for the week-long shoot-offs that would be necessary to find the winner.

The side-by-side double was the dominant type of shotgun in use in America at the time of the invention of the clay target in 1880 and remained so until about 1930, and guns of this type were used by many prominent trapshooters (and, later, skeet shooters) until the mid-1930's. However, from the day (before 1900) that serviceable repeaters appeared on the market they were the choice of some clay target shooters (and even a few live-pigeon trapshooters) and the number and proportion of clay target shooters whose choice they were grew steadily as time went on. The fact that repeaters were somewhat cheaper than double guns of equal quality had little to do, ever, with the rise of the repeater in North American clay target shooting, for double guns were far from expensive and clay target shooting is not and never has been a sport for the poor. It would be difficult to demonstrate, either, that these earlier, generally ribless, repeaters with their discreet little frontsights, were easier to point straight for direction or elevation than were the competition models of American side-by-side double guns, most of which sported high, flat, matted ribs, and a variety of prominent frontsights borrowed from the live pigeon trapshooter.

What the repeater did have, however, was what the double-gun makers (and their customers) described as ''bad balance'', which is to say that in comparison with the double-guns they had more weight forward, which helped to keep the gun moving with the target, and the comb from rotating upward in recoil to an extent which became uncomfortable when shooting was sustained (which it speedily became from the earliest days of clay target shooting in America). Whether there was any general, articulate, realisation of the virtues of such ''loginess'' in a gun for clay target shooting, especially in the American games with relatively slow targets, is doubtful. Increasing numbers of people bought repeaters with which to shoot trap and skeet (even putting up with the necessarily ''creepy'' trigger-pull of long-recoil autoloaders in some cases) because it was increasingly obvious that high scoring was easier with a 7½ lb gun having its weight well spread out along its length, than with a gun of similar weight and the ''better balance'' that American side-by-side double gun makers had now achieved in their products, in common with those of a similar type from other parts of the world.

American makers of double-barrelled side-by-side guns mostly went on turning out guns with the weight ''well between the hands'' in models intended for clay target trapshooting and for skeet shooting, and thus labelled, until virtually everyone knew better than to buy these for such purposes, at which point they went off the market.

Between the end of World War I and 1930 most of America's leading trapshooters were using repeaters. They were also going to international competitions, and winning, watched by the shooters of other nations. The publicity given to clay target shooting, at home and abroad, had its effect on what guns people in North America bought for *hunting*.

The Depression did give an added fillip to the progress of the repeating shotgun in America, and sounded the death knell of all but a few makes of American side-by-side doubles for general, *field*, use. The relative prices of a repeater and a double gun of a certain quality (about one to three) mattered to most North American *hunters* in the money-short 1930's.

American (and other) clay target shooters were beginning to have thrust under their noses increasing numbers of an excellent American-designed, Belgian-built, over-and-under gun, a gun which at the shoulder looked *and felt* to the shooter like the repeaters to which, if an American (and he usually was) he was used.

By the 1950's only a couple of makes of American side-by-side double-barrelled guns remained, one quite expensive, the other (purely a hunting gun) quite cheap. The former was made in trap and skeet, as well as field, models. But though the former were better adapted in weight, balance and ribbing for these games, most clay target shooters, fully cognisant of what the champions were using, would buy only over-and-unders, single shot trap guns, and repeaters. And increasingly a technique was being evolved in American-rules trap which was incompatible with the use of the side-by-side double gun, as we shall see below.

By now the dominance of America in international clay target competition was over, but the influence of American choice of guns remained. Though the repeater gained little ground elsewhere (until now, when gas-operated autoloaders are becoming more prominent everywhere) when the post World War II upsurge in clay target shooting took place in the rest of the world, the maker of the American-designed, Belgian-made, over-and-under gun mentioned above was ready, with already tried and refined models for all kinds of clay target shooting. Except perhaps in Italy, whose gunmakers have always been able to produce whatever kind of shotgun is required for any purpose, this over-and-under gun at once became the norm over much of the world outside America for clay target shooting, and only recently is its supremacy being challenged by the over-and-under guns from other countries, notably Italy and Japan. In America it was at first "the over-and-under gun among the repeaters", and now is *one* of the over-and-under guns vying for the clay target market with the repeaters!

However, its effect in the post World War II period on gunmakers all over the world was to force them to follow suit with similar over-and-under guns if they wanted a share of the growing clay target shooting market. And this they have done, as we all know. All except the British gunmakers that is, who to this day have been unable to co-operate sufficiently among themselves to provide a worthwhile order for over-and-under actions in the rough, for distribution to the British gun trade, and so have missed the boat.

Nowadays a side-by-side double gun built specifically for clay target shooting of any kind would be a special-order item anywhere in the world, and there seems scant chance of such a thing being ordered by more than one or two people, let alone its becoming a common item on gundealers' shelves! One Japanese firm did list 12 and 20-gauge skeet guns of this type for a while, but now they seem to have disappeared.

In fact, for most forms of clay target shooting, there is no reason that a side-by-side double gun should not be as successful as the over-and-under. It is ironic that it was the influence of the American trapshooter (then the majority clay target shooter in the world) which pushed the side-by-side gun out of the clay target shooting picture *before* most of his kind adopted a method (a preliminary-point high over the traphouse) which made the side-by-side gun less than suitable for American-rules trap, a game scarcely shot outside North America, and whose variants in other English-speaking countries are unlikely to spread farther.

To be successful as a clay target gun the side-by-side double would have to be of full weight (suited to the particular game being shot) and to have its weight spread out more along its length than is usual even on live pigeon trap guns of this kind (let alone game guns). A beavertail fore-end (to keep fingers off hot barrels, and the ends of glove-fingers out of the line of sight on cold days), a prominent matted rib of suitable pitch and standing well up between the muzzles, and a single-trigger for use wherever the climate made gloves required (even sometimes) would be necessities. Given these things, there is no reason to believe that such guns would not be a success.

Never have there been the results published of any tests which showed that the side-by-side gun is not capable of being pointed as accurately as a repeater or an over-and-under gun (and this in a world where some manufacturers make *only* repeating and/or over-and-under guns . . .). Nor can there be, for no one points the side-by-side gun less consistently than they do any other type. And a small proportion of shooters points the side-by-side gun more accurately than they do the over-and-under, *perhaps* because with the side-by-side gun the greatest width of the barrel assembly is displayed to the eye which is over them, rather than to the other eye.

The majority of today's American-rules trapshooters hold high (up to 4 feet) above the house when calling for a target. These are people who shoot with both eyes open (the shooter who closes one eye has to hold below the traphouse roof or he misses the early flight of the target) but the side-by-side gun blots out too much of the area beneath it for them, no matter how far back the forward hand is held, or how low either (by means of a deep fore-end) and the early part of the target's flight, again, is lost to view. A handful of American shooters still use the side-by-side gun on doubles targets, holding a preliminary point that lets them see the track of the first target they intend to shoot, yet one that allows them to shoot it with a short movement of the muzzles. This practice is made possible by the virtually fixed track of doubles targets.

Side-by-side doubles include in their number the most-fired shotgun known to the author, a plain, boxlock, shooting-school try-gun, that had been fired over seven million times when he shot with it some 10 years ago. Its tally must be nearer 10 million by now, and I believe it is still in daily use firing hundreds of shots each day. Repairs at the time I shot with it had amounted to two springs and one firing pin. Some other British side-by-side doubles have been shot over a million times in the field and at the patterning plate. However, some over-and-under guns, pumpguns, and single-barrel trap guns demonstrate comparable durability. If these seem of mere academic interest it should be remembered that a gun used for tuition at a shooting school may be fired 500 to 1000 times *a day*. Two hundred such days a year means a consumption of 100,000 to 200,000 shells in that gun per year.

Despite the evidence before them (perhaps they never look at it) certain older British shooting commentators endlessly repeat that the light, side-by-side, double game gun is the only gun in the world worth considering for *any purpose*. Over-and-under guns are said by these writers to be unwieldy, unbalanced, heavy, unreliable, ugly and unnecessary. They speak of the repeater as a kind of aberrant curiosity, not to be taken seriously, and likely soon to disappear. Reading what some of them say it is hard to believe that there have been successful repeaters in use for the whole of their considerable lifetimes, and that some models of repeater have sold over two million each, including in their purchasers hundreds of thousands of people who are expert shooters, who bought them from choice, and are satisfied with their purchase. These writers are the only real enemies of the side-by-side gun as a type, for many of their readers, knowing what they write about the over-and-under gun and the repeater to be ill-informed at best (and plain wrong at worst) also class what they write about the side-by-side gun as also probably inaccurate, and hence become biased against the latter as a *type*. This applies particularly to those British shooters who have come into the sport in the last 20 or 25 years, many of them via clay target shooting.

These last are the people who in the 1970's "discovered" the over-and-under gun, there being by then numerous European and Japanese models on the market in forms perfectly suited to playing a dual role as Sporting Clay target (and skeet) guns and guns for game and wildfowl. We saw above why the type has not become a normal product of British gunmakers in general, even in the period since World War II. The first good, hammerless, over-and-under guns were English, but the type failed to gain general popularity among their customers until all but one of those British gunmakers who made the occasional over-and-under gun as a special item had lost by death or retirement (and had failed to replace) those of their workers capable of making these guns. Though several British gunmakers produced their own design of over-and-under gun, only a few thousand have been made in total in the 80 or so years of their production. Until the 1960's and the upsurge of clay target shooting in Britain, the average British shooter seemed to think of the over-and-under gun as a blatant attempt by gunmakers to produce "something different" just to sell guns. He was encouraged in this belief by many of the older generation of writers mentioned. Increasing numbers of British driven game shooters are to be seen with one or a pair of non-British over-and-under guns. As a group they are by no means so conservative as the older British shooting commentators.

The only way that the typical, light, British side-by-side double game gun (and imitations thereof) can be used with comfort (and hence reasonable accuracy) over a series of shots is from that rigid framework of bone and muscle described in Chapter 2 for the "British" styles. Development of these styles allowed the use of relatively light guns, but things have gone too far when many of these guns are so light that recoil is too punishing for many people if much shooting is indulged in, even with such loads as 1 oz in the 12-gauge gun. Full-length 12-gauge ammunition with but $1\frac{5}{16}$ oz of shot has been a standard product of some British cartridge loaders for many years, and increasingly the Eley 12-gauge "Trainer" load with but ⅞ oz of shot, and intended for use on clay targets at shooting schools, is used as a driven-game load.

Considerations of recoil apart, many of these guns are too light for consistently accurate gun-pointing in any style. The most respected coach of what I have termed the "Standard British" style recommends a 7 lb gun for game shooting, but many British commentators, particularly the older generation, write as if a 6 lb, or even lighter, gun was the desirable thing for general game shooting. The standard product of British gunmaking today (1982) is a side-by-side, 12-gauge gun with barrels 25 to 28 inches long, 2¾ inch chambers, nearly always two triggers, and weighing 5 lb 14 oz to 6 lb 12 oz. Very few smaller gauge guns are made and none larger. Twenty-gauge guns with 2¾ inch or 3 inch chambers weigh 5½ lbs at most. Total production is a few hundred guns per year.

OVER-AND-UNDER GUNS

Successful designs of hammerless over-and-under guns date from before World War I. There are now very many different makes and models on the market, and new designs appear every year. The market is a very competitive one and rapid evolution of this kind of gun is taking place. In any gauge the over-and-under gun *tends* to be heavier than the side-by-side double, due to the U-section receiver. However, there are now on the market a number of models of steel-receivered, 2¾ inch chambered, 12-gauge over-and-under guns weighing as little as 6¾ lbs, and 20-gauge guns under 6 lbs. Twelve-gauge over-and-under guns with titanium-alloy receivers weigh as little as 6lbs.

Those who favour the side-by-side gun rather than the over-and-under, have raised a variety of objections to the latter. It does indeed, for example, have to be opened more widely to load and unload, but this does not make it any more of a nuisance to use in cramped quarters (in a hide or blind, say) than is the side-by-side gun. To say that it does is mere hair splitting, and from this viewpoint either gun compares ill in such surroundings with the repeater, which is not broken to load, and can be replenished while pointing straight up (let alone any other angle) if need be. Further: wide opening of the over-and-under gun, which is no inconvenience at all in ordinary surroundings, usually means easy closing because the actual effort of this is usually spread over a wider angle.

Some models of over-and-under gun have gone through "teething troubles" of misfires in the lower barrel when they first appeared. None seems to have been hard to cure of this habit. Their firing pins are usually at an angle to the barrel axes, but they are not the only kind of firearm with this feature. Over-and-under actions with firing pins virtually, or actually, in line with the barrel-axes exist, and have existed for 50 years or more, but the feature has not presented sufficient advantage to cause it to be widely, let alone universally, adopted.

Nor are rebound locks (see below) universal, nor withdrawal of lower (or both) firing pins by the first part of the movement of the opening lever. Such features when present do prevent drag of the tip of the firing pin on the fired primer of the lower barrel when the gun is opened. However, the dent in the primer is rounded anyway, and the firing pin is pushed upward and backward pretty smoothly by the primer itself when the gun is opened. In those guns which have:

a) A low hinge (wholly beneath the lower barrel),
b) A well-timed cocking mechanism which starts to lift the hammers (tumblers) immediately the gun begins to open, and
c) Spring-loaded firing pins,

drag of the firing pin of the lower barrel on the fired primer is too slight to matter to anyone or anything.

Low-hinge designs of over-and-under guns are a little deeper through the receiver than are those with higher, divided, hinges. However, except for traditional ideas of "beauty" based on the side-by-side double, there is no reason for the quest of some companies to make their over-and-under guns as shallow as possible. Unless care is taken in design and manufacture, this quest for shallowness can lead to poor support for the rim of the cartridge in the lower barrel. This, in turn, can give rise to misfires, particularly if the firing pin of the lower barrel is quite oblique to the barrel-axis (as can easily happen in a design of this kind) and the trouble may be aggravated if such a pin is combined with a rebound lock. In such a lock the hammer lifts a little off the firing pin after delivering the blow that fires the cartridge, thus freeing the pin to be pushed back into the face of the breech by a slight nudge from the fired primer in opening the gun (or to be withdrawn by a spring around the pin). However, though overcoming drag on the fired primer of the cartridge in the lower barrel (otherwise inherent in high-hinge, shallow, over-and-under guns) rebound locks in general do not give as solid a blow to the firing pin as do locks lacking this feature. This is especially true if the hammer is slowed by the rebound mechanism beginning to come into play before the firing pin is hit. Sophisticated adjustment of such things cannot be done by unskilled workers, nor by someone working against the clock.

The preceding paragraph reads rather like a catalogue of the ills that the supporters of the side-by-side double say that the over-and-under gun is heir to! The reader will notice that they can be due to trying to make the latter as shallow through the receiver as is the former, which is to say through trying to please most of the people all of the time. It must be said, however, that despite the cautions noted above, excellent and completely reliable "shallow" over-and-under guns are made in which all the potential pitfalls are avoided. They include some excellent, very famous, and expensive competition and game guns, as well as other inexpensive models.

The truth is that the over-and-under gun is now undergoing the same kind of period of rapid evolution and development that the side-by-side hammerless gun went through for some 30 years beginning about 100 years ago. Parallel kinds of criticism for the newer, and emotional support for the older type, are apparent as when hammerless guns were replacing those with outside hammers. In the not-too-distant future the over-and-under will be the dominant type of double-barrelled gun everywhere, including Britain and Eastern Europe.

The author knows of one inexpensive, Czech, over-and-under gun which has had more than two million shots fired through it at a British shooting school, for the replacement of a few minor parts. Potentially and actually the over-and-under can be as durable as any other type of gun. One famous Turkish duck shooter has found that the only double guns which will stand up to continual use with the heavy, 3 inch, 12-gauge loads he favours to be over-and-under sidelock guns of a well-known Italian marque.

REPEATING SHOTGUNS

Since no new lever-action shotguns are now being made, the pumpgun is the oldest type of repeating shotgun still being manufactured. In America the pumpgun may still be the largest-selling repeater, though the gas-operated autoloader must now be vying for first place, if indeed it doesn't occupy it. The pumpgun is the cheapest, effective multi-shot shotgun. Though it has never achieved more than a toehold in Britain or Europe for any purpose, including clay target shooting, it is so effective as a multi-shot gun that huge numbers of North American gunners use nothing else, and have no intention of doing so. It exists in qualities from the cheapest (in which everything possible has been done to decrease manufacturing costs and still leave a reasonably durable gun) to others (some of them sporting figured wood and some engraving) which with some minor replacement of parts as the years go by, will go on shooting for hundreds of thousands of shots. Some guide to durability, and to things like achievable quality of trigger-pull, is to look what models are used in trap and skeet. However, good models exist which do not have trap and skeet models among their variations (or do not any longer) and the trap and skeet models of some otherwise excellent pumpguns have their trigger and lock mechanisms routinely replaced by custom-built items by serious competition shooters (who do the same thing with the pumpgun's "sister" gas-operated autoloader). Some other models of pumpgun include variants meant by their makers specifically for trap and skeet, but which are used by hardly any trap and skeet shooters!

Many people find that having to pump the gun for each repeat shot steadies them, and as a consequence they hit better with such shots than with any other type of gun. People who are not pumpgunners usually fail to realise that, having opened slightly, automatically, when fired (the fall of the hammer unlocking the breechblock, and the gun "bouncing" a little forward from the shoulder after recoil while the fore-end remains put, as it were) the well-smoothed pumpgun needs only to be "assisted" to open fully and eject the fired shell, and then closed on a new one. After a while only the sensation of closing the gun remains, pumping becomes swift and automatic, and part of pointing correctly for the next shot. It does not take the gun off the line of a missed bird.

The pumpgun is used by millions of North American hunters and retains a small, loyal, highly-successful following among American-rules skeet shooters (particularly in gauges smaller than 12) and among American-rules trapshooters for 16 yard singles and handicap shooting. Doubles-trap shooters of an older generation who use the pumpgun for this, as for every other facet of the game, appeared to be labouring under no difficulties when compared to other shooters who used other types of guns. However, it is difficult to convince today's younger doubles shooters of this when they see no need to even try the gun for this purpose when excellent gas-operated autoloaders in trap models are available for the competitor who favours the repeater. Since these offer minimum disturbance of the gun at the shoulder by the first shot, and minimum apparent recoil to the shooter, no doubt these shooters are right.

To give some idea of the time that elapses in the actuation of the action of a pumpgun by practised hands, it may be noted that pumpguns have been known to fail to load a shell from the magazine when the magazine spring was a little weak (I do not mean in any sense feeble, mind you) the gunner having opened and closed the gun again before the spring had time to push the next shell onto the carrier to be lifted into line with the chamber! I should add that with a spring up to strength this doesn't happen.

The pumpgun is apt to be a little heavier than many double guns built to fire the same ammunition, particularly side-by-side doubles. However, some 12-gauge models weigh but 6½ to 7 lbs and we now have two 20-gauge models with steel receivers and weighing between 5¾ and 6¼ lbs, depending on the detailed specification. One 20-gauge model with an aluminium-alloy receiver tips the scales at only 4¾ lbs despite the ventilated rib on its barrel! Thus every requirement for the man who prefers a pump may be said to be covered, except, unfortunately, those of the would-be user of a lightweight 28-gauge or .410, presently available models in these sizes weighing 6 lbs or more.

The latest variant of the pumpgun is a single-shot, 12-gauge model for American-rules trap singles, which incorporates recoil reduction by trapping gas from the barrel to drive a piston rearward against spring pressure. The piston is situated in a cylinder that takes the place of the magazine tube on more conventional pumpguns. This gun was mentioned in Chapter 1 in connection with recoil reduction.

Turning now to the long-recoil autoloader, this is represented on today's market by only two or three makes (each closely resembling the others) having been largely supplanted by the gas-operated guns. In spite of a trigger having, inherently, a lot of movement in firing the gun (to adjust it to less means a risk of full-automatic fire!) the long-recoil autoloaders, from the lightest 20-gauge at 5 lbs to the 9½ lb 12-gauge Magnum, are easy guns to hit with, as durable as any autoloader in terms of wear and tear on replaceable parts, and full of satisfaction as a hunting gun for many people, particularly perhaps in North America, where the type is beginning to have an air of nostalgia and tradition about it! They do not reduce recoil-sensation as much as do the gas-operated guns, and some people (not including the author) don't like to feel the mechanism working after they pull the trigger. I expect them to be around a long time yet.

Gas-operated autoloading shotguns first came into prominence in the 1950's and have gone from strength to strength since then as models have improved in functioning and durability, and more and more shooters experience the advantages of the type. Little more expensive than a pumpgun (though less durable due to greater wear on the parts in the repeating function by friction, gas-erosion, and concussion) their strong suit is recoil-attenuation to a point where many people shoot better with this than any other type of gun when shooting is prolonged or intensive or both. All other things being equal, the gun is simply more comfortable to shoot than is any other type. This makes for a particularly good showing on shots fired subsequent to the first.

This type of gun is the dominant one in American-rules 12-gauge skeet. It is increasingly prominent in American trap, where, in doubles, the fact that the face is left firmly on the comb after the first shot goes far to make up for not having the flatter-shooting second barrel of the over-and-under gun well-adjusted for doubles. Though used by some of the most successful competitors, the gas-operated autoloader has not yet made much inroad into the ranks of over-and-under guns used in International Trap nor is it yet much seen in live pigeon trap.

But for the hunter in many parts of the world there seems little doubt that the gas-operated autoloader is the gun of the future, though, following the North American example, it seems likely that its capacity will be restricted by legislation to one shell in the chamber plus one, or at most two, in the magazine. In practical shooting this deprives it of virtually none of its advantages.

A NOTE ON GUN RIBS

A rib on the barrel of a repeater (or that of a single-shot gun) or on the top barrel of an over-and-under gun, showing a matt surface to the eye when the gun is at the shoulder, is as much use to the game shooter in ensuring correct elevation as it is to the competition shooter. However, when set against the extra weight of the rib, extra trouble in cleaning (ventilated ribs are great gatherers of dirt, foreign matter and water), it is doubtful if the rib, on balance, is worth it to the game shooter and wildfowler. If he chooses a gun of one of these types without a rib he should make sure that the frontsight is large enough and eye-catching in colour, even going to the extent of cementing a plastic bead over the usual small metal one if this is necessary to ensure this. If he can secure guns of these types having the upper side of the barrel (or the top barrel) matted over its whole surface (i.e. half its circumference, not just a narrow strip) or can have this work done on his barrels (I have no suggestions how) then ribs would certainly seem to be superfluous on guns of these types for game and water-fowl shooting.

Chapter 6
Choosing the Gun

GENERAL

In this chapter I shall assume an understanding on the part of the reader that what are under discussion are guns which are neither the lowest, cheapest quality of their type, nor models which have not been on the market long enough to get over any "teething troubles" (or to have been withdrawn if these proved incurable).

This is not to imply that some quite inexpensive guns of all types are not well made of durable materials (a good example is the Czech over-and-under gun mentioned in the previous chapter). Nor that some new models are not almost or quite free of faults from the outset. However, with the two provisos in the first paragraph, neither lack of durability nor tendency to malfunction are factors in choosing a *type* of shotgun.

There is really only one question to be answered: Does this gun allow you to hit to your full potential in the circumstances in which you shoot? Presumed are that the gun fits the user, that it complies with the rules if the shooting is of the competition variety, and that the use of such a gun is acceptable to other shooters present. Answering the question calls for serious analysis on a personal basis, rather than simply buying what takes one's fancy, or what other people use (for sometimes what is fashionable has no very good reason for its popularity).

For example: if in your shooting you often fire a lot of ammunition in a relatively short time, then if recoil is at all noticeable to you, it will begin to affect your performance in a remarkably short time. As we noticed earlier in this book, recoil as felt by the shooter can be decreased by:

a) **Adopting stocks with a minimum usable heel-drop.**

b) **Gunmounting in a way that cradles the gun in a fairly rigid framework of bones and muscles.**

c) **Using a relatively heavy gun, thus decreasing its recoil velocity. It is quite unusual to have to carry a gun in such a way that one is ready to stop and shoot at any time *and* to have to shoot a lot of ammunition in a short time too. Hence a heavy gun is often neither nuisance nor handicap.**

d) **Using the lightest-recoiling, effective load. In competition shooting few people would be happy using a shot-load under the allowed maximum, though many adopt loads giving less than the maximum allowed velocity (if such a thing is specified).**

e) **Using the gas-operated autoloader for its recoil-attenuating properties. Many such guns are relatively heavy, too, thus further helping to reduce apparent recoil.**

The solution to a problem can depend very much on the type of shooting. In the example above, the solution of b) is not one open to the competition shooter, nor that of e) to the British driven-game shooter, whose companions would usually feel that such a gun was quite unsuitable for such shooting.

Another example: if your shooting entails your carrying the gun a long way, yet being ready to shoot at any time for long periods at a stretch as you go (so that "resting" the gun can cause you to lose chances to shoot) then the actual weight of the gun becomes very important. Thus, if you shoot over flushing dogs (usually spaniels) or if you walk up and flush birds without a dog (for example, snipe, or in North America, ruffed grouse) the weight of the gun becomes very obvious to the arms. If these are fatigued, shooting performance is certainly affected. Thus, in such circumstances the optimum gun is considerably lighter in weight than the ones you would shoot best with if you *didn't* have to carry the gun always ready for use (as you don't, for example, in competition shooting, and shooting decoyed ducks and driven game). Note that in shooting over pointing dogs you can carry the gun in any way that is safe and comfortable when not actually going up to a point.

Now for some specific examples.

WATERFOWLING

The jump-shooting of ducks apart, waterfowling means hides or blinds, no matter how temporary and flimsy. Since the gun can always be rested somewhere while waiting for birds, a heavy gun is no disadvantage. Loads are heavy. All these things point to the gas-operated autoloader as the ideal gun for most shooters. As with all repeaters, such a gun is easily loaded in the more-or-less cramped quarters of a hide (all break-action guns are quite inconvenient by comparison). The thick-walled barrel of this kind of gun is far more resistant to denting than are the relatively thin-walled barrels of double-barrelled guns. Also, in current models these barrels are virtually unaffected by the use of steel shot (required by law in some parts of the United States, and perhaps soon in other parts of the world). The gas-operated autoloader is inherently low in apparent recoil, making it especially suitable for use with heavy loads, and giving with these (because of the low apparent recoil and the quick recovery of the shooter) more accurate shots after the first than any other type of gun. If the autoloader is restricted by law to *two* shots (three is the usual legal capacity in North America) it is still a superior gun to the double for most waterfowling and most waterfowlers. There is no need to put into any gun any greater amount of ammunition than one feels is "sporting" of course, though it must be pointed out that many North American shooters never fire the third shot they are allowed except as a "cripple-stopper" to prevent the escape of a wounded bird. Which is worth thinking about.

The "Churchill-style" shooter is pretty well restricted to the use of a short-barrelled, double gun in this kind, as in all other kinds, of shooting for reasons we examined at length in Chapter 2. However, for other people the obvious choice of a gun for waterfowl will be between the 10-gauge 3½ inch Magnum, the 12-gauge 3 inch Magnum and the 12-gauge 2¾ inch chambered gas-operated autoloaders. Traditionally such guns have 30 inch or even longer barrels, but in a 12-gauge gun for shooting over decoys (the big 10 is artillery too heavy for such a purpose) it is doubtful if there is any advantage in barrels over 26 or 28 inches. In flighting (American:

pass shooting) barrels 30 or 32 inches long enforce a steadier swing on distant birds for the "majority method" and "sustained" leaders.

In Britain most woodpigeon shooting is from hides. Though ordinary game loads are ideal ammunition, the autoloader is still the best gun for such shooting, being easier to load in such surroundings and less liable to be damaged by the inevitable "hard knocks" sustained by a gun in such shooting.

GAME SHOOTING

Except for driven game shooting in Britain and Europe, game shooting (much of it in the rest of the world would be classified as "rough shooting" by the British shooter) generally means a lot of walking. If you hunt birds with pointing dogs, the weight of the gun is not a factor of prime importance, as we saw earlier. Thus many American bob-white quail hunters, for example, use a 12-gauge autoloader rather than a dinky, 28-gauge double gun. Conversely, if you have to walk *and* be ready to shoot at virtually any time, the weight of the gun is on the arms continually, and makes its presence felt in no uncertain terms towards the end of a day. However, except when crossing and quartering birds are virtually always close to the shooter when shot at (for example woodcock and ruffed grouse in their usual thickets) few people shoot well with guns much under 6 lbs as they simply do not swing steadily enough when the length of such a swing is perceptible. On the other hand, few people are able to carry a gun much over 7 lbs all day (or even half a day) and still shoot well with it, either over flushing dogs or when walking out cover without dogs (except perhaps at heel). Exceptions to this are those snipe shooters, and others, who go out day after day, the length of the season.

Thus, the right weight of gun for most British rough shooters, and for the American upland game hunter who favours spaniels or retrievers over the pointing breeds, will be somewhere in the range from 5¾ to 7¼ lbs. Into this range fall a lot of 12, 16 and 20-gauge side-by-side doubles, some 12-gauge over-and-under guns, most 16 and 20-gauge over-and-unders, the newer models of 20-gauge gas-operated autoloaders, some (not all) 20-gauge and 16-gauge pumpguns, some 12-gauge pumpguns, and most of the few remaining 20-gauge long-recoil autoloaders. Thus the choice is virtually endless. The extra difficulty in *unloading* repeating shotguns, as compared with the double-barrelled gun, becomes a nuisance when seeking game in a landscape of small fields where this procedure has to be gone through repeatedly to cross fences and ditches. This has played no little part in restricting the popularity of the repeating shotgun in Britain and Europe.

Many of the currently manufactured 20-gauge guns have 3 inch chambers. The 16-gauge retains its popularity in German-speaking countries, runs a distant second to the 12 in other European countries (including Britain) and lags behind the second-place 20-gauge in North America (where it may be on the way to extinction despite attempts at revival). The 28-gauge gun is favoured as a quail and woodcock gun by some American hunters, and as a gun for game and for woodpigeons over decoys by some Britons. Two loads are generally available: the ¾ oz American load and the lighter $\frac{9}{16}$ oz British load. In my experience, long-time users of the 28-gauge gun know the circumstances of their own shooting and the range limitations of their chosen gun very well and govern themselves accordingly.

Regardless of the gauge he chooses, the "Churchill-style" shooter will wisely stick to the short-barrelled double gun. Other shooters will find themselves better suited by barrels of at least 28 inches on double guns. The 28 inch barrel is also well suited to general use on the repeater. However, most repeater barrels bored at the factory with less choke than "Modified" are 26 inches long. Since these equate to a barrel-length of 29 inches or so on a double-barrelled gun, due to the length of the repeater's receiver, the result is a fairly long gun that moves pretty steadily.

There are three "special cases" in game shooting (two of them strictly "rough shooting" I suppose) that seem to me important. These are:

1. *Towards the end of the year, game-birds in open terrains, or where cover is scattered and sparse, tend to become very "wild" indeed.* Long shots (if the birds afford any shots at all!) become the rule rather than the exception. Birds will generally not lie at all to a dog, but get up a long way off and clear off under full steam. If shooting alone the only thing one can do is to use what amounts to some kind of heavily choked duck or suitably stocked trap gun, with the farthest-killing loads procurable or loadable, and to hope that sufficient strength will remain to mount and move it properly when the birds rise within its very considerable range. One often has a good idea where the birds are, anyway, having first spotted them from some distance away perhaps, and done a little "stalking" to get near them. If this is so, one doesn't have to carry that 9 lb cannon in the ready-to-shoot mode for too long. Shooters in couples or groups can often arrange minor impromptu "drives" of such previously-spotted, highly nervous birds, with gratifying results.

2. *Some shooting is at really-short range.* For example: woodcock and rabbits in close cover, and in North America ruffed grouse and even bobwhite quail in similar situations. By really-short range I mean that one has to shoot at, say, 7 to 12 yards or the bird (or rabbit) will be lost to view behind cover. Among several solutions perennially proposed for this situation: cubic shot, discoid shot, rifled shotgun barrels, and spreader loads, what you find for sale in the local gun shop depends on where you live in the world, and usually you will not find any of them. I must add that spreader loads other than those with a more-or-less thick rod attached to the wad and running forward through the centre of the shot-load along the long-axis of the shotshell, have produced such unreliable and irregular patterns for me that I cannot recommend them. Further, the whole list above is of things intended for use in or on guns of the usual weight-range of game guns, and what this kind of circumstance really calls for is a very light gun. Weight, inertia, and barrel-length to smooth the swing and to help keep it going on crossing birds at medium to long range are simply irrelevant. Most birds distant beyond 40 feet are invisible behind cover! For 40 years in such situations I have used British and European, side-by-side double .410 guns, about 4 lbs in weight, with 26 to 28 inch barrels, and chambered for the 2½ inch case, with satisfaction. The width of the muzzles on the side-by-side .410 is sufficient for quick shooting.

3. *Driven game shooting in Britain and Europe, traditionally, is carried out with double-barrelled guns.* Until recently almost all of the guns used for this kind of shooting were the side-by-side type, and these remain a (decreasing) majority. A continuous, steady, high rate of fire, when such is necessary, is more easily sustained from hammerless, ejector double guns (particularly if one has two of them and a loader to help) than from repeaters (often, ironically, felt to be "unsporting" because of their supposedly greater fire-power!). Repeaters have therefore never been popular anywhere for driven game shooting. The vast majority of guns used for driven game shooting are 12-gauges. The usual weight of new side-by-side double-barrelled 12-gauge guns being built today for mainly driven game shooting (most of them are

Spanish or British) is 6 to 6½ lbs. The average (and a usual) barrel-length is 27 inches, which is really too long for the "Churchill-style" shooter (the muzzles tending to obtrude into the field of vision too early in gunmounting) and too short to give the steady gunmounting and slower final acceleration required by the "majority method" lead in any style of shooting. The standard load is $1\frac{1}{16}$ oz, but increasing numbers of people use the 1 oz load (or even a little less) and such decreased loads are adequate for the ranges at which most driven game is shot if barrels are not more open than about Quarter choke. A few hardy souls use loads of 1⅛ oz from these light guns when birds will be farther off (generally these will be high pheasants, less frequently mallard or late-season red grouse) and usually fewer shots will be fired. The usual cartridges these days are 2⅝ inches long. The logical thing would be to use guns a pound heavier than present standards, say 7 to 7½ lbs. The gun doesn't have to be carried around ready for use any more than a clay target competition gun does, every ounce of gun-weight helps in cutting down recoil (an important thing when a lot of ammunition will be got through), second shots are more accurate (the first one disturbing the shooter less) and actions, hinges, barrel lumps and bolts can be made to dimensions such that "tightening" of the action of a gun kept properly lubricated would hardly be necessary in a lifetime. Currently such work is a major part of the repairs carried out on British guns and foreign imitations of these. Coaches of what is termed in this book the "Standard British" style consistently recommend guns heavier in weight and longer in the barrels than the 6 lb, 25 to 27 inch barrelled "featherweights" that many of their clients have in mind. But under the influence of the flood of articles from many British (and anglophile American) journalists encouraging them to believe that the lighter the shotgun, and the smaller its inertia, the better will they shoot with it, these clients often go away and seek such guns anyway (followed by 12-gauge loads of 1 oz, $\frac{15}{16}$ oz, and often finally ⅞ oz). However, increasing numbers of driven game shooters in Britain are to be found using 12-gauge, factory-built over-and-under guns, 7 to 7½, or even 8 lbs in weight, sometimes in the "American classic" style, though more often in what is called in this book the "Modern British" style. Usually these guns have the standard, castless, American-style field stock, though a minor gunsmithing industry has arisen restocking them to measure. Such guns have all the virtues of the heavier gun listed above, except that durability varies very much from model to model. It seems likely that within a few years the over-and-under gun will outnumber the side-by-side double in British game and waterfowl shooting.

INTERNATIONAL SKEET

The most popular guns for International-rules skeet are 28 inch barrelled over-and-unders of 7½ to 9 lbs. Barrels of 26 inches have proved too short for best results. The gun-weight currently favoured by most experts on the eastern side of the Atlantic is about 8¼ lbs, and the current fashion in this area is for cylinder barrels or "bell" "chokes". In America, chokes about "Improved Cylinder" (100 per cent of the shot load in the circle at 21 yards) and somewhat heavier guns, are the choice of an increasing number of the leading shooters. Stocks of the American "field and skeet" and the East European types are most prominent everywhere, but some American shooters favour virtually or quite castless stocks with high, level combs. Some (but not many) shooters use 26 inch barrelled, skeet model, gas-operated autoloaders. The small number may have something to do with fashion!

ENGLISH SKEET

The most popular guns for this game are "skeet models" of various, 7½ to 8 lb, 12-gauge over-and-under guns, with gas-operated autoloaders becoming more prominent due to the influence of American skeet shooters on military service in Britain, and to a lesser extent that of British shooters with American experience. Since English skeet is a (purely) 12-gauge game, as scores improve and shootoffs become more frequent and longer, there seems little doubt that an ever-greater proportion of autoloaders will be seen.

AMERICAN-RULES (NSSA) SKEET

This game is shot wherever in the world there are a fair number of Americans, particularly American servicemen. The 12-gauge division is dominated by the gas-operated autoloader. The length of the ever-present shootoffs make this type of gun especially suitable in this gauge. For competitions in the three smaller gauges some shooters stick to the same type of gun (with added weights to bring them to the weight and balance of their sister 12-gauge). However, other alternatives are more popular. One of these is the over-and-under gun with four sets of barrels (generally 28 inches long) in 12, 20 and 28-gauges, and .410. The gun weighs and balances exactly the same with any set of barrels. Some shooters do use this kind of gun in 12-gauge competitions too (fitted with the 12-gauge barrels of course). The other alternative is a 12-gauge over-and-under gun with pairs of easily-interchangeable full-length tubes in the two smaller gauges and the .410, that fit inside the 12-gauge barrels. The popular barrel-length is, again, 28 inches. The gun weighs and balances the same with any pair of tubes in place, but minus any tubes obviously weighs and balances differently, and (minus tubes) is rarely used as a 12-gauge in skeet competition!

The more successful 20 and 28-gauge skeet guns (or barrels, or tubes!) are bored what would be described as "Improved Cylinder" were they field models. The choke in the most successful .410 skeet barrels is between Quarter and Half.

Most American-rules skeet shooters adopt a "gun up" ready position, and, reflecting this, the "traditional" stock may be said now to be one with a length of 14½ inches and drops of 1½ and 2 inches at comb and heel. More and more people are using level-comb stocks with a drop of 1½ inches or so. Favoured gun-weights are tending to increase, and 8 to 9 lbs is now the norm in all gauges (thus requiring some guns to have weight added to them in various ways).

SPORTING CLAY TARGETS

The favourite kind of gun for this kind of shooting is the 7½ to 8 lb, 12-gauge over-and-under, suitably choked. However, increasing numbers of gas-operated auto-loaders are seen in competitions both in Britain and Europe, their users walking off with more than their proportionate share of wins. Barrel-lengths of 28 to 30 inches are most popular on over-and-under guns, and 26 to 28 inches on repeaters.

BRITISH DTL TRAP

British trapshooters as a whole favour the over-and-under gun for all games, and 30 inch barrels are currently the most popular with a few 32 inch barrelled guns in evidence. Record-keeping shows that full choke in both barrels is the best boring for most shooters, even for 16 yard DTL clays. Methods and equipment in British DTL lag somewhat behind those in the relatively-similar American-rules trap game in sophistication, and average scores in each in terms of percentages of targets broken (even though two shots are allowed at each singles and handicap target, except in specific "single barrel" competitions) reflect this. For example, the British trap-shooter often uses the same (approximately 8 lb) gun for both DTL and International clays, scoring as well in the single-trap variant of the latter (Ball Trap) as he does on the slower DTL targets with their constant elevation! This indicates that his usual gun is far from well-adapted to the latter, a suspicion that would appear to be confirmed by the use of guns weighted to 10 to 11 lbs by many leading American-rules trapshooters.

AMERICAN-RULES TRAP

Combinations of a single barrel (or barrels) for 16 yard singles and handicap targets, with a pair of over-and-under barrels for doubles shooting, interchangeable on the same action, are the current choice of many of the most successful American-rules trapshooters. The most popular lengths for barrels are 34 inches for the single tubes and 32 inches for the over-and-under barrels. We are also witnessing an upsurge in popularity of the gas-operated autoloader (usually with a 30 inch barrel) both for its mild recoil, and because of its suitability for shooting all facets of the American trap game. The pumpgun (also usually with a 30 inch barrel) retains some following for singles and handicap, and this following may increase with the appearance of a model with built-in recoil-attenuation. Few shooters favour a gun under 8 to 8½ lbs, and many constant and consistent winners have whatever guns they use weighted to 10 to 11 lbs.

As we saw in previous chapters, the high comb typical of trap stocks gives built-in high-shooting to help in hitting the rising trap targets. In doing this, unless the pitch of the rib is altered by raising its rear end, such a stock allows the shooter to see more of the rib, which will seem strange to him until he gets used to it, particularly if his previous shooting experience has been with game or skeet guns. It may be appropriate to note here, again, that anyone who indulges in different kinds of shotgun shooting, needing different guns, and who wishes to shoot really consistently (as which of us doesn't) should ensure that all of his guns present the same picture to the eye as regards how much rib he sees when the gun is properly mounted. This regardless of the slope (pitch) on each rib with respect to the axis of the barrel required to cause the gun to shoot with the desired elevation for the kind of shooting that particular gun is used for. Thus, the rib on a trap gun would usually be higher above the breech than are those on game or skeet guns, causing the trap gun, desirably, to shoot higher than the others for the same "picture" of the rib for the eye above the breech. This may need removal and replacement of the ribs on some trap guns, but if it is needed, and you can find someone to do it, it is well worth the trouble. It will bear reiterating that difficulties in pointing for the experienced shooter are generally matters of elevation rather than lead. A similar "picture" of the rib on each gun used, when the gun shoots where desired for elevation, lessens any such difficulties, while dissimilar "pictures" increase them. Trap guns with ribs (and hence stock-combs) raised high above the barrel/s (Figure 133) are becoming increasingly popular for reasons discussed in Chapter 2.

Stocks for American-rules trap have, on average, the highest combs of all shotgun stocks. As a whole, North American trapshooters take advantage of the constant rate of climb, and constant elevation, of the targets in this game by building almost all the vertical lead the targets need *into the gun itself* by the use of stocks which place the eye high above the breech (the breech end of the *rib* may or may not be raised to bring it close up under the line of sight, as suggested above). This allows the shooter to pull (or release, page 253) the trigger on all targets with the targets clearly visible above the muzzle. Since they are able to see under the gun, those who point the gun with both eyes open take further advantage of constant target-elevation by holding 2 to 4 feet above the roof of the traphouse before calling for a target. This decreases the distance the muzzle has to be raised to the target to shoot it. The shorter this distance, the more controlled is the movement, and the less likely is it to be an over-fast swing (or even, at worst, a sharp jerk) going beyond the relatively slow target, leading to a stopped gun and a miss. Smoothness is essential in all trapshooting.

Barrel-bending to produce high-shooting is less in vogue than formerly. It never was wholly satisfactory.

Extremely high-shooting in a gun is of no use where a second shot is fired, or may be fired, as in British DTL singles, American and British doubles, and International Trap, as it confers as much disadvantage in shooting the second shot as advantage in hitting with the first one. Over-and-under trap guns that shoot higher with the first barrel fired than with the other one, fired second, go part way to having the best of both worlds.

INTERNATIONAL TRAP

The usual gun for all kinds of International Trap (Olympic Trench, Universal Trench, and Ball Trap) all of which show fast targets over a wide lateral arc and with variable elevation, is the over-and-under. The usual barrel-length is 29 to 30 inches. Stocks tend to be somewhat shorter and lower-combed than the norm for American rules trap singles (the other, and second, "great class" of trapshooting on a participant numbers basis, making comparisons inevitable!). In fact, the stock suited to trap doubles (American, or British DTL) for any shooter is usually right for him, too, for International Trap. However, whereas guns of 9 to 10 lbs, or even more, are thoroughly suitable for American trap, few International-rules trapshooters would choose a gun weighing even 9 lbs, and most feel that a gun of about 8 lbs is the right thing. Chokes should be such as to give the smallest, densest patterns obtainable, and shooters should test in their gun every type of ammunition loaded for these games that they can secure to make sure they are getting the optimum in this regard. A barrel and cartridge combination that merely reduces first-barrel targets centred in the pattern to a relatively few pieces will inevitably let some equally well-centred clays slip through unbroken. Unfortunately there are at the present time some so-called trap and trench over-and-under guns on the market that will do no better than that kind of break on a, say, 35 yard clay, with *either* barrel, and with these a second-barrel shot is a gamble indeed. Let us hope the pendulum swings back soon to full chokes in all guns purporting to be suited to International trapshooting (and indeed most trapshooting). Knowledge of how to bore such chokes has been common for 80 years or more and there can be no excuse when a modern trapgun throws loose, feeble patterns with good ammunition.

Only limited vertical lead can be built into the gun for these games by means of a high stock-comb (with or without a rib correspondingly raised an extra amount at the breech end) or the lower targets, which climb but little, are apt to be missed by shooting over them. The reader will, I hope, excuse the author for repeating that it is important that the barrel fired first shoot *at least* as high as the one fired second, and many people like it to shoot 6 inches to a foot higher when tested at 40 yards. Guns with variable barrel-convergence allow the shooter's desires in this regard to be achieved with any choice of ammunition.

A small, increasing, number of gas-operated autoloaders are now seen in International trap, but they cannot achieve prominence in the prize lists unless and until the better shots adopt them!

LIVE PIGEON TRAP

The broad muzzle-end of the side-by-side double gun, easily registered by the eye, would probably have made it the preferred type of gun for live-pigeon trapshooting when rules enforced a gun-down position before calling for the bird, even if other types of multi-shot gun had been readily available. In this kind of trapshooting, the speed with which the first shot can be fired (with accuracy) pays greater dividends than in any other. Since about 1900 live-pigeon trapshooting rules everywhere have allowed a pre-mounted gun, and though the side-by-side double retains some following (as well it might with nearly 200 years of tradition behind it in this field) the influence of clay target shooting, and the ready availability of over-and-under guns as suited to live-pigeon trapshooting in weight, balance and stocking as they are to International clay target trapshooting, have resulted in these being the current choice of most shooters. The desire of some live pigeon shooters is for a gun which shoots to one point with both barrels with their chosen ammunition, but, like the International clay target trapshooter, most prefer a gun which shoots higher with the barrel which is fired first. Each kind gets what he wants from those gunmakers familiar with live-pigeon trapshooting.

In the matter of chokes for live pigeon trapshooting, the reader may note that the gas-operated autoloaders which are beginning to creep into the game, and to figure in the prize lists, can by their nature only have one choke (at once) and this is always "Full".

GENERAL

Not all guns sold outside their country of manufacture are backed up by adequate parts service wherever they are sold. I am thinking now of the "factory made" shotgun. For the true "custom", "hand-made" (or hand finished) gun there are, obviously, *no* spare parts. This bears thinking about. Some guns have mechanisms unfamiliar to gunsmiths outside their country of origin, and hence can require a first-principles study before they can be repaired. Some importers do keep a good stock of spare parts, and have gunsmiths highly qualified to service what they sell (including the top-grade, custom-built guns). The customer deserves no less. Satisfy yourself about these things wherever you live in the world before handing over your cash for an imported gun. I do realise that in many countries the *only* guns are imported guns!

Chapter 7
Cleaning and Maintenance

BARRELS

To put any kind of wiping material (cloth, fibre, or industrial wiping tissue, say) through a fouled barrel before giving it a good scrub with a soft wire brush dripping with powder solvent to loosen that fouling, is a waste of time, energy, and wiping material. In scrubbing, and in subsequent wiping out, pay particular attention to the chamber if plastic-cased ammunition has been used, or later rusting in that area is a virtual certainty unless the chambers are chromed.

Lead is best removed by wrapping finest steel-wool around your cleaning jag, making a little cylinder. Oil it thoroughly and try it in the bore. It should be an easy push-fit. Adjust its size until it is. Keep it thoroughly wet with oil when in use and it will never bind and scratch the bore. A few strokes will shift the worst leading like magic.

In cleaning the outsides of barrels be careful to make a good job of the long, narrow grooves down each side of the barrel-joining ribs of double guns. Pay attention, too, to the slots under ventilated ribs. A thorough cleaning of barrels from break-action guns means removal and cleaning of the extractors and cleaning of the holes or grooves they run in. This may require the removal of one or more screws. If you don't know how, ask your gunmaker or gunsmith to show you.

The final stage is to put a thin film of suitable rust-preventive oil on all surfaces, inside and out. On barrels from break-action guns **a smear of grease** is needed, too, on:

a) The surface of the forward lump (lug) that contacts the hinge-pin (on some over-and-under guns this lug is divided, half being each side of the breech-end of the barrels).

b) Those surfaces of the lumps and/or breeches which enter and slide on surfaces of the receiver.

c) Bolting surfaces (in slots, make sure you grease the surface the bolt actually contacts. It is only too easy to grease the other one!).

ACTIONS

It is relatively easy (sometimes childishly simple) to remove the mechanism from the receiver of most repeaters (but examine the manual for details) and everyone who owns one of these guns should learn how to do it. Mechanisms in autoloaders get

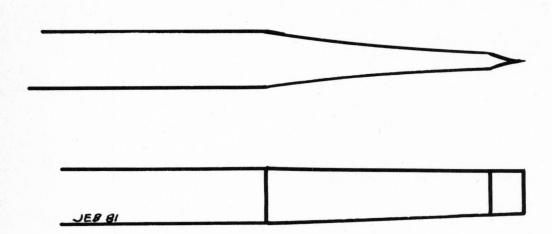

Figure 143   Screwdriver for narrow slots

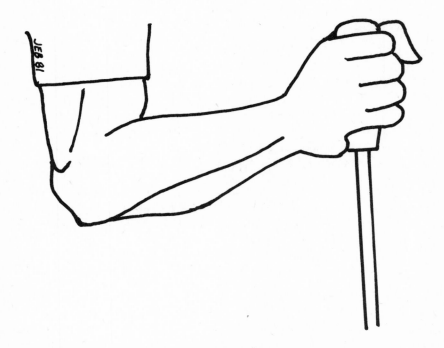

Figure 144   Using the Screwdriver

dirtier than those in pumps. Either can be cleaned very easily by shaking in a closed, screw-topped jar with suitable solvent-cum-lubricant (Hoppe's No. 9 gun cleaner is excellent) or in a mixture of gasoline and a very little lubricating gun oil (mix what you need and get rid of the residue safely after use). Allow the mechanism to drip, wipe off the excess, if any, and replace in the gun.

It is easy to remove the locks from sidelock guns and the bottom plate from the usual type of true boxlock (there is a sloppy modern terminology which calls the mechanism of any type of break-action gun which is not a sidelock, a "boxlock") thus giving access to the lock parts. The type of screwdriver used on the narrow-slotted screws of many European (and virtually all British) guns is shown in Figure 143. They are knife-edged and carefully tempered. Figure 144 shows the way they are used. If there is any chance of the blade jumping from the slot, or if the screw is a large one, the user adds weight to the top of the tool by resting his chest on his hand. Access to the locks of most modern, non-sidelock, over-and-under guns is gained by simply removing the stock. Locks of all kinds of break-action guns can be lubricated with one of the spray-type lubricants which also leave a rust-preventing film. A current example is G96 Gun Treatment. Wipe off all excess before reassembling things.

The breech-face of every kind of gun should be carefully cleaned after use, especially around the firing pin holes. If you can get at the tip/s of the firing pin/s (you usually can) clean these too. To get the breech-face thoroughly clean may take scrubbing with an old toothbrush plus solvent. The corroded and pitted breech faces of many used guns bear witness to neglect of this area. Corrosion + Stress = Stress Corrosion, and I have seen more than one *cracked* breech-face (the crack having one extremity in the firing-pin hole) due to chronic lack of simple cleaning.

As with barrels, the exposed metal of receivers (I am referring here to the, majority, steel ones) should have a thin film of oil applied. Keep it off the woodwork. On break-action guns a smear of grease should be applied to hinge pins (or trunnions on that kind of over-and-under) to contact-surfaces of bolts, and to the sides of slots and other surfaces where lugs and breeches enter the receiver. This ensures lubrication if you forget to grease the appropriate areas on the barrels on occasion. Read the manual on such matters as the lubrication of cocking levers and so on.

GAS-OPERATED AUTOLOADERS

Pistons, gas-cylinders, magazine tubes, and actuating rods or bars can be cleaned with finest steel-wool soaked with powder solvent. Simply clean everything that gathers fouling. A small cylindrical brass-wire brush, chucked in an electric drill, makes cleaning of some parts (particularly the inside of cylinders) of some models easier. Some popular models require thorough cleaning of these areas, and of the mechanism within the receiver as described above, every 200 to 300 shots if the gun is used in competition where repeat shots are required, to ensure certainty of function in this respect. It is ironic that, despite the fact that they shoot better with it than with any other type of gun, some competition shooters have forsaken the autoloader on the grounds of unreliability in repeating, simply caused by lack of necessary, regular, rigorous, cleaning as outlined. They didn't realise it was necessary, didn't imagine it could be the cause of the trouble, and the makers didn't tell them.

WATER

If a gun is wet inside the water *must* be got out of it. Take everything apart as far as you can, or dare, bearing in mind the subsequent job of reassembly. Dry everything, and follow with the usual application of rust-preventive oil. Water-displacing oils (e.g. WD-40) are able to chase water out of places you cannot otherwise get at.

WOODWORK

Oiled stocks should have two drops of boiled linseed oil rubbed into them a few times a year, oiled fore-ends one drop. Varnished and lacquered stocks usually just need wiping, though deep scratches in any kind of finish should be touched up with the same kind of finish.

Chapter 8
Safety

BASIC RULES

1. NEVER point a gun at anyone except:
   a) A shooting instructor who asks you to point at his eye, after both of you have made doubly sure that the gun is not loaded.
   b) If you mean business (I am trying to cover *all* circumstances).
2. The first thing you do on picking up or being handed a gun is to make sure it is empty while continuing to point it in a safe direction.
3. While not actually looking for, waiting for, or shooting at game or targets, the gun must be empty and open. This particularly applies if more than one person is present.
4. When climbing a fence or jumping a ditch the chamber/s of the gun must be empty, as must the magazine of a repeater unless it has an effective cut-off device.
5. At shooting clubs, the only time a gun may properly be closed when it is not in its case (except for a break-action gun in the rack) is when it is your turn to shoot and you are about to call for a target or a bird. If a breakdown in·equipment, or a pause in proceedings, finds you with a loaded gun, ready to shoot, it must be unloaded at once and remain open until things start up and it is again your turn to shoot.
6. Never put down a gun which is closed on a loaded chamber, not for a second, let alone lean it against something while you tie your bootlace, or whatever. Open it, empty it, and put it down open if laying it flat. One of my friends leaned a loaded gun against the inside of a hide when he went out to pick up a pigeon he had shot with the right barrel, the chamber of the left barrel containing a live cartridge. His girl friend, who was also in the hide, picked up the gun and in doing so accidentally pulled the left trigger while the gun was pointing at him. She did not put the gun to her shoulder, she was merely holding it sideways across her chest. As he received most of the load in the head he was killed instantly. An acquaintance laid down a loaded gun against a steep little grassy slope behind his parked car, the muzzle pointing at the back of the car. While he was putting the ducks he had shot into the boot (trunk) of the car, his retriever came gambolling along, trod on the trigger of the gun, and shot him in the side from a few yards range. He lived long enough to relate how it happened. An applied safety catch would have saved the lives of both these people, but put not your trust in safety catches — see below!

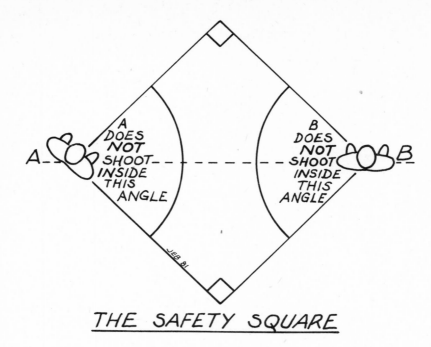

THE SAFETY SQUARE

Figure 145　The Safety Square

7. Never carry a loaded gun in a vehicle (I am here writing for sportsmen not police-men). Never mind whether it is illegal or not: don't do it.

8. Always be certain of the whereabouts of your companions when shooting with others, so that you will never discharge a gun within 45 degrees or so of the line that joins you (see the Safety Square of Figure 145). When firing at birds at high angles, say within 20 degrees of the vertical, the rule about not shooting within 45 degrees of the line between you and someone else is waived. Spent pellets raining down after such high-angle shots have a quite low velocity. Only a hit on an unprotected eye would be unpleasant. For this to happen one would have to be looking upward at exactly the right place and time, without glasses, to catch one of the widely scattered pellets. I have never heard of anyone being thus hit in the eye, and the chances must be very small. It is, however, another reason to wear shooting glasses at all possible times.

9. Never shoot unless you can see what you are shooting at sufficiently clearly to be quite certain what it is, and unless the background is safe to shoot into. In a populated countryside, if the rabbit you are going to shoot runs behind cover as you are about to pull the trigger — don't. In similar circumstances, hold your fire on birds less than three person-heights above the ground. Pellets don't kill very well through brush anyway.

10. Whether or not your eyesight needs correction, you should wear shooting glasses with hardened lenses at all times when you are shooting, unless rain is actually blowing into your face. Then, the brim of hat or cap ceases to be protection for the glasses, and either nothing, or contact lenses if you need correction, are the only solutions if you are to continue shooting, as in competition (for example) you must. But, this circumstance apart, shooting glasses are a very good idea. If you

shoot enough you are eventually going to get a blast of gas in the face from a pierced primer, a split case, or even excess pressure, unless you are very lucky, and without proper glasses the damage to your eye or eyes may be permanent. There is always the possibility, too, of ricochet pellets (possibly fired by *you*) hitting you in the face. Nor is that all. Coming from a family of congenital "brush hunters", *two* of the author's uncles each lost the sight of one eye from thorns piercing the eyeball. In both these cases it was the eye opposite the gun. However, such a thing leaves one with no depth-perception, and but one eye remaining this side of total blindness. It is also, they told me, incredibly painful. Wear your shooting glasses. If your seeing days come to an end, so do your shooting days. For further details of shooting glasses, see the last chapter.

11. Always be certain that the ammunition you put into a gun is in every way the stuff it was intended to shoot. Not all guns are built to withstand the pressures produced by the highest-pressured examples of the range of ammunition that will fit their chamber/s. Guns built for use with black powder (gunpowder) are an obvious example. Some British 12-gauge guns built since World War II are chambered for 2¾ inch cartridges, but are neither built nor proved for use with other than the lowest-pressured of smokeless loads in this cartridge.

12. Always be certain that the gun itself is safe to shoot, both with that ammunition and in general. This includes consideration not only of its mechanical condition, but also whether or not the barrel or barrels are quite clear of even partial obstructions. If there might be mud or snow in a barrel: check. If there is: get it out before you shoot.

13. (A suitable number for this perhaps!). "Safety" catches are safe in name only. Some safety mechanisms are as "safe" as they could possibly be, and still allow the gun to be fired, yet there is not one of them quite incapable of failure under more or less extreme circumstances. They do NOT remove the necessity never to point a gun (whether or not you believe it to be loaded) at anyone except in the circumstances of 1) above, nor the requirement that guns should only be loaded when they *need* to be loaded. They have, however, prevented many accidental discharges. There is neither necessity nor requirement for them on competition guns, due to rules as to when a gun may be loaded.

A virtue is made by many writers on the shotgun of the possession by virtually all bar-action sidelock guns of secondary, "safety", sears, which catch the hammer and prevent it hitting the firing pin if the nose of the main sear is jarred, or otherwise dislodged, from the notch in the tumbler (hammer) without the trigger being pulled. They fail to note that the presence of these secondary sears is actually a reflection of the relative ease with which the main sears of many designs of bar-action sidelock can be thus jarred free! This is something far harder to do with, for example, a boxlock gun of the usual British design and with average weights of trigger pull. In fact, the usual British design of bar-action sidelock might be something of a menace without such secondary sears. If boxlocks needed them, they would be fitted. They were, unnecessarily, fitted to some high-grade British boxlock guns of the late 19th century. One of these, before me as I write, has secondary "safety" sears above and behind the tumblers, and two further safety devices actuated by the safety catch: one bolting the triggers, the other the tails of the sears. Secondary sears have been omitted from even the very highest grade of British boxlock guns (in the building of which expense is no object) for about 80 years.

Nor are the secondary sears of the typical bar-action sidelock the complete answer to the jarring-off problem. It is noteworthy that when Jeffreys of London were building double-barrelled .600 Nitro rifles they chose the boxlock action for these. It is little use to the shooter if the tumbler of the lock of the second barrel, jarred off by the discharge of the mighty .600 cartridge in the first barrel, *is* caught by the safety sear, if the elephant (or whatnot) is still advancing with murder in mind. First, one would have to realise that the tumbler had indeed partly fallen (from the refusal of the second lock to fire). Then one would have to open and close the rifle again to cock the second tumbler (actually both tumblers of course) to get the weapon to fire again. Far better to use a boxlock action (or a sidelock of the same geometry, as most European ones are) in the first place and avoid all this! Which is what Jeffreys did.

14. Guns should not be stored, or kept, with all the parts required to make them functional in the same place. Always one can find a way to remove a part, or parts, without which the gun cannot be used, and often nothing could be simpler. These should be carefully hidden, away from the rest of the gun. Ammunition should be stored separately too. If this is done, the chance of accidents happening to children playing with guns in the absence of the owner (and stranger things have happened) is reduced to near-zero. Nor will criminals usually steal incomplete guns (if they realize they lack parts) though they may damage them from spite. In some countries if your complete, stolen, gun is subsequently used in crime, rightly or wrongly, you are liable to prosecution. It is best, then, to be able to show parts, still in your possession, without which your stolen gun or guns will not function.

Chapter 9
Miscellanea

TRIGGERS

If a trigger has a "creepy", grating, pull-off, your finger cannot learn exactly what it takes to make the gun fire, because this varies from shot to shot. In these circumstances your shooting will never be as good as it might be with a better pull-off. Nearly all mechanisms can produce a good pull when adjusted by a competent gunsmith (its excellence depending on the geometry of the lock and trigger mechanism, and the amount of tolerance in the parts he has to work with). With a certain mechanism, there is a limit to how *short* the trigger movement to fire the gun can be made. It should be adjusted to be as short as is possible with safety, and it must be made to move *smoothly*. The consistency of the pull from shot to shot (regardless of its shortness) depends on the lack of sloppy tolerances in the fit of the parts. If much tolerance exists anywhere, the parts can "set" themselves a little differently relative to each other each time, giving a pull-off inconsistent in weight, length, and smoothness. This can sometimes only be remedied by making one or more new parts. And the least frustrating thing with some otherwise excellent repeaters is to discard the factory lock and trigger mechanism complete (salvaging the springs and other "bits" for spares) and replace it with a "custom" job built on a steel floorplate. These are well advertised, and worth every penny of their cost in the makes I have used.

Triggers should not be made too light (under 3 to 3½ lbs, say). They all vary a *little* in pull-off from shot to shot, and a variation of a few ounces that is unnoticeable, and unimportant, with a 4 lb trigger, is very apparent (and hence very important) with a 2 lb one (an example of something called Weber's Law). For this reason very light pull-triggers (yes, pull-triggers) are no solution for the trigger-shy trapshooter: the tiniest variation in pull-off seems enormous, this makes the trigger seem unreliable, and this leads to more trigger-shyness. In fact, the use of a light pull-off can be the actual, fatal, first step leading to this kind of flinch (which is what it is, and one particularly prevalent among trapshooters). If you shoot trap, and cannot get a smoothly-released shot with a pull-trigger through no fault of the trigger, then go to a release-trigger you must (or give up the game altogether). A release-trigger is one which fires the gun, not when it is pulled, but when it is subsequently released. In other words, you put the gun to shoulder and face, point over traphouse or trench, pull the trigger and hold it back, call for the target/s, go after the target, and *release* the trigger when you want the gun to fire. The action is a bit like releasing an arrow in archery. The gun seems to fire more quickly than when using a normal, pull-trigger, and consultations are usually necessary between a release-trigger user and his gunsmith in getting the right length of release-movement on the trigger before it releases the tumbler (which it does directly) hence giving the exact timing of discharge of the gun that is satisfactory to the shooter. On over-and-under guns used for trap doubles, International trap, and live pigeons, a single-trigger which is a release for the first shot and a pull for the second shot suits a great many people.

Double triggers on double guns are something easily got used to, simple, and reliable. However, they are to be avoided if you shoot where gloves are sometimes required. Gloves are *not* required where the glove-finger covering the trigger-finger, or even part of it, can be cut off, and that finger not then freeze, *actually*, and quite quickly. The second shot with properly placed and set double triggers is, I think, faster than with a single-trigger that has to be pulled twice, slower than when a single release/ pull trigger is used, but as the time taken in aligning the gun for that second shot is many times that taken in placing the finger and pulling the trigger with any of these alternatives, this is really only of academic interest. Double triggers should be placed and set so that there is no need to move the hand when the finger moves from one trigger to the other, and the hand should not be so moved. Ideally the stock should have a pistol grip that anchors the hand in such a position that the trigger finger has easy and equal access to both triggers.

GUNS FOR "LEARNING ON"

Trapshooting apart, the best gun to use to teach anyone to shoot is a gas-operated autoloader in 20-gauge, with a 26 inch Improved Cylinder barrel. Obviously, if this is a model with a tube of relatively large diameter within, and running the length of, the stock, the stock usually will be castless or nearly so. Early shooting (at least) then will usually have to be what is called in this book "American classic" style. However, if the targets shown to the beginner in these early sessions are at angles of elevation no lower than those on a skeet field, a later transition to other styles (if this is desired and desirable) will present no difficulties. The beginner should not be allowed to cant either head or gun, or to shoot off shoulder-joint or arm. Having learned to hit, what style he adopts later for whatever shooting he does is his own affair, including the accepting or not of advice from any source. Loads with ⅞ oz (or less) of shot should be used at first (the 20-gauge skeet load of No. 9 shot is excellent to 30 yards on clay targets from the Improved Cylinder barrel). If appropriate, a shorter stock than standard should be substituted, and as we saw in Chapter 2, downpitch has to be looked at very carefully for youthful beginners. The 20-gauge autoloader has very little apparent recoil, yet produces patterns large and dense enough for total success at realistic ranges. Rather than start with the .410, which needs more choke than the 20-gauge, it is better that the child should wait until he or she weighs 80 lbs or so, and can use the 20-gauge gas gun. The 28-gauge gas-operated autoloader, with ¾ oz skeet loads in that gauge, is equally good, but a rarity in most parts of the world, I think.

All trapshooters should begin their careers with a gas-operated autoloader, fitted with a suitable stock (and a good trigger, whether or not it came thus equipped from the factory). A proportion will never change to a different type of gun.

In the (later) period of search for just the right stock for different kinds of clay target shooting (at least) it is useful to have a pumpgun, the drop and cast on the stock of which can be altered by substitution of washers ahead of the stock, in the recess behind the receiver. A selection of these washers are filed so as to be wedge-shaped in cross-section, each thinning in a different direction and by a different amount. Thus, one of them can be selected so that when the head of the stock is tightened against it it moves the butt of the stock to give the desired drop and cast. Turning the washer over from side to side gives cast-on one way and cast-off the other. The top and bottom ends of such washers are not shaped similarly, so they cannot be "flipped" in that sense to alter the drop of the stock. The tenon around the head of the stock should be cut back a trifle to prevent its contacting the lip surrounding the recess behind the receiver. If this is not done, splitting of the wood is a possibility.

Some gas-operated autoloading shotguns will function quite normally with the tube which runs longitudinally through the stock bent *slightly* out of line, right or left, to produce cast. The head of the stock has to be reshaped slightly to fit the back of the receiver. Slight changes of drop can be produced in a similar fashion.

BENT BARRELS

Barrel-bend can be seen quite easily if the inside of the barrel is viewed with the eye close to the breech. It is best if the light entering the muzzle is reflected from an evenly-lit pale surface such as a sheet of paper. A barrel which is virtually straight throws its internal reflections as a series of concentric circles; one with a noticeable bend as a series of ovals, with long axes in the plane of the bend, and the muzzle displaced towards the direction of bending.

Few barrels, even those of the finest target rifles, are perfectly straight. The author remembers an erudite controversy as to whether or not bent rifle barrels give any poorer accuracy in practice than do straight ones, that when on for months in the letter columns of an excellent American magazine devoted to bench-rest rifle shooting. The correspondence ended when a specialist, target-rifle barrel-maker, a man in the very topmost elite of his trade, wrote to say, musingly, that he had been interested in the letters, and that of the thousands of target-rifle barrels he had examined (of his own make and others) he had seen one that he thought was indeed probably straight (at least he could find no bend in it) and one that was nearly so. The bends that had been under discussion were, of course, very slight, and not something apparent to the casual observer!

A SHORT-CUT TO SUCCESS (IN ONE PLACE ANYWAY!)

Birds flushed by a dog, or by the shooter himself (sometimes walking out ahead of a pointing dog) normally rise from the ground (rather than flying out of a tree for example, though some species can do that too!). It would seem, therefore, to be an advantage to be watching the ground so as to see the bird, or birds, as they flush, hence giving the shooter the maximum time in which to shoot. Except perhaps for the experienced shooter, who has been in this situation very many times and knows to ignore the early part of the flight of the bird or birds except as indication of *where* they are, this is not so.

Apart from the occasional glance downward when the going is rough (so as to be sure of the footing) the shooter should look *ahead*, his gaze passing at a minimum of head-height above the nearby ground in the direction he expects the bird or birds to flush, his eyes relaxed in "distant focus". Flushing birds rise into the horizontal plane containing his line of sight, and are shot there, or thereabouts, with a minimum of head-movement by the shooter, and a short, controlled, movement of the gun (both of which are important). If this is not already your modus operandi, try it.

SHOOTING GLASSES

If your distant vision can be improved by glasses or contact lenses, then you need one or the other to shoot your best with the shotgun. The prescription should be that giving you the clearest-possible distant vision. To try to shoot with a degree of uncorrected short-sightedness that makes the muzzle-end of the gun clearer to the eye than is the bird or target, is a far greater handicap than is readily believable. The eye loves to focus on what it sees easily, and when shooting the shotgun there must be no easier focus available to it than the distant object. Do not feel handicapped if you need a pretty large correction: more than one shooting champion is legally blind without his glasses.

Tinted glasses of a variety of shades and densities are often a definite help in combating glare and in helping one to see the object being shot at, particularly in clay-target trap shooting. What suits you best is something you will have to find for yourself.

Because of the possibility of being struck in the eye by fragments of clay target, or even the rare stray pellet, skeet and Sporting Clay shooters should be even more careful than other shotgunners to wear hardened glasses at all possible times when shooting.

Unfortunately, if the rain is driving into one's face, glasses soon become too obscured to be useful. For the shooter who needs sight-correction, contact lenses plus glasses without correction leave him able to see and shoot when the glasses are removed in such conditions.

SEEING THE SHOT

In teaching others to shoot it is necessary to be able to see the shot-charge in the air when the pupil shoots. The knack of this seemingly-miraculous "trick" is easy to acquire. Start by doing all you can to prevent yourself hearing the noise of the shot. If this is not done, the noise causes an involuntary blinking of the eyes at the precise split-second you need them open to see the shot-charge in flight! Plug your ears, and wear ear-muffs too if you have them. Pick an overcast day and recruit a shooter. Have him shoot at straightaway clays which are climbing a little into the grey sky. Stand a little behind the shooter, looking over his shoulder, in line with the gun, your line of vision above the rib.

At first you are likely to see nothing, especially when the target is hit. Ask the shooter to shoot to just miss it, or to see if he can just get it in the edge of the pattern (top, bottom, and each side: this is a challenge to him). Eventually, probably within 10 to 20 shots, you will see the shot-charge as a kind of little "cloud" (or a "glassy" area, it is difficult to describe). Soon you will see it virtually every time. To my vision, what one sees seems to be about a foot or 15 inches across, not larger. Soon you will be able to see it when the shooting is at quartering and crossing birds, without your ear-coverings (but keep an effective measure in place to protect your hearing) on fairly bright days, and finally when a little out of line with the shooter. The truth of the adage that the larger pieces of a struck clay target normally fly away from the centre of the pattern will become apparent to you.

Knowing where the pupil put the pattern in missing (or even nearly missing) the target is not the same as knowing why he or she shot there. That is something you can only be sure of by watching the actions of the pupil. The miss at the target is caused by a mistake at the shooter's end of things, if I may be excused for stating the obvious. Coaching will teach you a lot about shooting, including your own. It is a lot of fun. Perhaps the most fun there is in shooting indeed, and that's saying plenty. Remember that the pupil, in the end, must hit the target in *his* way, and that when he is doing this competently and consistently, it may not be just like *your* way of doing it. When you get over that early hurdle you are on your way to being a real instructor.

FOOT POSITION AND
THE CLAY TARGET SHOOTER

A position of the feet relative to the direction of shooting like that shown in Figure 146 is advocated by a good many clay target shooters, who demonstrate its suitability by shooting 100 straights! The shooter stands facing some 60 degrees from the direction of fire, with his feet a comfortable distance apart, toes turned slightly outward. The weight is largely on the front foot, and the heel of the rear foot is often slightly raised from the ground. Gunmounting turns the body another 15 degrees or so toward the direction of shooting. This is, in fact, an excellent foot position for clay target shooting, and equally well suited to driven game shooting, and to such things as duck shooting from blinds (hides) when the wildfowler has the luxury of shooting from the unmodified standing position. No matter what style of gunmounting the gun is fitted for, and used in, this remains true. The reader may wonder, therefore, why the author has not put forward the possibility of using a foot position like that in Figure 146 as part of the "American" and "British" styles described earlier, for it is a perfectly sound base for all of them.

The reason is that *most* shooters the world over are neither clay target specialists nor driven game shooters. The chief concern of most shotgunners is with birds that rise in front of them when the shooter is in mid-stride. A foot position like that in Figures 47 and 91 is easily assumed by the shooter taking one, or two, steps across his erstwhile line of progress, the feet then "automatically" taking the position shown in those two figures. The foot position shown in Figure 146 is *not* so easily or quickly assumed from the walk. The shooter has to first stop, then adjust his feet, then shoot. Considering that shooting from the foot position shown in Figures 47 and 91 is not less accurate than from the position shown in Figure 146, the author has given the former prominence in this book as being more generally useful. In assuming the position shown in the two earlier figures from the walk, the reader may find his feet farther

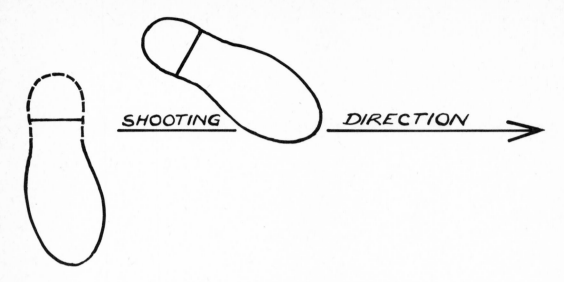

Figure 146   Foot position, Clay Target Shooting

apart than shown in them. This is really no matter if the weight is kept on the forward foot. He will be in good company as he may see by looking at the drawings by Will Garfit of that deadly and stylish shot David Olive, in the "How to Shoot" series in *The Shooting Times and Country Magazine*, October 1983 to January 1984.

Nevertheless, those whose shooting is virtually all at clay targets and/or driven game should try a stance like that shown in Figure 146. They may find that it suits their purpose perfectly.

The foot position associated with the "Churchill" style (Figure 105) is still "squarer" to the direction of shooting, and perhaps reflects the tremendous amount of clay target shooting, driven game, and live pigeon trapshooting in Churchill's experience. The author believes it is too "square-on" for most shooters.

EXTRA-LARGE SHOT

There is a belief, particularly prevalent among wildfowlers, that when large shot are used the fewness of the pellets in the load is compensated for by the gun throwing them into a smaller-diameter pattern, one, therefore, in which little density is lost when compared to patterns made with the same weight of a smaller shot-size. The truth is that such a tendency is but slight until shot sizes far larger than those of interest for shooting ducks, or even geese, are reached (Figure 147). The density compensation is always merely partial, and there is no sense in using a shot-size of more than adequate penetration. The power of penetration required on large, heavily-feathered waterfowl is, however, a good deal more than is commonly supposed.

Really large shot are used, still, in some parts of the world for deer and boar-sized game, for such exciting events as finishing off a wounded leopard, and by law-enforcement officers and prison guards. The patterning behaviour at the left, upper, end of the curve in Figure 147 is therefore of more than academic interest.

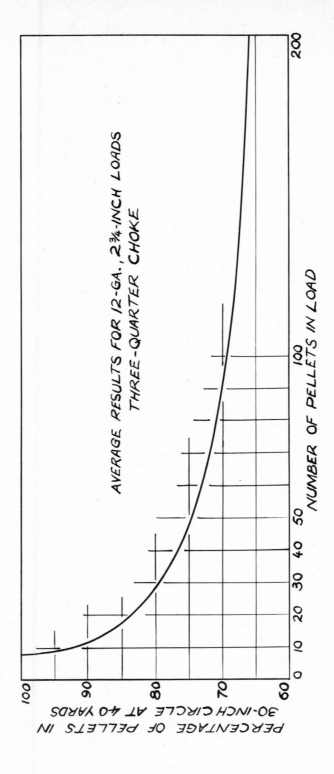

Figure 147 Number of Pellets in Load vs. Pattern Percentage

CLAY TARGET SHOOTING —
THE "DEAD GUN" PROBLEM

In all shotgun competition except ISU Skeet and FITASC Sporting it is now (1984) permitted to put the gun to the shoulder before calling for targets. All such rules have their origin in solving the referees' problem with shooters who try to cheat on rules which require the gun to be out of the shoulder until the target is in the air, and in this they are successful. For the shooters concerned they also solve the problem of the inconsistency in gunmounting which can result when this has to be performed quickly, after the target is in the air. For this reason, when allowed to put up the gun fully before calling for the target, practically all shooters will do so.

However, while solving one problem for the shooter, the premounted gun creates another one for him — that of the so-called "dead gun".

When the gun is already at the shoulder when the target appears, since its weight is well out in front of the shooter, its inertia (its resistance to being moved) is much greater than it is before it is mounted, when its weight is much closer to the shooter's body. With a premounted gun, the shooter is apt to overcome this greater inertia by starting the gun on its way with a sharp "jerk". This jerk is the very antithesis of the smooth movement of the gun necessary to good shooting. However, if one knows how, it is easy to get rid of it.

In Skeet and Sporting, the path of the targets is known to the shooter before they appear. In American and English Skeet, and in English Sporting, the shooter should "back-track" the muzzle of the shouldered gun a short extra distance along the line it will travel after the target appears. Trapshooters should point a little *below* where they feel the muzzle should ideally be when the target appears. The shooter then *starts the gun moving gently* (along the expected path of the target in Skeet and Sporting, upward in trapshooting) *at the same time as he calls*. Accelerating the already moving gun when the target is seen produces much less of a jerk than does starting a stationary ("dead") gun moving. Indeed, with practice, most shooters can altogether eliminate that jerk. Scores rise accordingly.

INDEX